taste of home
SOUTHERN
favorites

taste of home
BOOKS

taste of home

A TASTE OF HOME/READER'S DIGEST BOOK
© 2012 Reiman Media Group, LLC
5400 S. 60th St., Greendale WI 53129
All rights reserved.

Taste of Home and Reader's Digest are registered trademarks of The Reader's Digest Association, Inc.

EDITORIAL

EDITOR-IN-CHIEF	Catherine Cassidy
EXECUTIVE EDITOR, PRINT AND DIGITAL BOOKS	Stephen C. George
CREATIVE DIRECTOR	Howard Greenberg
EDITORIAL SERVICES MANAGER	Kerri Balliet
EDITORS	Janet Briggs, Sara Rae Lancaster
ASSOCIATE CREATIVE DIRECTOR	Edwin Robles Jr.
ART DIRECTOR	Jessie Sharon
CONTENT PRODUCTION MANAGER	Julie Wagner
LAYOUT DESIGNER	Catherine Fletcher
COPY CHIEF	Deb Warlaumont Mulvey
PROJECT PROOFREADER	Valerie Berg Phillips, Victoria Soukup Jensen
RECIPE ASSET SYSTEM BUSINESS ANALYST	Colleen King
RECIPE TESTING & EDITING	Taste of Home Test Kitchen
FOOD PHOTOGRAPHY	Taste of Home Photo Studio
EXECUTIVE ASSISTANT	Marie Brannon
EDITORIAL ASSISTANT	Marilyn Iczkowski

BUSINESS

VICE PRESIDENT, PUBLISHER	Jan Studin, jan_studin@rd.com
REGIONAL ACCOUNT DIRECTOR	Donna Lindskog, donna_lindskog@rd.com
EASTERN ACCOUNT DIRECTOR	Jennifer Dietz
MIDWEST & WESTERN ACCOUNT DIRECTOR	Jackie Fallon
MIDWEST ACCOUNT MANAGER	Lorna Phillips
WESTERN ACCOUNT MANAGER	Joel Millikin
MICHIGAN SALES REPRESENTATIVE	Linda C. Donaldson
CORPORATE INTEGRATED SALES DIRECTOR	Steve Sottile
VICE PRESIDENT, DIGITAL SALES AND DEVELOPMENT	Dan Meehan
DIGITAL/INTEGRATED DIRECTOR	Kelly Paxson
GENERAL MANAGER, TASTE OF HOME COOKING SCHOOLS	Erin Puariea
DIRECT RESPONSE	Katherine Zito, David Geller Associates
EXECUTIVE DIRECTOR, BRAND MARKETING	Leah West
VICE PRESIDENT, CREATIVE DIRECTOR	Paul Livornese
MARKETING MANAGER	Katie Gaon Wilson
ASSOCIATE MARKETING MANAGER	Emily Moore
PUBLIC RELATIONS MANAGER	Heidi Frank
VICE PRESIDENT, MAGAZINE MARKETING	Dave Fiegel

READER'S DIGEST NORTH AMERICA

PRESIDENT	Dan Lagani
PRESIDENT, CANADA	Tony Cioffi
PRESIDENT, BOOKS AND HOME ENTERTAINING	Harold Clarke
CHIEF FINANCIAL OFFICER	Howard Halligan
VICE PRESIDENT, GENERAL MANAGER, READER'S DIGEST MEDIA	Marilynn Jacobs
CHIEF MARKETING OFFICER	Renee Jordan
VICE PRESIDENT, CHIEF SALES OFFICER	Mark Josephson
VICE PRESIDENT, GENERAL MANAGER, RD MILWAUKEE	Lisa Karpinski
VICE PRESIDENT, CHIEF STRATEGY OFFICER	Jacqueline Majers Lachman
VICE PRESIDENT, MARKETING AND CREATIVE SERVICES	Elizabeth Tigne
VICE PRESIDENT, CHIEF CONTENT OFFICER	Liz Vaccariello

THE READER'S DIGEST ASSOCIATION, INC.

PRESIDENT AND CHIEF EXECUTIVE OFFICER	Robert E. Guth

"Timeless Recipes from Trusted Home Cooks" is a registered trademark of Reiman Media Group, LLC.
"Cooking, Caring, Sharing" is a registered trademark of Reiman Media Group, LLC.

For other Taste of Home books and products, visit us at tasteofhome.com.

For more Reader's Digest products and information, visit
rd.com (in the United States)
or see rd.ca (in Canada).

INTERNATIONAL STANDARD BOOK NUMBER (10)	1-61765-037-4
INTERNATIONAL STANDARD BOOK NUMBER (13)	978-1-61765-037-6
LIBRARY OF CONGRESS CONTROL NUMBER	2012935011

COVER PHOTOGRAPHY

PHOTOGRAPHER: Rob Hagen
FOOD STYLIST: Joylyn Trickel
SET STYLIST: Jennifer Bradley Vent

PICTURED ON FRONT COVER	Top: Sage Cornmeal Biscuits, page 177; Lemon-Filled Coconut Cake, page 273; Marvelous Shells 'n' Cheese, page 197; Raspberry Sweet Tea, page 26; Main: Nutty Oven-Fried Chicken, page 120
PICTURED ON BACK COVER	Crawfish Fettuccine, page 101; Ham 'n' Corn Fritters, page 187; Slow-Cooked Pork Barbecue, page 53; Butterscotch Peach Pie, page 254

Printed in China.
1 3 5 7 9 10 8 6 4 2

TABLE OF CONTENTS

GATHER 'ROUND THE TABLE, Y'ALL!

If there's anything that rivals Southern hospitality, it has to be the food. Nothing makes a stranger feel like family more than a plateful of old-fashioned Southern comfort food.

But you don't need to travel south of the Mason-Dixon Line to savor the comforting dishes that put Southern cuisine on the culinary map. *Taste of Home Southern Favorites* lets you bring the taste of the South into your kitchen with more than 380 homestyle favorites.

The lip-smackin' collection explores the culinary delights from every region—the Deep South, New South, Gulf South and Appalachia—that beckon you to pull up a chair and dig in. *Southern Favorites* is packed with all the classics—crispy fried chicken, saucy barbecues, fried green tomatoes, cheesy grits and greens—and even a few newfangled creations. Sweet Potato Cheese Ball (p. 23), Chorizo-Stuffed Turkey Breast with Mexican Grits (p. 112), and Cajun Shrimp Lasagna Roll-Ups (p. 84) are just a few new dishes sure to tickle your fancy.

And because no self-respecting Southern cook would dream of sending folks from the table without dessert, you'll find plenty of sweet treats. Old-Fashioned Jam Cake (p. 266), Southern Sweet Potato Pie (p. 244), Mississippi Mud Cake (p. 269), Brownie Bourbon Bites (p. 292) and more will provide the perfect ending to your meal.

Sprinkled throughout this book, you will also find inspiring photographs of the finished recipes, plus handy tips, kitchen secrets and convenient prep and cook times.

Grab your cast-iron skillet, tie your apron and **GET READY** to **CELEBRATE** the very best Southern eats in all their **FINGER-LICKIN' GLORY!**

AVOCADO SHRIMP SALSA, PG. 22

APPETIZERS & BEVERAGES

In the South, food is big! It's the focal point of every gathering, large or small. After one taste of these scrumptious Southern bites and sweet sips, you'll know why this region is home to some of the tastiest vittles anywhere.

RASPBERRY SWEET TEA, PG. 26

VIRGIN HURRICANES

PREP/TOTAL TIME: 10 min. | **YIELD:** 9 servings (3/4 cup each).

Revelers of all ages can enjoy this non-alcoholic version of the punch-like refresher, often called "Mardi Gras in a glass." (Adults who want a more authentic flavor can mix in rum.) **TASTE OF HOME TEST KITCHEN**

2 cups passion fruit juice

1 cup unsweetened pineapple juice

1 cup orange juice

3/4 cup lemon juice

2 cups carbonated water

Ice cubes

Pineapple wedges and maraschino cherries

Combine the juices in a pitcher. Just before serving, stir in carbonated water.

Pour into hurricane or highball glasses filled with ice. Garnish with pineapple wedges and cherries.

SPICED PEANUTS

PREP: 10 min. | **BAKE:** 20 min. | **YIELD:** 3 cups.

Liven up plain peanuts with a sweet-and-spicy blend of flavors from sugar, cumin and cayenne pepper. You'll want to double—or triple—the recipe! **HOLLY KUNKLE** WALTON, KENTUCKY

- 1 jar (16 ounces) unsalted dry roasted peanuts
- 2 tablespoons canola oil
- 2 tablespoons sugar
- 1-1/2 teaspoons ground cumin
- 1 teaspoon salt
- 1/2 teaspoon cayenne pepper
- 1/2 teaspoon garlic powder

Place peanuts in a small bowl; drizzle with oil and toss to coat. Combine sugar and seasonings; sprinkle over nuts and toss to coat. Transfer to an ungreased 15-in. x 10-in. x 1-in. baking pan. Bake at 300° for 20-25 minutes or until lightly browned, stirring occasionally.

Spread on waxed paper to cool. Store in an airtight container.

CHEESE STRAWS

PREP: 20 min.
BAKE: 15 min. + cooling
YIELD: 2-1/2 dozen.

Five ingredients create these tempting, crisp cracker sticks. The hand-held snacks make for easy mingling at parties.
ELIZABETH ROBINSON CONROE, TEXAS

- 1/2 cup butter, softened
- 2 cups (8 ounces) shredded sharp cheddar cheese
- 1-1/4 cups all-purpose flour
- 1/2 teaspoon salt
- 1/4 teaspoon cayenne pepper

In a large bowl, beat butter until light and fluffy. Beat in cheese until blended. Combine the flour, salt and cayenne; stir into cheese mixture until a dough forms. Roll into a 15-in. x 6-in. rectangle. Cut into thirty 6-in. strips. Place strips 1 in. apart on ungreased baking sheets.

Bake at 350° for 15-20 minutes or until lightly browned. Cool for 5 minutes before removing from pans to wire racks to cool completely. Store in an airtight container.

WATERMELON SALSA

PREP: 20 min. + chilling | **YIELD:** 3 cups.

When I'm in the mood for some Southern fare that's also light, I make this fruity, fresh-tasting salsa.

CAROLYN BUTTERFIELD LAKE STEVENS, WASHINGTON

- 2 cups seeded finely chopped watermelon
- 1/2 cup finely chopped peeled cucumber
- 1/4 cup finely chopped red onion
- 1/4 cup finely chopped sweet red pepper
- 1 jalapeno pepper, seeded and minced
- 1/4 cup minced fresh cilantro
- 1 tablespoon minced fresh basil
- 1 tablespoon minced fresh mint
- 2 tablespoons honey
- 1 teaspoon lime juice

Baked tortilla chip scoops

In a large bowl, combine the watermelon, cucumber, onion, peppers and herbs. Drizzle with honey and lime juice; gently toss to coat.

Refrigerate for at least 1 hour. Serve with chips.

EDITOR'S NOTE: Wear disposable gloves when cutting hot peppers; the oils can burn skin. Avoid touching your face.

BACON-WRAPPED CAJUN JALAPENOS

PREP: 20 min. | **BAKE:** 25 min. | **YIELD:** 16 appetizers.

These peppers are so addictive that if I want any for myself, I either need to make a double batch or hide some from my family. The jalapenos are not too spicy after they are baked (I take out the seeds and white membrane), but still have a wonderful flavor.

LINDA FOREMAN LOCUST GROVE, OKLAHOMA

- 8 large jalapeno peppers
- 1 package (3 ounces) cream cheese, softened
- 1/2 cup finely shredded cheddar cheese
- 1 teaspoon Cajun seasoning
- 8 thick-sliced peppered bacon strips

Cut jalapenos in half lengthwise; remove seeds and center membranes. In a small bowl, combine the cream cheese, shredded cheddar cheese and Cajun seasoning. Stuff about 1-1/2 teaspoonfuls into each pepper half.

Cut bacon strips in half widthwise. In a large skillet, cook bacon until partially cooked. Wrap a bacon piece around each pepper; secure with a toothpick.

Place jalapenos on a wire rack in a shallow baking pan. Bake, uncovered, at 350° for 25-30 minutes or until bacon is crisp. Discard toothpicks. Serve immediately.

EDITOR'S NOTE: Wear disposable gloves when cutting hot peppers; the oils can burn skin. Avoid touching your face.

MARINATED CHEESE

PREP: 30 min. + marinating | **YIELD:** about 2 pounds.

Don't expect this special appetizer to last long. It's always the first starter to make an appearance on the buffet table, and the first to disappear. It's attractive and delicious. **LAURIE CASPER** CORAOPOLIS, PENNSYLVANIA

- 2 blocks (8 ounces *each*) white cheddar cheese
- 2 packages (8 ounces *each*) cream cheese, softened
- 3/4 cup chopped roasted sweet red peppers
- 1/2 cup olive oil
- 1/4 cup white wine vinegar
- 1/4 cup balsamic vinegar
- 3 tablespoons chopped green onions
- 3 tablespoons minced fresh parsley
- 2 tablespoons minced fresh basil
- 1 tablespoon sugar
- 3 garlic cloves, minced
- 1/2 teaspoon salt
- 1/2 teaspoon pepper

Toasted sliced French bread *or* assorted crackers

Slice each block of cheddar cheese into twenty 1/4-in. slices. Cut each block of cream cheese into 18 slices; sandwich between cheddar slices, using a knife to spread evenly. Create four 6-in.-long blocks of cheese; place in a 13-in. x 9-in. dish.

In a small bowl, combine the roasted peppers, oil, vinegars, onions, herbs, sugar, garlic, salt and pepper; pour over cheese.

Cover and refrigerate overnight, turning once. Drain excess marinade. Serve cheese with bread or crackers.

TEXAS CAVIAR

PREP: 20 min. + chilling | **YIELD:** 5 cups.

I adapted this recipe from a cookbook I received a long time ago, and now I can't imagine a get-together at my house without it.
BECKY OLIVER FAIRPLAY, COLORADO

> 2 cans (15-1/2 ounces *each*) black-eyed peas, rinsed and drained
> 1 can (10 ounces) diced tomatoes and green chilies, drained
> 1 medium green pepper, finely chopped
> 1 small red onion, finely chopped
> 1/2 cup fat-free Italian salad dressing
> 2 tablespoons lime juice
> 1/4 teaspoon salt
> 1/4 teaspoon pepper
> 1 medium ripe avocado, peeled and cubed

Tortilla chips

In a large bowl, combine the peas, tomatoes, green pepper and onion. In a small bowl, whisk the dressing, lime juice, salt and pepper. Pour over black-eyed pea mixture and stir to coat. Cover and refrigerate for at least 1 hour.

Stir in avocado just before serving. Serve with chips.

BOTTOMS-UP CHERRY LIMEADE

PREP/TOTAL TIME: 10 min.
YIELD: 8 servings.

My guests enjoy this refreshing cherry-topped drink. It's just right on a hot Southern summer evening.
AWYNNE THURSTENSON
SILOAM SPRINGS, ARKANSAS

> 3/4 cup lime juice
> 1 cup sugar
> 2 liters lime carbonated water, chilled
> 1/2 cup maraschino cherry juice
> 8 maraschino cherries with stems
> 8 lime slices

In a large bowl, combine lime juice and sugar. Cover and refrigerate. Just before serving, stir carbonated water into lime juice mixture.

For each serving, place 1 tablespoon cherry juice in a glass. Add crushed ice and about 1 cup of lime juice mixture. Garnish with a maraschino cherry and a lime slice.

BENEDICTINE DIP

PREP/TOTAL TIME: 15 min. | **YIELD:** 1-3/4 cups.

Benedictine is a creamy spread studded with chopped cucumbers. It was originally used for cucumber sandwiches but makes a great dip.
TASTE OF HOME TEST KITCHEN

> 4 ounces cream cheese, softened
> 1 log (4 ounces) fresh goat cheese
> 2 tablespoons minced fresh parsley
> 1 tablespoon mayonnaise
> 1/4 teaspoon salt
> 1/8 teaspoon cayenne pepper
> 1/8 teaspoon pepper
> 1 drop green food coloring, optional
> 3/4 cup finely chopped peeled cucumber, patted dry
> 1/4 cup finely chopped green onions

Assorted crackers

In a small bowl, combine the cheeses, parsley, mayonnaise, salt, cayenne, pepper and food coloring if desired; beat until smooth. Stir in cucumber and onion. Chill until serving. Serve with crackers.

CRISPY CHICKEN FINGERS

PREP: 20 min. | **COOK:** 5 min./batch
YIELD: 7 servings.

My kids love these tender, moist chicken strips! My husband and I like to cut up the chicken and add it to a lettuce salad with eggs, tomatoes and cheese.

RACHEL FIZEL WOODBURY, MINNESOTA

- 1 cup all-purpose flour
- 1 cup dry bread crumbs
- 2 tablespoons grated Parmesan cheese
- 1 teaspoon salt
- 3/4 teaspoon garlic powder
- 1/2 teaspoon baking powder
- 1 egg
- 1 cup buttermilk
- 1-3/4 pounds boneless skinless chicken breasts, cut into strips

Oil for deep-fat frying

In a large resealable plastic bag, combine first six ingredients. In a shallow bowl, whisk egg and buttermilk. Dip a few pieces of chicken at a time in buttermilk mixture, then place in bag; seal and shake to coat.

In an electric skillet, heat oil to 375°. Fry chicken, a few strips at a time, for 2-3 minutes on each side or until no longer pink. Drain on paper towels.

CREAM CHEESE DEVILED EGGS

PREP/TOTAL TIME: 25 min. | **YIELD:** 16 appetizers.

Peas and bacon give this traditional Southern appetizer a nice little twist. A family favorite, these deviled eggs are always first to disappear from the table.

ABI MCMAHON SHERMAN OAKS, CALIFORNIA

- 8 hard-cooked eggs
- 1 package (8 ounces) cream cheese, softened
- 2 teaspoons Dijon mustard
- 1/4 teaspoon salt
- 1/4 teaspoon pepper
- 1/4 cup frozen peas, thawed
- 3 bacon strips, cooked and crumbled

Cut eggs in half lengthwise. Remove yolks; set whites aside. In a small bowl, mash yolks. Add the cream cheese, mustard, salt and pepper; beat until blended. Stir in peas.

Stuff or pipe mixture into egg whites. Sprinkle with bacon. Refrigerate until serving.

EGGNOG

PREP: 15 min. | **COOK:** 20 min. + chilling | **YIELD:** 20 servings (3/4 cup each).

Store-bought eggnog just can't compete with my homemade version. Apricot brandy is my secret ingredient!
SHELIA WEIMER BLUEFIELD, WEST VIRGINIA

1-3/4 cups sugar
1/4 cup all-purpose flour
1/2 teaspoon salt
2 quarts 2% milk
6 eggs, beaten
1 cup apricot brandy *or* brandy
1/2 cup rum
2 tablespoons bourbon
2 tablespoons vanilla extract
1 quart half-and-half cream
1/2 teaspoon ground nutmeg

In a Dutch oven, combine the sugar, flour and salt. Gradually whisk in milk until smooth. Cook and stir over medium-high heat until thickened and bubbly. Reduce heat; cook and stir 2 minutes longer. Remove from the heat.

Stir a small amount of hot mixture into eggs; return all to the pan, stirring constantly. Cook and stir over medium heat until mixture is slightly thickened and coats the back of a spoon.

Transfer to a large bowl; cool quickly by placing bowl in ice water and stirring for 2 minutes. Stir in the brandy, rum, bourbon and vanilla. Cool completely. Cover and refrigerate for at least 3 hours. Just before serving, stir in cream and nutmeg.

COCONUT FRIED SHRIMP

PREP/TOTAL TIME: 20 min. | **YIELD:** 4 servings.

These crisp and crunchy shrimp make a tempting appetizer or a fun change-of-pace main dish. The coconut coating adds a little sweetness, and the tangy orange marmalade and honey sauce is great for dipping. It's impossible to stop munching these once you start! ANN ATCHISON O'FALLON, MISSOURI

1-1/4 cups all-purpose flour
1-1/4 cups cornstarch
6-1/2 teaspoons baking powder
1/2 teaspoon salt
1/4 teaspoon Cajun seasoning
1-1/2 cups cold water
1/2 teaspoon canola oil
2-1/2 cups flaked coconut
1 pound uncooked large
   shrimp, peeled and deveined

Additional oil for deep-fat frying
1 cup orange marmalade
1/4 cup honey

In a large bowl, combine the first five ingredients. Stir in water and oil until smooth. Place coconut in another bowl. Dip shrimp into batter, then coat with coconut.

In an electric skillet or deep-fat fryer, heat oil to 375°. Fry shrimp, a few at a time, for 3 minutes or until golden brown. Drain on paper towels.

In a small saucepan, heat the marmalade and honey; stir until blended. Serve sauce with shrimp.

TEST KITCHEN TIP
Only fry two to three shrimp at a time or the temperature of the oil will lower and the shrimp will not be as crisp. **TASTE OF HOME TEST KITCHEN**

COCONUT FRIED SHRIMP

GRITS 'N' SHRIMP TARTS

PREP/TOTAL TIME: 30 min. | **YIELD:** 2-1/2 dozen.

People can't get enough of this deliciously different appetizer that showcases two Mississippi staples: shrimp and grits! Crispy phyllo shells create a tasty hand-held bite. **ELIZABETH LATADY** JACKSON, MISSISSIPPI

1 cup water
1/4 cup quick-cooking grits
2 ounces cream cheese, softened
1/4 cup shredded cheddar cheese
3 tablespoons butter, *divided*
1/4 teaspoon garlic salt
1/8 teaspoon salt
Pepper to taste

1 pound uncooked small shrimp, peeled and deveined
3 green onions, sliced
2 packages (1.9 ounces *each*) frozen miniature phyllo tart shells

In a small saucepan, bring water to a boil. Gradually stir in grits. Reduce heat; cover and simmer for 4 minutes. Stir in the cheeses, 1 tablespoon butter, garlic salt, salt and pepper.

In a large skillet, saute shrimp and onions in remaining butter until shrimp turn pink. Fill tart shells with grits; top with shrimp mixture. Refrigerate leftovers.

OYSTERS ROCKEFELLER

PREP: 1-1/4 hours. | **BAKE:** 10 min. | **YIELD:** 3 dozen.

Delight guests with this classic starter. Even those who are a bit hesitant to eat oysters soon learn they enjoy this recipe.
BETH WALTON EASTHAM, MASSACHUSETTS

- 3 dozen fresh oysters in the shell, washed
- 1 medium onion, finely chopped
- 1/2 cup butter, cubed
- 1 package (9 ounces) fresh spinach, torn
- 1 cup grated Romano cheese
- 1 tablespoon lemon juice
- 1/8 teaspoon pepper
- 2 pounds kosher salt

Shuck oysters, reserving bottom shell; set aside. In a large skillet, saute onion in butter until tender. Add spinach; cook and stir until wilted. Remove from the heat; stir in the cheese, lemon juice and pepper.

Spread kosher salt into two ungreased 15-in. x 10-in. x 1-in. baking pans. Lightly press the oyster shells down into the salt. Place one oyster in each shell; top each with 2-1/2 teaspoons spinach mixture. Bake, uncovered, at 450° for 6-8 minutes or until oysters are plump. Serve oysters immediately.

ICED COFFEE SLUSH

PREP: 10 min. + freezing | **YIELD:** 12 servings (2-1/4 quarts).

We have a tradition of hosting a game night during the holidays with nine other couples. Our guests come for the camaraderie, but they sure love washing down delicious buffet items with this sweet slush. Even non-coffee drinkers enjoy it. **IOLA EGLE** BELLA VISTA, ARKANSAS

- 3 cups hot strong brewed coffee
- 1-1/2 to 2 cups sugar
- 4 cups milk
- 2 cups half-and-half cream
- 1-1/2 teaspoons vanilla extract

In a freezer-safe bowl, stir coffee and sugar until sugar is dissolved. Refrigerate until thoroughly chilled. Add the milk, cream and vanilla; freeze. Remove from the freezer several hours before serving. Chop mixture until it becomes slushy; serve immediately.

PIMIENTO CHEESE SPREAD

PREP: 10 min. + chilling
YIELD: 1-1/4 cups.

A classic Southern comfort food, Pimiento Cheese Spread is used as an appetizer with crackers, corn chips or celery. It is also smeared between two slices of white bread for sandwiches and as a topping for hamburgers and hot dogs.
EILEEN BALMER SOUTH BEND, INDIANA

- 1-1/2 cups (6 ounces) shredded cheddar cheese
- 1 jar (4 ounces) diced pimientos, drained and finely chopped
- 1/3 cup mayonnaise
- Assorted crackers

In a small bowl, combine the cheese, pimientos and mayonnaise. Refrigerate for at least 1 hour. Serve with crackers.

CANDIED PECANS

PREP: 20 min. | **BAKE:** 40 min. | **YIELD:** about 1 pound.

I give family and friends these crispy pecans in jars tied with pretty ribbon. Everyone who tries them says they are too good to be true!

OPAL TURNER HUGHES SPRINGS, TEXAS

- 2-3/4 cups pecan halves
- 2 tablespoons butter, softened, *divided*
- 1 cup sugar
- 1/2 cup water
- 1/2 teaspoon salt
- 1/2 teaspoon ground cinnamon
- 1 teaspoon vanilla extract

Place pecans in a shallow baking pan in a 250° oven for 10 minutes or until warmed. Grease a 15-in. x 10-in. x 1-in. baking pan with 1 tablespoon butter; set aside.

Grease the sides of a large heavy saucepan with remaining butter; add sugar, water, salt and cinnamon. Cook and stir over low heat until sugar is dissolved. Cook and stir over medium heat until mixture comes to a boil. Cover and cook for 2 minutes to dissolve sugar crystals.

Cook, without stirring, until a candy thermometer reads 236° (soft-ball stage). Remove from the heat; add vanilla. Stir in warm pecans until evenly coated.

Spread onto prepared baking pan. Bake at 250° for 30 minutes, stirring every 10 minutes. Spread on a waxed paper-lined baking sheet to cool.

EDITOR'S NOTE: We recommend that you test your candy thermometer before each use by bringing water to a boil; the thermometer should read 212°. Adjust your recipe temperature up or down based on your test.

EASY CITRUS SLUSH

PREP: 15 min. + freezing
YIELD: about 6 quarts (about 25 servings).

Try using different flavored gelatins to color-coordinate this slushy, refreshing beverage with the decor of the occasion. It's simple to prepare and always a winner.

JOY BRUCE WELCH, OKLAHOMA

- 2-1/2 cups sugar
- 1 package (3 ounces) lemon gelatin
- 1 package (3 ounces) pineapple gelatin
- 4 cups boiling water
- 1 can (12 ounces) frozen pineapple juice concentrate, thawed
- 1 cup lemon juice
- 1 envelope (0.23 ounce) unsweetened lemonade soft drink mix
- 10 cups cold water
- 2 liters ginger ale, chilled

In a large container, dissolve sugar and gelatins in boiling water. Stir in the pineapple juice concentrate, lemon juice, drink mix and cold water. If desired, place in smaller containers. Cover and freeze, stirring several times.

Remove from freezer at least 1 hour before serving. Stir until mixture becomes slushy. Just before serving, place 9 cups slush mixture in a punch bowl; stir in 1 liter ginger ale. Repeat with remaining slush and ginger ale.

MARINATED MOZZARELLA

PREP: 15 min. + marinating | **YIELD:** 8-10 servings.

I always come home with an empty container when I bring this dish to a party. It can be made ahead to free up time later. I serve it with pretty party picks for a festive look. **PEGGY CAIRO** KENOSHA, WISCONSIN

1/3 cup olive oil

1 tablespoon chopped oil-packed sun-dried tomatoes

1 tablespoon minced fresh parsley

1 teaspoon crushed red pepper flakes

1 teaspoon dried basil

1 teaspoon minced chives

1/4 teaspoon garlic powder

1 pound cubed part-skim mozzarella cheese

In a large resealable plastic bag, combine the first seven ingredients; add cheese cubes. Seal bag and turn to coat; refrigerate for at least 30 minutes.

Transfer to a serving dish; serve with toothpicks.

CRUNCHY CARAMEL CORN

PREP: 10 min. + cooling | **YIELD:** about 2 quarts.

Kids of all ages will gobble up this sweet and crunchy popcorn. It's really a quick snack to prepare and has wonderful homemade goodness. **SHELY GROMER** LONG BEACH, CALIFORNIA

6 cups popped popcorn
3/4 cup salted peanuts
1/2 cup packed brown sugar
1/4 cup butter, cubed
2 tablespoons light corn syrup
1/4 teaspoon salt
1/2 teaspoon vanilla extract
1/4 teaspoon baking soda

Place popcorn and peanuts in a large microwave-safe bowl; set aside. In another microwave-safe bowl, combine the brown sugar, butter, corn syrup and salt. Cover and microwave on high for 30-60 seconds; stir. Microwave 1-1/2 minutes longer.

Stir in vanilla and baking soda. Pour over popcorn mixture. Microwave, uncovered, on high for 2 minutes, stirring several times. Spread on greased baking sheets to cool. Store in an airtight container.

EDITOR'S NOTE: This recipe was tested in a 1,100-watt microwave.

GEORGIA PEANUT SALSA

PREP: 25 min. + chilling | **YIELD:** about 6-1/2 cups.

Former President Jimmy Carter gave First Place to this zippy salsa at the Plains Peanut Festival in his Georgia hometown. My daughter and I came up with the recipe just days before the competition. Although we weren't allowed in the judging room, we later saw a tape of President Carter tasting our salsa and saying, "Mmmmmm, that's good!" **LANE MCLOUD** SILOAM SPRINGS, ARKANSAS

3 plum tomatoes, seeded and chopped
1 jar (8 ounces) picante sauce
1 can (7 ounces) white *or* shoepeg corn, drained
1/3 cup Italian salad dressing
1 medium green pepper, chopped
1 medium sweet red pepper, chopped
4 green onions, thinly sliced
1/2 cup minced fresh cilantro
2 garlic cloves, minced
2-1/2 cups salted roasted peanuts *or* boiled peanuts
Hot pepper sauce, optional
Tortilla chips

In a large bowl, combine the first nine ingredients. Cover and refrigerate for at least 8 hours.

Just before serving, stir in peanuts and pepper sauce if desired. Serve with tortilla chips.

EDITOR'S NOTE: This recipe was tested with salted peanuts, but the original recipe used boiled peanuts, which are often available in the South.

THE SKINNY ON SEEDING TOMATOES

Seeding tomatoes isn't always necessary, but it can improve the dish's appearance or eliminate excess moisture. To remove the seeds from a tomato, cut it in half horizontally and remove the stem. Holding a tomato half over a bowl or sink, scrape out seeds with a small spoon or squeeze the tomato to force out the seeds. Then slice or dice as directed in the recipe.
TASTE OF HOME TEST KITCHEN

GEORGIA PEANUT SALSA

AVOCADO SHRIMP SALSA

PREP/TOTAL TIME: 25 min. | **YIELD:** 6 cups.

Southern-style salsa at its best! Try this medley of shrimp, tomatoes and avocado scooped up with tortilla chips or atop grilled chicken. You can even eat it as a chunky side dish. **MARIA SIMMONS** RIO RANCHO, NEW MEXICO

- 1 pound cooked small shrimp, peeled, deveined and chopped
- 2 medium tomatoes, seeded and chopped
- 2 medium ripe avocados, peeled and chopped
- 1 cup minced fresh cilantro
- 1 medium sweet red pepper, chopped
- 3/4 cup thinly sliced green onions
- 1/2 cup chopped seeded, peeled cucumber
- 3 tablespoons lime juice
- 1 jalapeno pepper, seeded and chopped
- 1 teaspoon salt
- 1/4 teaspoon pepper

Tortilla chips

In a large bowl, combine the first 11 ingredients. Serve with tortilla chips.

EDITOR'S NOTE: Wear disposable gloves when cutting hot peppers; the oils can burn skin. Avoid touching your face.

SWEET POTATO CHEESE BALL

PREP: 10 min. + chilling | **YIELD:** about 3 cups.

My husband and I farm 300 acres of sweet potatoes. I promote our product at fairs, ag expos and school functions. When I pass out recipes, this distinctive cheese ball is one of the favorites.

EDWINA HARPER BASTROP, LOUISIANA

- 1 package (8 ounces) cream cheese, softened
- 2 cups cold mashed sweet potatoes
- 1/4 cup finely chopped onion
- 2 tablespoons finely chopped jalapeno pepper
- 1 teaspoon seasoned salt
- 1 teaspoon Worcestershire sauce
- 1 teaspoon Louisiana hot sauce
- 1/2 to 1 teaspoon hot pepper sauce
- 1/4 cup chopped pecans

Assorted crackers, breadsticks *or* raw vegetables

In a bowl, beat cream cheese and sweet potatoes until smooth. Add the next seven ingredients; mix well. Cover and refrigerate for 4 hours or until easy to handle. Shape into a ball; cover and refrigerate for 4 hours or until firm. Serve with crackers, breadsticks or vegetables.

EDITOR'S NOTE: Wear disposable gloves when cutting hot peppers; the oils can burn skin. Avoid touching your face.

HONEY CINNAMON MILK

PREP/TOTAL TIME: 10 min.
YIELD: 1 serving.

I enjoy this warm, soothing beverage on a bleak and dreary day. It's a nice alternative to hot cocoa or tea.

LEONY SANTOSO WINCHESTER, VIRGINIA

- 1 cup fat-free milk
- 1 cinnamon stick (3 inches)
- **Dash ground nutmeg**
- **Dash ground allspice**
- 1-1/2 teaspoons honey

In a small saucepan, combine the milk, cinnamon stick, nutmeg and allspice. Cook and stir over medium heat until heated through; whisk in honey.

Serve warm in a mug; garnish with cinnamon stick.

PASSION FRUIT HURRICANES

HEARTY ENGLISH MUFFINS

PREP/TOTAL TIME: 20 min. | **YIELD:** 2 servings.

My husband and I enjoy these quick bites for breakfast before we start work on our dairy farm. I suggest topping them with pizza sauce or a squirt of ketchup for a tasty breakfast that's ready in no time.
CHRISTINE WEBER PALMERSTON, ONTARIO

5 eggs, lightly beaten

1/2 cup shredded cheddar cheese

1/2 teaspoon minced chives

Salt and pepper to taste

4 bacon strips

2 English muffins, split and toasted

In a large bowl, whisk the eggs, cheese, chives, salt and pepper. Pour into a nonstick skillet; cook and stir over medium heat until eggs are completely set.

Meanwhile, cut bacon strips in half widthwise; cook until crisp. Place two bacon pieces on each English muffin half; top with eggs.

PASSION FRUIT HURRICANES

PREP/TOTAL TIME: 10 min. | **YIELD:** 6 servings.

This is our version of the famous Hurricane beverage that's so popular in New Orleans. They're so named because each sip packs a punch! TASTE OF HOME TEST KITCHEN

2 cups passion fruit juice

1 cup plus 2 tablespoons sugar

3/4 cup lime juice

3/4 cup light rum

3/4 cup dark rum

3 tablespoons grenadine syrup

6 to 8 cups ice cubes

Orange slices and maraschino cherries

In a pitcher, combine the fruit juice, sugar, lime juice, rum and grenadine; stir until sugar is dissolved.

Pour into hurricane or highball glasses filled with ice. Garnish with orange slices and cherries.

FUN CITRUS GARNISH

Orange spirals make an attractive and fragrant garnish for any type of dessert. To make them, use a citrus stripper to remove the peel of an orange in one continuous motion, working from end to end. Tightly wind the strip around a straw; trim and secure ends with waterproof tape. Use the remaining orange peel strip to wrap more straws. Let wrapped straws stand for at least 20 minutes. (The longer the strips are wrapped around the straw, the longer they'll hold their shape after the straw is removed.)
TASTE OF HOME TEST KITCHEN

CRAB CAKES WITH RED CHILI MAYO

PREP: 35 min. + chilling | **COOK:** 10 min./batch
YIELD: 2 dozen (1 cup sauce).

I make these attractive bites for every party I attend, and they're always a hit. The spicy mayo is just the right accent for the crab cakes.
TIFFANY ANDERSON-TAYLOR GULFPORT, FLORIDA

- 1-1/3 cups mayonnaise
- 2 tablespoons Thai chili sauce
- 2 teaspoons lemon juice, *divided*
- 1/4 cup *each* finely chopped celery, red onion and sweet red pepper
- 1 jalapeno pepper, seeded and finely chopped
- 4 tablespoons olive oil, *divided*
- 1/2 cup soft bread crumbs
- 1 egg, lightly beaten
- 1 pound fresh crabmeat
- 1/4 cup all-purpose flour

In a small bowl, combine the mayonnaise, chili sauce and 1-1/4 teaspoons lemon juice. Set aside.

In a small skillet, saute the celery, onion, red pepper and jalapeno in 1 tablespoon oil until tender. Transfer to a large bowl; stir in the bread crumbs, egg, 1/2 cup reserved mayonnaise mixture and remaining lemon juice. Fold in crab. Cover and refrigerate for at least 2 hours. Cover and refrigerate remaining mayonnaise mixture for sauce.

Place flour in a bowl. Drop crab mixture by 2 tablespoonfuls into flour. Gently coat and shape into a 1/2-in.-thick patty. Repeat with remaining mixture.

In a skillet over medium-high heat, cook patties in remaining oil in batches for 3-4 minutes until golden brown. Serve with reserved sauce.

EDITOR'S NOTE: Wear disposable gloves when cutting hot peppers; the oils can burn skin. Avoid touching your face.

RASPBERRY SWEET TEA

PREP: 20 min. + chilling
YIELD: 15 servings.

You only need a handful of ingredients to stir together this refreshing sipper. Its brilliant color and smile-fetching flavor will make it a popular thirst-quencher as the weather turns warm.
TASTE OF HOME TEST KITCHEN

- 4 quarts water, *divided*
- 1 cup sugar
- 10 individual tea bags
- 1 package (12 ounces) frozen unsweetened raspberries, thawed and undrained
- 3 tablespoons lime juice

In a large saucepan, bring 2 qts. of water to a boil. Stir in sugar until dissolved. Remove from the heat.

Add tea bags; steep for 5-8 minutes. Discard tea bags.

In another saucepan, bring raspberries and remaining water to a boil. Reduce heat; simmer, uncovered, for 3 minutes. Strain and discard pulp. Add raspberry and lime juices to the tea.

Transfer to a pitcher. Refrigerate until chilled.

SUGARED PEANUTS

PREP: 20 min. | **BAKE:** 30 min. + cooling | **YIELD:** 5 cups.

I tend to make these only for special occasions, such as holidays, because I cannot keep my husband and son (and myself!) away from them. They never last long, so you might want to make a double batch.

POLLY HALL ROCKFORD, MICHIGAN

5 cups unsalted peanuts

1 cup sugar

1 cup water

1/4 teaspoon salt

In a large heavy saucepan, combine the peanuts, sugar and water. Bring to a boil; cook until syrup has evaporated, about 10 minutes.

Spread peanuts in a single layer in a greased 15-in. x 10-in. x 1-in. baking pan; sprinkle with salt.

Bake at 300° for 30-35 minutes or until dry and lightly browned. Cool completely. Store in an airtight container.

CRISPY OVEN-FRIED OYSTERS

SWEET TEA CONCENTRATE

PREP: 30 min. + cooling | **YIELD:** 20 servings (5 cups concentrate).

Try this refreshingly sweet cooler that is a Southern classic. Whip up a batch to serve at your next party or picnic or make a single glass to sip slowly on a hot, sticky day. **NATALIE BREMSON** PLANTATION, FLORIDA

2 medium lemons

4 cups sugar

4 cups water

1-1/2 cups English breakfast tea leaves *or* 20 black tea bags

1/3 cup lemon juice

EACH SERVING:

1 cup cold water

Ice cubes

Remove peels from lemons; save fruit for another use.

In a large saucepan, combine sugar and water. Bring to a boil over medium heat. Reduce heat; simmer, uncovered, for 3-5 minutes or until sugar is dissolved, stirring occasionally. Remove from the heat; add tea leaves and lemon peels. Cover and steep for 15 minutes. Strain tea, discarding tea leaves and lemon peels; stir in lemon juice. Cool to room temperature.

Transfer to a container with a tight-fitting lid. Store in the refrigerator for up to 2 weeks.

TO PREPARE TEA: In a tall glass, combine water with 1/4 cup concentrate; add ice cubes.

CRISPY OVEN-FRIED OYSTERS

PREP/TOTAL TIME: 30 min. | **YIELD:** about 2-1/2 dozen (about 2/3 cup jalapeno mayonnaise).

These flavorful breaded and baked oysters, served with a zippy jalapeno mayonnaise, are just divine. I entered this recipe in a seafood contest and took first place in the hors d'oeuvres category. **MARIE RIZZIO** INTERLOCHEN, MICHIGAN

3/4 cup all-purpose flour

1/8 teaspoon salt

1/8 teaspoon pepper

2 eggs

1 cup dry bread crumbs

2/3 cup grated Romano cheese

1/4 cup minced fresh parsley

1/2 teaspoon garlic salt

1 pint shucked oysters *or* 2 cans (8 ounces *each*) whole oysters, drained

2 tablespoons olive oil

JALAPENO MAYONNAISE:

1/4 cup mayonnaise

1/4 cup sour cream

2 medium jalapeno peppers, seeded and finely chopped

2 tablespoons milk

1 teaspoon lemon juice

1/4 teaspoon grated lemon peel

1/8 teaspoon salt

1/8 teaspoon pepper

In a bowl, combine the flour, salt and pepper. In another shallow bowl, whisk eggs. In a third bowl, combine the bread crumbs, cheese, parsley and garlic salt.

Coat oysters with flour mixture, then dip in eggs and coat with crumb mixture. Place in a greased 15-in. x 10-in. x 1-in. baking pan; drizzle with oil.

Bake at 400° for 15 minutes or until golden brown. Meanwhile, in a small bowl, whisk the jalapeno mayonnaise ingredients. Serve with oysters.

EDITOR'S NOTE: Wear disposable gloves when cutting hot peppers; the oils can burn skin. Avoid touching your face.

NOW THAT'S USING YOUR MELON

Use a melon baller to easily scrape out the seeds and membranes from a jalapeno pepper. It speeds the job along and keeps you from accidentally slicing your gloves. **TASTE OF HOME TEST KITCHEN**

PARMESAN CHEESE STRAWS

PREP/TOTAL TIME: 30 min.
YIELD: 6 dozen.

These rich and buttery breadsticks are a fun change from regular dinner rolls, and they are fairly easy to make. Enjoy them alongside salads and soups.

MITZI SENTIFF ANNAPOLIS, MARYLAND

- 1/2 cup butter, softened
- 2/3 cup grated Parmesan cheese
- 1 cup all-purpose flour
- 1/4 teaspoon salt
- 1/8 teaspoon cayenne pepper
- 1/4 cup milk

In a small bowl, beat butter and Parmesan cheese until well blended. Add the flour, salt and cayenne; mix well. Divide dough in half. On a lightly floured surface, roll each portion into an 18-in. x 3-in. rectangle. Cut into 3-in. x 1/2-in. strips.

Place 1 in. apart on greased baking sheets; brush with milk. Bake at 350° or 8-10 minutes or until lightly browned. Remove to wire racks to cool. Store in an airtight container.

BLOODY MARY

PREP/TOTAL TIME: 10 min. | **YIELD:** 1 serving.

Horseradish makes this Bloody Mary special. Without the horseradish, you'll have a more traditional drink, and without the alcohol, you'll have a Virgin Mary. Serve it with a stalk of celery, dill pickle spear or green olives. **TASTE OF HOME TEST KITCHEN**

- 1-1/2 to 2 cups ice cubes, *divided*
- 2 ounces vodka
- 1 cup tomato juice, chilled
- 1 tablespoon lemon juice
- 1-1/2 teaspoons lime juice
- 3/4 teaspoon Worcestershire sauce
- 1/2 teaspoon prepared horseradish, optional
- 1/8 teaspoon celery salt
- 1/8 teaspoon pepper
- 1/8 teaspoon hot pepper sauce

GARNISHES:

Celery rib, pickle spear, green and ripe olives, cucumber slice and/*or* cocktail shrimp

Fill a shaker three-fourths full with ice. Place remaining ice in a highball glass; set aside.

Add the vodka, juices, Worcestershire sauce, horseradish if desired, celery salt, pepper and pepper sauce to shaker; cover and shake for 10-15 seconds or until condensation forms on outside of shaker. Strain beverage into prepared glass. Garnish as desired.

EDITOR'S NOTE: To make a batch of Bloody Marys (4 servings), place 1 cup ice in a 2-qt. pitcher. Add 1 cup vodka, 4 cups tomato juice, 1/4 cup lemon juice, 2 tablespoons lime juice, 1 tablespoon Worcestershire sauce, 2 teaspoons prepared horseradish if desired, 1/2 teaspoon celery salt, 1/2 teaspoon pepper and 1/2 teaspoon hot pepper sauce; stir to combine. Serve over ice.

HEARTY RYE MELTS

PREP/TOTAL TIME: 30 min. | **YIELD:** 2 dozen.

When we moved from the Midwest to Kentucky, we were invited to a neighborhood gathering, where this appetizer was served. Hanky panky, as it's often called around here, is traditionally served at Derby Day parties, but at our home it's become a year-round favorite. **MELANIE SCHLAF** EDGEWOOD, KENTUCKY

1/2 **pound lean ground beef
(90% lean)**

1/2 **pound bulk pork sausage**

1-1/2 **teaspoons chili powder**

8 **ounces process cheese
(Velveeta), shredded**

24 **slices snack rye bread**

Fresh parsley sprigs, stems removed

In a large skillet, cook the beef and sausage over medium heat until no longer pink; drain. Add chili powder and cheese; cook and stir until cheese is melted. Spread a heaping tablespoonful onto each slice of bread. Place on a baking sheet.

Bake at 350° for 12-15 minutes or until edges of bread begin to crisp. Garnish with parsley. Serve warm.

SAUSAGE HASH SKILLET, PG. 40

SUNSHINE CREPES, PG. 41

BREAKFAST & BRUNCH

Southern cooking conjures images of rich, luscious foods—and breakfast is no different. Biscuits smothered in gravy, golden griddle cakes and fried potatoes...these home-style specialties and more will leave you feeling bright-eyed and bushy-tailed.

BENEDICT EGGS IN PASTRY

PREP: 30 min. | **BAKE:** 20 min. | **YIELD:** 4 servings.

Here's a new twist on an old favorite. Inside these puffy golden bundles is an omelet-like filling of eggs, ham, cheese and rich, lemony hollandaise sauce. **CATHY SLUSSLER** MAGNOLIA, TEXAS

  2 **egg yolks**
  2 **tablespoons lemon juice**
  1 **teaspoon Dijon mustard**
  1/2 **cup butter, melted**
Dash cayenne pepper
  2 **cups cubed fully cooked ham**
  2 **green onions, chopped**
  1 **tablespoon butter**
  6 **eggs, lightly beaten**
  2 **tablespoons 2% milk**
  1 **package (17.3 ounces) frozen puff pastry, thawed**
  1 **cup (4 ounces) shredded cheddar cheese**
  1 **egg**
  1 **tablespoon water**
Minced fresh tarragon, optional

In a double boiler over simmering water or a small heavy saucepan, constantly whisk the egg yolks, lemon juice and mustard until mixture begins to thicken and reaches 160°. Reduce heat to low. Slowly drizzle in warm melted butter, whisking constantly. Whisk in cayenne.

Transfer to a small bowl if necessary. Place bowl in a larger bowl of warm water. Keep warm, stirring occasionally, until ready to use.

In a large skillet over medium heat, cook and stir ham and onions in butter until onions are tender. In a large bowl, whisk six eggs and milk. Add egg mixture to the pan; cook and stir until set. Remove from the heat; stir in 1/3 cup reserved hollandaise sauce. Set aside.

On a lightly floured surface, unfold puff pastry. Roll each sheet into a 12-in. x 9-1/2-in. rectangle; cut each in half widthwise. Place 1 cup egg mixture on half of each rectangle; sprinkle with cheese.

Beat egg and water; brush over pastry edges. Bring an opposite corner of pastry over the egg mixture; pinch seams to seal. With a small sharp knife, cut several slits in the top.

Transfer to a greased baking sheet; brush with remaining egg mixture. Bake at 400° for 18-22 minutes or until golden brown. Serve with remaining hollandaise sauce. Sprinkle with tarragon if desired.

MOM'S FRIED APPLES

PREP: 5 min. | **COOK:** 30 min. | **YIELD:** 6-8 servings.

Mom often made these rich, cinnamon-sugar apples when I was growing up. It's a trip down memory lane when I make them. The recipe is very dear to me. **MARGIE TAPPE** PRAGUE, OKLAHOMA

- 1/2 **cup butter, cubed**
- 6 **medium unpeeled tart red apples, sliced**
- 3/4 **cup sugar,** *divided*
- 3/4 **teaspoon ground cinnamon**

Melt butter in a large skillet. Add apples and 1/2 cup sugar; stir to mix well. Cover and cook over low heat for 20 minutes or until apples are tender, stirring frequently.

Add cinnamon and remaining sugar. Cook and stir over medium-high heat for 10 minutes or until apples are tender.

HAM GRIDDLE CAKES

PREP/TOTAL TIME: 30 min. | **YIELD:** 8 pancakes.

Looking for a different way to use up leftover ham? Try these golden pancakes. I serve them to company, and I'm always asked for the recipe.
VIRGINIA CULLEN SARASOTA, FLORIDA

- 1 **cup all-purpose flour**
- 1-1/2 **teaspoons baking powder**
- 2 **eggs**
- 3/4 **cup milk**
- 1 **cup ground fully cooked ham**

Pancake syrup

In a large bowl, combine flour and baking powder. In another bowl, beat the eggs and milk. Stir into dry ingredients just until moistened. Fold in ham.

Pour the batter by 1/4 cupfuls onto a lightly greased hot griddle. Turn when bubbles form on top. Cook until the second side is golden brown. Serve with syrup.

FREEZING SLICED APPLES

Sliced apples freeze well if properly prepared. Peel and slice the apples, then drop into Fruit Fresh to keep them from discoloring. Place the slices in boiling water for 2 minutes, then cool in ice water for 2 minutes. Drain. Pack slices into plastic freezer bags in the amounts needed for your favorite recipes. Seal, label and freeze. **TASTE OF HOME TEST KITCHEN**

SPICY SAUSAGE PATTIES

PREP/TOTAL TIME: 20 min.
YIELD: 4 servings.

Jazz up any breakfast with these subtly spiced sausage patties. They're sure to perk up your taste buds, plus they only take 20 minutes to make.
ATHENA RUSSELL
FLORENCE, SOUTH CAROLINA

- 1/2 **teaspoon salt**
- 1/2 **teaspoon dried sage leaves**
- 1/4 **teaspoon ground coriander**
- 1/4 **teaspoon pepper**
- 1/8 to 1/4 **teaspoon crushed red pepper flakes**
- 3/4 **pound ground pork**

In a bowl, combine the first five ingredients. Crumble pork over mixture and mix well. Shape into four 3-in. patties.

In a large skillet, cook patties over medium heat for 5-6 minutes on each side or until a thermometer reads 160°. Drain on paper towels.

BUTTERMILK PECAN PANCAKES

PREP/TOTAL TIME: 25 min. | **YIELD:** 16 pancakes.

With flecks of pecans in each bite, these light, tasty pancakes are an elegant morning entree. I find them to be so flavorful that they can be enjoyed with or without syrup. **JANN BRAUN** CHATHAM, ILLINOIS

3 eggs, *separated*

3 tablespoons butter, melted

1-1/2 cups all-purpose flour

1/2 to 1 cup chopped pecans

1 tablespoon sugar

1 teaspoon baking powder

1 teaspoon baking soda

1/2 teaspoon salt

1-2/3 cups buttermilk

In a large bowl, beat egg yolks and butter. Combine the flour, pecans, sugar, baking powder, baking soda and salt; add to the egg mixture alternately with buttermilk. Beat egg whites until stiff peaks form; fold into batter.

Pour batter by 1/4 cupfuls onto a lightly greased hot griddle; turn when bubbles form on top of pancakes. Cook until second side is golden brown.

HAM AND LEEK PIES

PREP: 40 min. | **BAKE:** 20 min. | **YIELD:** 4 servings.

This is my favorite recipe for leftover ham. I freeze the individual dishes and they are great for a quick meal.
BONNY TILLMAN ACWORTH, GEORGIA

4 cups sliced leeks
(white portion only)

1/2 pound sliced fresh
mushrooms

1-1/2 cups sliced fresh carrots

1/4 cup butter, cubed

1/2 cup all-purpose flour

1-1/4 cups vegetable broth

1-1/4 cups milk

1-3/4 cups diced fully cooked ham

2 tablespoons minced
fresh parsley

1/4 to 1/2 teaspoon
ground nutmeg

Dash pepper

1 sheet frozen puff pastry, thawed

1 egg, lightly beaten

In a large saucepan, saute the leeks, mushrooms and carrots in butter until tender. Stir in flour until blended. Gradually stir in broth and milk. Bring to a boil over medium heat. Cook and stir for 2 minutes or until thickened. Remove from the heat; stir in the ham, parsley, nutmeg and pepper.

On a lightly floured surface, roll puff pastry to 1/4-in. thickness. Using a 10-oz. ramekin as a template, cut out four tops for pies.

Fill four greased 10-oz. ramekins with leek mixture; top with pastry. Cut slits in pastry. Cut decorative shapes out of pastry scraps if desired; arrange over pies. Brush tops with egg.

Bake at 425° for 18-22 minutes or until golden brown. Let stand for 5 minutes before serving.

LOVELY LEEKS

Leeks often contain sand between their many layers, so it's important to clean them thoroughly. First, remove any withered outer leaves and trim root end. Cut off and discard the green upper leaves at the point where the pale green becomes dark green. Then cut the leek open lengthwise down one side and rinse under running water, separating the leaves. **TASTE OF HOME TEST KITCHEN**

HAM AND LEEK PIES

greased 15-in. x 10-in. x 1-in. baking pan. Bake at 400° for 7-1/2 minutes on each side; turning gently.

Meanwhile, in a small saucepan, combine the sugar, cornstarch and salt. Gently whisk in orange juice and water until smooth. Bring to a boil; cook and stir for 1-2 minutes or until thickened. Reduce heat; stir in oranges and blueberries. Cook for 5 minutes or until heated through. Serve with French toast; sprinkle with almonds.

BLUEBERRY-STUFFED FRENCH TOAST

PREP: 35 min. | **BAKE:** 15 min. | **YIELD:** 8 servings.

I came across this recipe in a local newspaper several years ago. The fruity French toast is great for company.
MYRNA KOLDENHOVEN SANBORN, IOWA

- 1-1/2 cups fresh *or* frozen blueberries
- 3 tablespoons sugar, *divided*
- 8 slices Italian bread (1-1/4 inches thick)
- 4 eggs, lightly beaten
- 1/2 cup orange juice
- 1 teaspoon grated orange peel

Dash salt

BLUEBERRY ORANGE SAUCE:

- 3 tablespoons sugar
- 1 tablespoon cornstarch
- 1/8 teaspoon salt
- 1/4 cup orange juice
- 1/4 cup water
- 1-1/2 cups orange segments
- 1 cup fresh *or* frozen blueberries
- 1/3 cup sliced almonds

In a small bowl, combine blueberries and 2 tablespoons sugar. Cut a pocket in the side of each slice of bread. Fill each pocket with about 3 tablespoons berry mixture.

In a shallow bowl, whisk the eggs, orange juice, orange peel, salt and remaining sugar. Carefully dip both sides of bread in egg mixture (do not squeeze out filling). Place in a

TROPICAL FRUIT SALAD

PREP/TOTAL TIME: 25 min. | **YIELD:** 8 servings.

This recipe makes an excellent breakfast or dessert. Toasted coconut, mango and more bring the flavor of the tropics indoors.
KATIE COVINGTON BLACKSBURG, SOUTH CAROLINA

- 1 medium mango, peeled and cubed
- 1 medium green apple, cubed
- 1 medium red apple, cubed
- 1 medium pear, cubed
- 1 medium navel orange, peeled and chopped
- 2 medium kiwifruit, peeled and chopped
- 10 seedless red grapes, halved
- 2 tablespoons orange juice
- 1 firm medium banana, sliced
- 1/4 cup flaked coconut, toasted

In a bowl, combine the first seven ingredients. Drizzle with orange juice; toss gently to coat. Refrigerate until serving. Just before serving, fold in banana and sprinkle with coconut.

NEW ORLEANS BEIGNETS

PREP: 15 min. | **COOK:** 35 min. | **YIELD:** 4 dozen.

These sweet French doughnuts are square instead of round and have no hole in the middle. They're a traditional part of breakfast in New Orleans.

BETH DAWSON JACKSON, LOUISIANA

- 1 package (1/4 ounce) active dry yeast
- 1/4 cup warm water (110° to 115°)
- 1 cup evaporated milk
- 1/2 cup canola oil
- 1/4 cup sugar
- 1 egg
- 4-1/2 cups self-rising flour

Oil for deep-fat frying

Confectioners' sugar

In a large bowl, dissolve yeast in warm water. Add the milk, oil, sugar and egg and 2 cups flour. Beat until smooth. Stir in enough remaining flour to form a soft dough (dough will be sticky). Do not knead. Cover and refrigerate overnight.

Punch dough down. Turn onto a floured surface; roll into a 16-in. x 12-in. rectangle. Cut into 2-in. squares.

In an electric skillet or deep-fat fryer, heat oil to 375°. Fry squares, a few at a time, until golden brown on both sides. Drain beignets on paper towels. Roll warm beignets in confectioners' sugar.

EDITOR'S NOTE: As a substitute for cup of self-rising flour, place 1-1/2 teaspoons baking powder and 1/2 teaspoon salt in a measuring cup. Add all-purpose flour to measure 1 cup.

SAUSAGE JOHNNYCAKE

PREP: 20 min. | **BAKE:** 35 min. | **YIELD:** 6 servings.

Here's a nice, hearty breakfast with plenty of Southern flavor. People love the cake's savory middle and maple syrup topping. It's a great way to start the day!

LORRAINE GUYN CALGARY, ALBERTA

- 1 cup cornmeal
- 2 cups buttermilk
- 12 uncooked breakfast sausage links
- 1-1/3 cups all-purpose flour
- 1/4 cup sugar
- 1-1/2 teaspoons baking powder
- 1/2 teaspoon baking soda
- 1/2 teaspoon salt
- 1/3 cup shortening
- 1 egg, lightly beaten
- 1/2 teaspoon vanilla extract

Maple syrup

In a large bowl, combine cornmeal and buttermilk; let stand for 10 minutes.

Meanwhile, in a skillet over medium heat, cook sausage until no longer pink; drain on paper towels. Arrange eight links in a spoke-like pattern in a greased 9-in. deep-dish pie plate. Cut remaining links in half; place between whole sausages.

In a large bowl, combine the flour, sugar, baking powder, baking soda and salt. Cut in shortening until the mixture resembles coarse crumbs.

Stir egg and vanilla extract into cornmeal mixture; add to dry ingredients and stir just until blended. Pour the batter over sausages.

Bake at 400° for 35-40 minutes or until a toothpick inserted near the center comes out clean. Serve warm with syrup.

SAUSAGE HASH SKILLET

PREP/TOTAL TIME: 30 min. | **YIELD:** 2 servings.

I created this recipe by trying to work with what I had in the refrigerator. Regular or spicy sausage can be used and red potatoes make it more colorful. **KARI CAVEN** POST FALLS, IDAHO

- 1/2 pound bulk pork sausage
- 2-1/2 cups cubed cooked potatoes
- 1 cup thinly sliced sweet onion
- 1 cup sliced fresh mushrooms
- 2 tablespoons butter
- 1/4 teaspoon salt
- 1/4 teaspoon pepper

In a large heavy skillet over medium heat, cook the sausage until no longer pink; drain and set aside.

In the same skillet, cook the potatoes, onion and mushrooms in butter until potatoes are lightly browned. Stir in the sausage, salt and pepper; heat through.

SUNSHINE CREPES

PREP: 15 min. + chilling | **COOK:** 15 min. | **YIELD:** 6 servings.

When I was in charge of hosting a family brunch, I whipped up these sweet and fruity crepes. Everyone loved the creamy citrus filling.
MARY HOBBS CAMPBELL, MISSOURI

- 2/3 cup milk
- 2 eggs
- 1 tablespoon canola oil
- 1/2 cup all-purpose flour
- 1 teaspoon sugar
- 1/4 teaspoon salt

FILLING:

- 1 can (20 ounces) crushed pineapple, drained
- 1 can (11 ounces) mandarin oranges, drained
- 1 teaspoon vanilla extract
- 1 carton (8 ounces) frozen whipped topping, thawed

Confectioners' sugar

In a large bowl, beat the milk, eggs and oil. Combine the flour, sugar and salt; add to milk mixture and mix well. Cover and refrigerate for 1 hour.

Coat an 8-in. nonstick skillet with cooking spray; heat over medium heat. Stir crepe batter; pour 2 tablespoons into center of skillet. Lift and tilt pan to coat bottom evenly. Cook until top appears dry; turn and cook 15-20 seconds longer. Remove to a wire rack. Repeat with remaining batter, coating skillet as needed. When cool, stack crepes with waxed paper or paper towels in between.

For filling, in a large bowl, combine the pineapple, oranges and vanilla; fold in whipped topping. Spoon 1/3 cup down the center of each crepe; roll up. Dust with confectioners' sugar.

PLAN AHEAD

Make extra crepes to fill and enjoy later. Place waxed paper between cooked, cooled crepes, cover and store in the fridge for up to 24 hours or in an airtight container in the freezer for up to 1 month. Throw in the fridge for 6 hours or overnight to thaw.
TASTE OF HOME TEST KITCHEN

BACON 'N' EGG GRAVY

PREP/TOTAL TIME: 20 min.
YIELD: 2 servings.

My husband created this breakfast gravy. It's a home-style and old-fashioned Southern favorite. Sometimes we ladle the gravy over tender homemade biscuits.
TERRY BRAY WINTER HAVEN, FLORIDA

- 6 bacon strips, diced
- 5 tablespoons all-purpose flour
- 1-1/2 cups water
- 1 can (12 ounces) evaporated milk
- 3 hard-cooked eggs, sliced

Salt and pepper to taste

- 4 slices bread, toasted

In a skillet, cook bacon over medium heat until crisp; remove to paper towels. Stir flour into the drippings until blended; cook over medium heat until browned, stirring constantly.

Gradually add water and milk. Bring to a boil. Cook; stir for 2 minutes or until thickened. Add bacon, eggs, salt and pepper. Serve over toast.

FRIED POTATOES

PREP/TOTAL TIME: 15 min. | **YIELD:** 3-4 servings.

Fried potatoes are a wonderful way to use up leftovers. Ready in just a few minutes, they taste great with breakfast or as a side dish for a homestyle supper. **TASTE OF HOME TEST KITCHEN**

> 3 cups diced cooked potatoes
> 1/2 cup diced onion
> 2 tablespoons butter
> Salt and pepper to taste

In a skillet, cook potatoes and onion in butter over medium heat for 10 minutes or until golden brown. Season with salt and pepper.

ANDOUILLE EGG BURRITOS

PREP/TOTAL TIME: 30 min. | **YIELD:** 6 servings.

Give yourself a morning wake-up call with these spicy burritos. They make a great on-the-go breakfast, but try them weeknights for a delicious and different dinner. **FRANK MILLARD** JANESVILLE, WISCONSIN

> 1/4 cup chopped onion
> 1 tablespoon butter
> 3/4 pound fully cooked andouille sausage links, sliced
> 1 tablespoon chopped green chilies
> 1 jalapeno pepper, seeded and chopped
> 8 eggs, lightly beaten
> 1/8 teaspoon salt
> 1/8 teaspoon pepper
> Dash cayenne pepper
> 6 flour tortillas (8 inches), warmed
> 3/4 cup shredded pepper jack cheese
> Taco sauce, optional

In a skillet over medium heat, cook onion in butter until tender. Add the sausage, chilies and jalapeno; cook 4-5 minutes longer or until heated through. Add the eggs, salt, pepper and cayenne; cook and stir until the eggs are completely set.

Spoon filling off center on each tortilla. Sprinkle each with 2 tablespoons cheese. Fold sides and ends over filling and roll up. Serve with taco sauce if desired.

SAUSAGE EGG BURRITOS: Omit the jalapeno pepper. Substitute bulk pork sausage for the andouille sausage and Monterey Jack cheese for the pepper jack cheese. Proceed as directed.

EDITOR'S NOTE: Wear disposable gloves when cutting hot peppers; the oils can burn skin. Avoid touching your face.

ANDOUILLE SAUSAGE 101

Unfamiliar with andouille sausage? This heavily smoked sausage is made of pork and garlic and is usually associated with Cajun dishes such as jambalaya and gumbo. It is sometimes referred to as "hot link" sausage because of its spicy flavor. If you can't find andouille sausage at your local grocery store, you can use kielbasa or any other smoked sausage. **TASTE OF HOME TEST KITCHEN**

ANDOUILLE EGG BURRITOS

APPLE FRITTERS

PREP: 15 min. | **COOK:** 30 min.
YIELD: 40 fritters.

My kids love these fritters year-round, but I get even more requests in the fall when there are plenty of apples in season. I like to serve them as a special breakfast treat when they have sleepovers.

KATIE BEECHY SEYMOUR, MISSOURI

- 2-1/2 cups all-purpose flour
- 1/2 cup nonfat dry milk powder
- 1/3 cup sugar
- 2 teaspoons baking powder
- 1 teaspoon salt
- 2 eggs
- 1 cup water
- 2 cups chopped peeled apples

Oil for deep-fat frying

Sugar

In a large bowl, combine the first five ingredients. Whisk eggs and water; add to dry ingredients just until moistened. Fold in apples.

In an electric skillet, heat oil to 375°. Drop batter by teaspoonfuls, a few at a time, in hot oil. Fry until golden brown, about 1-1/2 minutes on each side. Drain on paper towels. Roll warm fritters in sugar. Serve warm.

SWEET POTATO WAFFLES WITH NUT TOPPING

PREP: 20 min. | **COOK:** 5 min./batch | **YIELD:** 12 waffles.

Ready in just minutes, these deliciously different and tender waffles have a sweet and crunchy topping that's simply delectable. What a mouthwatering way to get your family out of bed in the morning!

CHRISTINE KEATING NORWALK, CALIFORNIA

- 2 cups biscuit/baking mix
- 2 tablespoons brown sugar
- 1/2 teaspoon ground cinnamon
- 1/4 teaspoon ground ginger
- 1/4 teaspoon ground nutmeg
- 1 egg
- 1-1/3 cups 2% milk
- 1 cup canned sweet potatoes, mashed
- 2 tablespoons canola oil
- 1 teaspoon vanilla extract

TOPPING:

- 1 tablespoon butter
- 1/2 cup chopped pecans
- 1/2 cup chopped walnuts
- 2 tablespoons brown sugar
- 1 tablespoon water
- 1/8 teaspoon ground cinnamon

Dash salt

Dash ground nutmeg

Maple syrup

In a large bowl, combine the biscuit mix, brown sugar and spices. In another bowl, whisk the egg, milk, sweet potatoes, oil and vanilla. Stir into dry ingredients just until combined.

Bake in a preheated waffle iron according to manufacturer's directions until golden brown.

Meanwhile, in a small skillet, melt butter over medium heat. Add pecans and walnuts. Cook and stir for 2 minutes. Add the brown sugar, water, cinnamon, salt and nutmeg. Cook and stir until sugar is dissolved. Serve waffles with topping and syrup.

SOUTHERN SCRAPPLE

PREP: 20 min. + chilling | **COOK:** 10 min.
YIELD: 8-10 servings.

When it comes to regional recipes, this certainly fits the bill. Scrapple is a breakfast staple in this area.
RUSTY LOVIN GREENSBORO, NORTH CAROLINA

- 1/2 **pound bulk pork sausage**
- 4 **cups water**
- 1 **cup grits**
- 1 **teaspoon salt**
- 1 **teaspoon pepper**
- Dash cayenne pepper
- 1/4 **cup butter, cubed**
- 1 **cup (4 ounces) shredded cheddar cheese**
- Additional butter
- Maple syrup

In a large skillet, cook sausage over medium heat until no longer pink; drain and set aside. In a large saucepan, bring water to a boil. Gradually add the grits, salt, pepper and cayenne, stirring constantly until thickened. Stir in butter and cheese until melted. Stir in sausage.

Press into a greased 9-in. x 5-in. loaf pan. Cover and refrigerate for 1 hour or until cool.

Remove scrapple from pan; cut into 1/2-in. slices. In a skillet, cook scrapple in butter until browned on both sides, adding more butter as needed. Serve warm with syrup.

SOUTHERN EGGS AND BISCUITS

PREP: 30 min. | **BAKE:** 25 min. | **YIELD:** 6-8 servings.

To me, nothing beats the flavor of Southern cooking, especially for breakfast! The rich flavor of these eggs served over homemade biscuits is a hearty way to start the day. **RUTH WARD** LEXINGTON, TENNESSEE

- 10 **hard-cooked eggs, sliced**
- 1 **pound sliced bacon, diced**
- 1/3 **cup all-purpose flour**
- 1/4 **teaspoon salt**
- 1/8 **teaspoon pepper**
- 4 **cups milk**
- 2 **cups cubed process cheese (Velveeta)**

BISCUITS:
- 1/2 **cup shortening**
- 3 **cups self-rising flour**
- 1-1/4 **cups buttermilk**

Place eggs in a greased 13-in. x 9-in. baking dish. In a large skillet, cook bacon until crisp. Drain, reserving 1/4 cup drippings. Sprinkle bacon over eggs.

Whisk the flour, salt and pepper into reserved drippings until smooth. Gradually add milk. Bring to a boil. Cook and stir for 2 minutes or until thickened and bubbly. Stir in cheese until melted; pour over eggs.

For biscuits, cut shortening into flour until mixture resembles coarse crumbs. Stir in buttermilk; gently knead six to eight times. Roll out on a lightly floured surface to 1/2-in. thickness. Cut with a 2-1/2-in. biscuit cutter and place on a greased baking sheet.

Bake biscuits and eggs at 400° for 25 minutes or until biscuits are golden brown. Serve eggs over biscuits.

CLUB SANDWICHES, PG. 63

BUTTER BEAN SALAD, PG. 58

SANDWICHES & SALADS

Kick back and relax with a no-fuss, casual meal that puts these Southern-style salads and sandwiches front and center. One bite and you'll agree: This duo is a match made in heaven.

CALICO BLACK BEAN SALAD

PREP: 15 min. + chilling | **YIELD:** 6 servings.

This salad reflects the Caribbean culture here in South Florida. The combination of black beans, tomatoes and onions with a vinaigrette is great alongside pork or chicken. It's perfect for picnics and convenient, too, since you can make it a day ahead. **LINDA HOLLAND** LANTANA, FLORIDA

2 cans (15 ounces *each*) black beans, rinsed and drained

4 green onions, thinly sliced

2 plum tomatoes, chopped

1 medium onion, chopped

1 large sweet red pepper, chopped

DRESSING:

2 tablespoons olive oil

2 tablespoons red wine vinegar

1 tablespoon lemon juice

1/2 teaspoon salt

1/4 teaspoon pepper

3/4 teaspoon minced fresh basil *or* 1/4 teaspoon dried basil

In a salad bowl, combine the black beans, green onions, tomatoes, onion and red pepper.

In a small bowl, whisk the dressing ingredients. Drizzle over vegetables and toss to coat. Cover and refrigerate for at least 1 hour before serving.

ITALIAN MUFFULETTA

PREP/TOTAL TIME: 25 min. | **YIELD:** 6 servings.

I first made this hearty sandwich for my husband, friends and family who were helping us build our deck. These sandwiches can be found all over New Orleans from delis to pool halls and the corner grocery stores. The olive spread is what makes it stand out. **DANA SCHMITT** AMES, IOWA

- 2/3 cup pimiento-stuffed olives, chopped
- 1 can (4-1/4 ounces) chopped ripe olives
- 6 tablespoons shredded Parmesan cheese
- 1/4 cup Italian salad dressing
- 2 teaspoons minced garlic
- 1 loaf (1 pound) Italian bread
- 1/2 pound sliced deli turkey
- 1/4 pound sliced Swiss cheese
- 1/4 pound thinly sliced hard salami
- 1/4 pound sliced provolone cheese
- 1/4 pound thinly sliced bologna

In a small bowl, combine the first five ingredients; set aside.

Cut bread in half horizontally; carefully hollow out top and bottom, leaving a 1-in. shell (discard removed bread or save for another use).

Spoon half of olive mixture over bottom half of bread. Layer with turkey, Swiss cheese, salami, provolone cheese, bologna and remaining olive mixture. Replace bread top. Cut into six wedges.

MARINATED TOMATOES

PREP: 10 min. + marinating
YIELD: 8 servings.

My niece introduced me to this colorful Southern specialty some time ago. I now make it when I have buffets or large gatherings because it can be prepared hours ahead.
MYRTLE MATTHEWS MARIETTA, GEORGIA

- 3 large fresh tomatoes, thickly sliced
- 1/3 cup olive oil
- 1/4 cup red wine vinegar
- 1 teaspoon salt, optional
- 1/4 teaspoon pepper
- 1/2 garlic clove, minced
- 2 tablespoons chopped onion
- 1 tablespoon minced fresh parsley
- 1 tablespoon minced fresh basil *or* 1 teaspoon dried basil

Arrange tomatoes in a large shallow dish. Combine remaining ingredients in a jar; cover tightly and shake well. Pour over tomato slices. Cover; refrigerate for several hours.

NEXT-GENERATION GERMAN POTATO SALAD

PREP/TOTAL TIME: 30 min. | **YIELD:** 14 servings.

My quick-cooking German-style potato salad is ideal for family reunions. Balsamic vinegar and bacon give it a different taste twist.

MARY SHIVERS ADA, OKLAHOMA

- 4 pounds small red potatoes, quartered
- 10 bacon strips, chopped
- 1 large onion, chopped
- 3 tablespoons chopped celery
- 2 tablespoons chopped green pepper
- 1 tablespoon all-purpose flour
- 1 tablespoon sugar
- 1 teaspoon salt
- 1/2 teaspoon pepper
- 1 cup water
- 1/3 cup white balsamic vinegar

Place the potatoes in a Dutch oven and cover with water. Bring to a boil. Reduce heat; cover and simmer for 15-20 minutes or until tender.

Meanwhile, in a skillet, cook bacon over medium heat until crisp. Using a slotted spoon, remove to paper towels. In the drippings, saute the onion, celery and green pepper until tender. Stir in the flour, sugar, salt and pepper until blended.

Combine water and vinegar; stir into vegetable mixture. Bring to a boil; cook and stir for 2 minutes or until thickened.

Drain potatoes and place in a large serving bowl. Pour dressing over potatoes. Add bacon and toss to coat. Serve warm or at room temperature. Refrigerate leftovers.

COUNTRY HAM SANDWICHES

PREP/TOTAL TIME: 5 min. | **YIELD:** 2 servings.

Perfect for lunches or a quick weeknight dinner when there's no time for a big meal. Smoked cheddar and a creamy garlic-infused spread lend special appeal to this hand-held dinner.

JENNIFER PARHAM BROWNS SUMMIT, NORTH CAROLINA

- 2 tablespoons mayonnaise
- 2 tablespoons sour cream
- 1/8 teaspoon garlic powder
- 4 slices whole wheat bread
- 2 ounces smoked cheddar cheese, sliced
- 4 slices tomato
- 4 ounces thinly sliced deli ham
- 2 lettuce leaves

In a small bowl, combine the mayonnaise, sour cream and garlic powder. Spread over two slices of bread. Layer each with cheese, tomato, ham and lettuce. Top with remaining bread.

HOT BROWN SANDWICHES

PREP/TOTAL TIME: 25 min. | **YIELD:** 8 servings.

You can prepare these open-faced turkey sandwiches with leftover turkey or cooked turkey from the deli counter.

TASTE OF HOME TEST KITCHEN

1/4 cup butter
1/4 cup all-purpose flour
1 cup milk
1 cup chicken broth
1/2 teaspoon Worcestershire
   sauce
3/4 cup shredded cheddar cheese
1/4 teaspoon salt
1/8 teaspoon white pepper
8 slices Italian bread
   (1/2 inch thick), toasted

1-1/2 pounds sliced cooked turkey
8 cooked bacon strips, halved
2 medium tomatoes, sliced
1 cup (4 ounces) shredded Parmesan cheese

In a large saucepan, melt butter over low heat. Stir in flour until smooth; gradually add milk, broth and Worcestershire sauce. Bring to a boil; cook and stir for 2 minutes or until thickened. Stir in the cheese, salt and white pepper until cheese is melted. Remove from the heat.

Place slices of toast on a baking sheet. Layer each with turkey, cheese sauce, bacon, tomatoes and Parmesan cheese. Broil 3-4 in. from the heat for 3-4 minutes or until cheese is melted.

AMBROSIA FRUIT SALAD

PREP/TOTAL TIME: 10 min.
YIELD: 6 servings.

I make this fresh, creamy salad with plenty of fruit, yogurt for dressing, then mix in just enough goodies (marshmallows and coconut) so it tastes like the rich version I grew up with.

TRISHA KRUSE EAGLE, IDAHO

- 1 can (8-1/4 ounces) fruit cocktail, drained
- 1 can (8 ounces) unsweetened pineapple chunks, drained
- 1 cup green grapes
- 1 cup seedless red grapes
- 1 cup miniature marshmallows
- 1 medium banana, sliced
- 3/4 cup vanilla yogurt
- 1/2 cup flaked coconut

In a bowl, combine all the ingredients.

SAUCY FISH SANDWICHES

PREP: 10 min. + chilling | **COOK:** 10 min. | **YIELD:** 6 servings.

You'll be hooked on these homemade fish sandwiches. The golden cornmeal breading coats the fillets nicely, and the sauce is tangy.

ELIZABETH LEBLANC BOURG, LOUISIANA

- 1 cup mayonnaise
- 1/3 cup ketchup
- 1 teaspoon dried parsley flakes
- 1 teaspoon dried minced onion
- 1/2 teaspoon Worcestershire sauce
- 1/4 to 1/2 teaspoon hot pepper sauce
- 1/8 teaspoon garlic powder
- 1/2 cup all-purpose flour
- 1/2 cup yellow cornmeal
- 1 teaspoon salt
- 1/8 teaspoon pepper
- 1/8 teaspoon cayenne pepper
- 1 egg
- 1/2 cup milk
- 6 panfish *or* cod fillets (about 1 pound)

Canola oil

- 6 hamburger buns, split

Lettuce leaves

In a small bowl, combine the first seven ingredients; cover and chill at least 1 hour. In a shallow bowl, combine the flour, cornmeal, salt, pepper and cayenne pepper. In another shallow bowl, beat egg and milk. Cut fish to fit buns; dip fillets into egg mixture, then coat with flour mixture.

In a skillet, brown fish in a small amount of oil for 3-5 minutes on each side or until fish flakes easily with a fork. Serve on buns with lettuce and sauce.

BLACK-EYED PEA SALAD

PREP/TOTAL TIME: 10 min. | **YIELD:** 4 servings.

I've had a lot of compliments and requests for this recipe over the years. It's especially great on hot days, and the Italian salad dressing keeps the avocado from turning dark. **NANCY CARIKER** BAKERSFIELD, CALIFORNIA

> 1 can (15-1/2 ounces) black-eyed peas, rinsed and drained
> 1 large tomato, diced
> 1 medium ripe avocado, peeled and diced
> 1/3 cup chopped green pepper
> 2 green onions, chopped
> 1 tablespoon minced fresh cilantro
> 1 jalapeno pepper, seeded and chopped
> 1/3 cup Italian salad dressing

In a large serving bowl, combine all the ingredients; toss to coat. Serve with a slotted spoon.

BLACK-EYED PEA CORN SALAD: Omit the tomato, avocado, green pepper and green onions. Add 2 cups corn and 1/4 cup chopped red onion to the salad mixture.

EDITOR'S NOTE: Wear disposable gloves when cutting hot peppers; the oils can burn skin. Avoid touching your face.

SLOW-COOKED PORK BARBECUE

PREP: 15 min. | **COOK:** 5 hours | **YIELD:** 10 servings.

I need only five ingredients to fix this sweet and tender pork for sandwiches. I think it's perfect just the way it is, but feel free to adjust the sauce ingredients to suit your family's tastes.

CONNIE JOHNSON SPRINGFIELD, MISSOURI

> 1 boneless pork loin roast (3 to 4 pounds)
> 1-1/2 teaspoons seasoned salt
> 1 teaspoon garlic powder
> 1 cup barbecue sauce
> 1 cup cola
> 10 sandwich buns, split

Cut roast in half; place in a 5-qt. slow cooker. Sprinkle with seasoned salt and garlic powder. Cover and cook on low for 4-5 hours or until meat is tender.

Remove meat; skim fat from cooking juices. Shred the meat with two forks ; return to the slow cooker. Combine barbecue sauce and cola; pour over meat. Cover and cook on high for 1-2 hours or until sauce is thickened. Serve on rolls.

SHRIMP 'N' SLAW PUFFS

PREP/TOTAL TIME: 15 min. | **YIELD:** 4 servings.

Coleslaw mix and bottled dressing cut the prep time for this colorful and delicious sandwich filling to practically nothing! Serving the shrimp mixture in cream puff shells gives the presentation a slightly upscale feel.

TASTE OF HOME TEST KITCHEN

- 1/2 pound cooked small shrimp, peeled, deveined and chopped
- 2 cups coleslaw mix
- 2 tablespoons chopped green onion
- 2 tablespoons chopped sweet yellow pepper
- 1/4 cup coleslaw salad dressing
- 1 tablespoon capers, drained and patted dry
- 1 teaspoon snipped fresh dill *or* 1/4 teaspoon dill weed
- 1/4 teaspoon salt
- 1/4 teaspoon pepper
- 4 cream puff shells

In a large bowl, combine the shrimp, coleslaw mix, onion and yellow pepper. In a small bowl, combine the coleslaw dressing, capers, dill, salt and pepper. Pour over shrimp mixture and gently toss to coat.

Refrigerate until serving. Just before serving, spoon 1/2 cup shrimp salad into each cream puff; replace tops.

RASPBERRY CONGEALED SALAD

PREP: 20 min. + chilling | **YIELD:** 6 servings.

My sisters and I especially enjoyed Mom's cool tangy side dish, which looks so lovely on the table. The pineapple and raspberries are a delectable duo, and pecans add a hearty crunch. **NANCY DUTY** JACKSONVILLE, FLORIDA

- 1 can (8 ounces) crushed pineapple
- 1 package (12 ounces) frozen unsweetened raspberries, thawed
- 1 package (3 ounces) raspberry gelatin
- 1 cup applesauce
- 1/4 cup coarsely chopped pecans

Mayonnaise, optional

Drain pineapple and raspberries, reserving juices. Place fruit in a large bowl; set aside. Add enough water to the juice to measure 1 cup. Pour into a saucepan; bring to a boil. Remove from the heat; stir in gelatin until dissolved.

Pour over the fruit mixture. Add the applesauce and pecans. Pour into a 1-qt. bowl. Chill until set. Spoon into individual dessert dishes; top with a dollop of mayonnaise if desired.

HOW TO PEEL & DEVEIN SHRIMP

Start on the underside by the head area to remove shell from shrimp. Pull legs and first section of shell to one side. Continue pulling shell up around the top and to the other side. Pull off shell by tail if desired. Remove the black vein running down the back of shrimp by making a shallow slit with a paring knife along the back from head area to tail. Rinse shrimp under cold water to remove the vein.

TASTE OF HOME TEST KITCHEN

RASPBERRY CONGEALED SALAD

HONEY PECAN & GOAT CHEESE SALAD

PREP/TOTAL TIME: 25 min. | **YIELD:** 4 servings.

Skip the ordinary house salad and try this innovative combination instead. The contrast of the sweet and crunchy pecans with the tangy, lightly toasted goat cheese is absolutely delectable. **GREG FONTENOT** THE WOODLANDS, TEXAS

- 1/2 cup chopped pecans
- 2 teaspoons plus 1 tablespoon honey, *divided*
- 1/3 cup plus 3 tablespoons olive oil, *divided*
- 2 tablespoons balsamic vinegar
- 1/2 teaspoon salt
- 1/8 teaspoon pepper
- 1/4 cup all-purpose flour
- 1 egg, beaten
- 3/4 cup seasoned bread crumbs
- 8 ounces fresh goat cheese
- 4 cups spring mix salad greens

In a shallow microwave-safe dish, combine pecans and 2 teaspoons honey; microwave, uncovered, on high for 1-1/2 to 2 minutes or until toasted, stirring twice. Immediately transfer to a waxed paper-lined baking sheet to cool. For dressing, in a small bowl, whisk 1/3 cup oil, vinegar, remaining honey, salt and pepper; set aside.

Place the flour, egg and bread crumbs in separate shallow bowls. Shape cheese into eight balls; flatten slightly. Coat cheese with flour, then dip in egg and coat with bread crumbs.

Heat remaining oil in a large skillet over medium-high heat. Fry cheese for 1-2 minutes on each side or until golden brown. Drain on paper towels.

Divide salad greens among four plates; top with cheese. Drizzle with dressing and sprinkle with honey pecans.

FRIED GREEN TOMATO SANDWICHES

PREP/TOTAL TIME: 20 min. | **YIELD:** 6 sandwiches.

This is one of my favorite quick-to-fix suppers. If you've never tried fried green tomatoes, give them a shot with these sandwiches.

MARY ANN BOSTIC SINKS GROVE, WEST VIRGINIA

- 1/4 cup all-purpose flour
- 1/4 teaspoon *each* garlic powder, salt, pepper and paprika
- 3 medium green tomatoes, sliced
- 12 bacon strips
- 12 slices sourdough bread, toasted
- 6 slices provolone cheese

Leaf lettuce, mayonnaise and Dijon mustard

In a shallow dish, combine flour and seasonings; dip tomatoes in the mixture and set aside. In a large skillet, cook bacon over medium heat until crisp.

Remove to paper towels to drain. In the drippings, cook tomatoes for 2 minutes on each side; drain on paper towels.

Place six slices of toast on a baking sheet. Layer with three tomato slices, two bacon strips and a cheese slice. Broil 3-4 in. from the heat for 3-4 minutes or until cheese is melted. Top with lettuce if desired.

Spread the mayonnaise and mustard on remaining toast if desired; place over lettuce.

HONEY MUSTARD SALAD DRESSING

PREP/TOTAL TIME: 5 min.
YIELD: about 1/2 cup dressing.

I remember when I first tried this flavorful dressing—it's been a favorite ever since and one I serve almost exclusively. It's quick to prepare and easily made.

PATTY BREWER KANSAS CITY, MISSOURI

- 6 tablespoons mayonnaise
- 2 tablespoons Dijon mustard
- 2 tablespoons honey

Assorted salad greens, tomatoes and croutons

In a bowl, combine the mayonnaise, mustard and honey; mix well. Store in refrigerator. Serve over salad.

SWEET 'N' SOUR COLESLAW

PREP/TOTAL TIME: 5 min. | **YIELD:** 4 servings.

My coleslaw is a cinch to make—it takes only five minutes and brings bright flavor and crunch to the menu. This was my mother's recipe; I'm reminded of her every time I make it. **BARBARA KEITH** FAUCETT, MISSOURI

- 5-1/2 cups coleslaw mix
- 1/2 cup heavy whipping cream
- 1/3 cup sugar
- 3 tablespoons white vinegar
- 1/2 teaspoon salt

Place coleslaw mix in a serving bowl. In a small bowl, combine the remaining ingredients. Pour over coleslaw mix and toss to coat. Chill until serving.

BUTTER BEAN SALAD

PREP/TOTAL TIME: 15 min. | **YIELD:** 8 servings.

Here's a nice summery side that includes flavorful olive oil and tastes fresh, even though it uses canned beans. It's sure to perk up any picnic spread.
SANDRA JACKSON MOBILE, ALABAMA

- 1 can (15-1/4 ounces) lima beans, rinsed and drained
- 1 can (16 ounces) butter beans, rinsed and drained
- 1 large sweet red pepper, chopped
- 1 medium green pepper, chopped
- 1 large onion, chopped
- 4 garlic cloves, minced
- 1/4 cup lemon juice
- 1/4 cup olive oil
- 2 tablespoons cider vinegar
- 2 teaspoons ground cumin
- 1/4 teaspoon pepper

In a large bowl, combine the beans, peppers, onion and garlic. In a small bowl, combine the remaining ingredients. Pour over bean mixture and toss to coat. Chill until serving.

AVOCADO CHICKEN SALAD

PREP/TOTAL TIME: 20 min. | **YIELD:** 5 servings.

This is the first time I've ever shared this recipe, but it's a dish that my family and friends request for every event we have! I sometimes serve it in pita bread for a filling grab-and-go lunch.
KARLENE JOHNSON MOORESVILLE, NORTH CAROLINA

- 1 medium ripe avocado, peeled and cubed
- 2 tablespoons lemon juice, *divided*
- 2 cups cubed cooked chicken
- 2 cups seedless red grapes, halved
- 1 medium tart apple, chopped
- 1 cup chopped celery
- 3/4 cup mayonnaise
- 1/2 cup chopped walnuts, toasted
- 1/2 teaspoon ground ginger

Lettuce leaves, optional

In a small bowl, toss avocado with 1 tablespoon lemon juice; set aside. In a large bowl, combine the chicken, grapes, apple, celery, mayonnaise, walnuts, ginger and remaining lemon juice. Stir in avocado. Serve on lettuce-lined plates if desired.

SHRIMP PO' BOYS

PREP: 30 min. | **COOK:** 15 min. | **YIELD:** 8 servings.

These sandwiches will add a touch of Louisiana flair to your next get-together. You can adjust the cayenne pepper to suit your taste. **BETTY JEAN JORDAN** MONTICELLO, GEORGIA

1/2 cup mayonnaise

1/2 cup finely chopped onion

1/2 cup chopped dill pickles

1-1/3 cups all-purpose flour

1 teaspoon salt

4 eggs, *separated*

1-1/3 cups 2% milk

2 tablespoons canola oil

8 French sandwich rolls, split

Additional oil for deep-fat frying

2 pounds uncooked large shrimp, peeled and deveined

Cayenne pepper to taste

4 cups shredded lettuce

16 tomato slices

In a bowl, combine the mayonnaise, onion and pickles; set aside. For batter, combine flour and salt in a bowl. Add the egg yolks, milk and oil; beat until smooth.

In a small bowl, beat egg whites until stiff peaks form; fold in batter.

Wrap sandwich rolls in foil. Bake at 350° for 10 minutes or until warmed. Meanwhile, in a large skillet or deep-fat fryer, heat 1/2 in. of oil to 375°. Dip shrimp in batter; fry for 2-3 minutes on each side or until golden brown. Drain on paper towels; sprinkle with cayenne.

Spread mayonnaise mixture over rolls; top with lettuce, tomato and shrimp.

ARKANSAS TRAVELERS

PREP/TOTAL TIME: 15 min. | **YIELD:** 6 servings.

I came across this club-style sandwich in a tearoom in Arkansas. I brought the recipe back home, much to the delight of my husband and our two sons. **ROBI KASTNER** SPRINGFIELD, MISSOURI

 1 pound turkey breast
 1 block (5 ounces) Swiss cheese
 1 avocado, peeled and pitted
 1 large tomato
10 bacon strips, cooked and crumbled
1/3 to 1/2 cup ranch salad dressing
12 slices whole wheat bread, toasted

Chop turkey, cheese, avocado and tomato into 1/4-in. cubes; place in a large bowl. Add bacon and dressing. Spoon 1/2 cup between two slices of toast.

TOMATO FETA SALAD

PREP/TOTAL TIME: 20 min. | **YIELD:** 4 servings.

One summer I combined onions with a bumper crop of tomatoes and a homemade balsamic dressing. The result was this salad that receives thumbs-up approval whenever it's served. **ROBERT GOLUS** GREER, SOUTH CAROLINA

 2 tablespoons balsamic vinegar
1-1/2 teaspoons minced fresh basil *or* 1/2 teaspoon dried basil
1/2 teaspoon salt
1/2 cup coarsely chopped sweet onion
 1 pound grape *or* cherry tomatoes, halved
 2 tablespoons olive oil
1/4 cup crumbled feta cheese

In a large bowl, combine the vinegar, basil and salt. Add onion; toss to coat. Let stand for 5 minutes. Add the tomatoes, oil and feta cheese; toss to coat. Serve with a slotted spoon.

FREEZE THE EXTRA

When I have a bunch of fresh basil that I can't use right away, I finely chop the extra, stir it into some oil and freeze the mixture. When I want some basil-seasoned oil in a recipe, I simply use a fork to remove some from the container.
FAYE H. GRESHAM, OREGON

TOMATO FETA SALAD

TUNA SALAD WRAPS

PREP/TOTAL TIME: 15 min. | **YIELD:** 6 servings.

Usually I make my tuna salad the night before, so the flavors have more time to blend. Plus, the sandwiches go together quickly for a neat and compact meal. **IVY ABBADESSA** LOXAHATCHEE, FLORIDA

- 1 large cucumber, seeded and finely chopped
- 1/4 cup finely chopped red onion
- 1 tablespoon minced fresh parsley
- 2 teaspoons grated lemon peel
- 1/4 teaspoon seasoned salt
- 1/4 cup reduced-fat Italian salad dressing
- 1 can (12 ounces) light water-packed tuna, drained and flaked
- 1/4 cup reduced-fat mayonnaise
- 1/4 cup chopped celery
- 1/4 cup chopped green onions
- 6 flour tortillas (8 inches), room temperature

In a small bowl, combine the first six ingredients. In another bowl, combine the tuna, mayonnaise, celery and green onions.

Spread 1/4 cup tuna mixture over each tortilla; top with 1/3 cup cucumber mixture. Fold in sides of tortillas and roll up.

CLUB SANDWICHES

PREP/TOTAL TIME: 25 min. | **YIELD:** 4 servings.

My family looks forward to having a sandwich we call "hunka munka." The layered sandwich is a satisfying, complete meal.

JANET MILLER MIDLAND, TEXAS

- 1/2 cup mayonnaise
- 4 French rolls, split
- 1 cup shredded lettuce
- 8 slices tomato
- 1 medium ripe avocado, peeled and sliced
- 1/4 cup prepared Italian salad dressing
- 1/2 teaspoon coarsely ground pepper
- 12 cooked bacon strips
- 1/2 pound sliced deli turkey
- 1/2 pound sliced deli ham
- 4 slices Swiss cheese

Spread mayonnaise over cut sides of rolls. On roll bottoms, layer the lettuce, tomato and avocado. Drizzle with dressing; sprinkle with pepper. Layer with bacon, turkey, ham and cheese. Replace roll tops.

HONEY POPPY SEED DRESSING

PREP/TOTAL TIME: 5 min.
YIELD: 3/4 cup.

We use this slightly sweet and tangy dressing on fresh fruit salads because it blends so well with the fruits' flavors. It's also delicious drizzled over assorted veggies.

ABIGAIL STAUFFER
PORT TREVORTON, PENNSYLVANIA

- 1/3 cup canola oil
- 1/4 cup honey
- 2 tablespoons cider vinegar
- 2 teaspoons poppy seeds
- 1/2 teaspoon salt

Fresh fruit *or* mixed greens

In a jar with a tight-fitting lid, combine the first five ingredients. Cover and shake well.

Store in the refrigerator until serving. Serve with fruit or mixed greens.

CAJUN CATFISH SANDWICHES

AVOCADO SALAD DRESSING

PREP/TOTAL TIME: 10 min. | **YIELD:** 2 cups.

Buttermilk and fat-free yogurt create the base for this creamy and delicious dressing. The avocado, parsley and dill add fresh flavor, making it an easy choice for topping pasta or veggie salads. **TASTE OF HOME TEST KITCHEN**

1 cup buttermilk

1/2 cup fat-free plain yogurt

1 ripe avocado, peeled and sliced

2 green onions, chopped

1/4 cup minced fresh parsley

1/2 teaspoon salt

1/2 teaspoon garlic powder

1/4 teaspoon dill weed

1/8 teaspoon pepper

In a blender, combine all ingredients; cover and process until blended. Transfer to a jar with a tight-fitting lid or small bowl. Serve immediately or refrigerate.

CAJUN CATFISH SANDWICHES

PREP/TOTAL TIME: 25 min. | **YIELD:** 4 servings.

This spicy bistro-style sandwich makes such a no-fuss summertime supper. Serve alongside your favorite vegetable side dish and enjoy. **SHAUNIECE FRAZIER** LOS ANGELES, CALIFORNIA

3/4 teaspoon seasoned pepper

1/2 teaspoon chili powder

1/2 teaspoon cayenne pepper

1/4 teaspoon seasoned salt

4 catfish fillets (4 ounces *each*)

2 teaspoons olive oil, *divided*

2 green onions, chopped

3 garlic cloves, minced

1/2 cup fat-free mayonnaise

4 French *or* kaiser rolls, split and toasted

4 romaine leaves

Combine the seasoned pepper, chili powder, cayenne and seasoned salt; sprinkle over fillets.

In a large skillet, cook fillets in 1 teaspoon oil for 4-6 minutes on each side or until fish flakes easily with a fork. Remove and keep warm.

In the same skillet, saute onions in remaining oil until onions are tender. Add garlic; cook 1 minute longer. Remove from the heat; stir in mayonnaise. Spread over rolls; top each with a romaine leaf and fillet. Replace tops.

IS IT DONE YET?

Overcooked fish loses its flavor and becomes tough. As a general guideline, fish is cooked 10 minutes for every inch of thickness. For fish fillets, check for doneness by inserting a fork at an angle into the thickest portion of the fish and gently parting the meat. When it is opaque and flakes into sections, it is cooked completely.

TASTE OF HOME TEST KITCHEN

OKRA AND BUTTER BEAN STEW, PG. 72

SOUPS, STEWS & CHILI

Ladle on the Southern hospitality with these soothing soups, stews and chili favorites. Enjoy everything from Cajun-style gumbo that delivers a fiery kick to old-fashioned chicken and dumplings that will remind you of dear ol' Grandma.

CREOLE JAMBALAYA, PG. 69

SWEET POTATO CHILI BAKE

PREP: 30 min. | **BAKE:** 20 min. | **YIELD:** 7 servings.

I'm a vegetarian and wanted to develop some dishes that are a little heartier than traditional meatless fare.

JILLIAN TOURNOUX MASSILLON, OHIO

- 2 cups cubed peeled sweet potato
- 1 medium sweet red pepper, chopped
- 1 tablespoon olive oil
- 1 garlic clove, minced
- 1 can (28 ounces) diced tomatoes, undrained
- 2 cups vegetable broth
- 1 can (15 ounces) black beans, rinsed and drained
- 4-1/2 teaspoons brown sugar
- 3 teaspoons chili powder
- 1 teaspoon salt
- 1/2 teaspoon pepper
- 1 package (6-1/2 ounces) corn bread/muffin mix
- 1/2 cup shredded cheddar cheese

Optional toppings: sour cream, shredded cheddar cheese and chopped seeded jalapeno pepper

In an ovenproof Dutch oven, saute sweet potato and red pepper in oil until crisp-tender. Add garlic; cook 1 minute longer. Add the tomatoes, broth, beans, brown sugar, chili powder, salt and pepper. Bring to a boil. Reduce heat; simmer, uncovered, for 15-20 minutes or until potatoes are tender.

Meanwhile, prepare corn bread batter according to package directions; stir in cheese. Drop by tablespoonfuls over chili.

Cover and bake at 400° for 18-20 minutes or until a toothpick inserted near the center comes out clean. Serve with toppings of your choice.

EDITOR'S NOTE: Wear disposable gloves when cutting hot peppers; the oils can burn skin. Avoid touching your face.

CREOLE JAMBALAYA

PREP: 20 min. | **COOK:** 35 min. | **YIELD:** 8 servings.

Creole jambalaya, also known as red jambalaya, is a traditional Louisiana dish with deep roots in French and Spanish cuisines. Tomatoes, seafood, rice, onions, green peppers and celery are the key ingredients in this Southern favorite. Most recipes also call for chicken or sausage, but mine uses ham for a unique taste twist.

RUBY WILLIAMS BOGALUSA, LOUISIANA

- 3/4 cup chopped onion
- 1/2 cup chopped celery
- 1/4 cup chopped green pepper
- 2 tablespoons butter
- 2 garlic cloves, minced
- 2 cups cubed fully cooked ham
- 1 can (28 ounces) diced tomatoes, undrained
- 1 can (10-1/2 ounces) condensed beef broth, undiluted
- 1 cup uncooked long grain white rice
- 1 cup water
- 1 teaspoon sugar
- 1 teaspoon dried thyme
- 1/2 teaspoon chili powder
- 1/4 teaspoon pepper
- 1-1/2 pounds fresh *or* frozen uncooked shrimp, peeled and deveined
- 1 tablespoon minced fresh parsley

In a Dutch oven, saute the onion, celery and green pepper in butter until tender. Add garlic; cook 1 minute longer. Add the next nine ingredients; bring to a boil. Reduce heat; cover and simmer until rice is tender, about 25 minutes.

Add shrimp and parsley; simmer, uncovered, for 7-10 minutes or until shrimp turn pink.

SUBSTITUTION SAVVY

Out of fresh garlic bulbs? No problem. You can substitute 1/4 teaspoon of garlic powder for each clove called for in the recipe. Next time you're shopping, look for convenient jars of fresh minced garlic in the produce section. Use 1/2 teaspoon of minced garlic for each clove.
TASTE OF HOME TEST KITCHEN

SUMMER STRAWBERRY SOUP

PREP: 15 min. + chilling
YIELD: 6 servings.

You'll be amazed that just five ingredients can create something so spectacular! This fruity chilled soup is certain to become a new summertime favorite.

VERNA BOLLIN POWELL, TENNESSEE

- 2 cups vanilla yogurt
- 1/2 cup orange juice
- 2 pounds fresh strawberries, halved (8 cups)
- 1/2 cup sugar
- Additional vanilla yogurt and fresh mint leaves, optional

In a blender, combine vanilla yogurt, orange juice, strawberries and sugar in batches. Cover; process until blended. Refrigerate for at least 2 hours. Garnish with additional yogurt and mint leaves if desired.

BAKED POTATO SOUP

PREP: 35 min. | **COOK:** 6 hours | **YIELD:** 10 servings.

The only thing that beats the comforting flavor of this thick and hearty potato soup is possibly the idea that it simmers on its own all day.

BARBARA BLEIGH COLONIAL HGTS., VIRGINIA

- 2 large onions, chopped
- 3 tablespoons butter
- 2 tablespoons all-purpose flour
- 2 cups water, *divided*
- 4 cups chicken broth
- 2 medium potatoes, peeled and diced
- 1-1/2 cups mashed potato flakes
- 1/2 pound sliced bacon, cooked and crumbled
- 3/4 teaspoon pepper
- 1/2 teaspoon salt
- 1/2 teaspoon dried basil
- 1/8 teaspoon dried thyme
- 1 cup half-and-half cream
- 1/2 cup shredded cheddar cheese
- 2 green onions, sliced

In a skillet, saute onions in butter until tender. Stir in flour. Gradually stir in 1 cup water. Bring to a boil; cook and stir for 2 minutes or until thickened. Transfer to a 5-qt. slow cooker.

Add the broth, potatoes, potato flakes, bacon, pepper, salt, basil, thyme and remaining water. Cover and cook on low for 6-8 hours or until potatoes are tender. Stir in cream; heat through. Garnish with cheese and green onions.

CREAM OF TOMATO SOUP

PREP: 30 min. + cooling | **COOK:** 5 min.
YIELD: 3 servings (3-1/2 cups).

I learned to make this comforting soup in my high-school home economics class. I've fixed it quite often since then, and I find it's wonderful made with ripe garden tomatoes. **GAIL HARRIS** RAMER, TENNESSEE

- 2-1/2 cups diced peeled tomatoes
- 1/4 cup diced celery
- 1/4 cup diced onion
- 1 tablespoon canola oil
- 2 tablespoons all-purpose flour
- 1 cup evaporated milk
- 1 teaspoon salt, optional
- 1/8 teaspoon pepper
- 3 tablespoons sour cream
- 3 teaspoons minced fresh parsley

In a saucepan, combine tomatoes, celery and onion; bring to a boil. Reduce heat; cover and simmer for 15 minutes, stirring often. Cool for 10 minutes; pour into a blender. Cover and process until smooth.

In a large saucepan, heat oil; stir in flour until smooth. Gradually add the milk; bring to a boil. Cook and stir for 2 minutes. Gradually stir in tomato mixture. Add salt if desired and pepper; heat through. Top individual servings with sour cream and parsley.

ANDOUILLE-SHRIMP CREAM SOUP

PREP: 20 min. | **COOK:** 30 min. | **YIELD:** 7 servings.

The bold flavor of andouille sausage blends beautifully with the shrimp and subtle spices in this variation on a creamy southern Louisiana corn stew. **JUDY ARMSTRONG** PRAIRIEVILLE, LOUISIANA

1/2 pound fully cooked andouille
    sausage links, thinly sliced

1 medium onion, chopped

2 celery ribs, thinly sliced

1 medium sweet red
    pepper, chopped

1 medium green pepper,
    chopped

1 jalapeno pepper, seeded
    and chopped

1/4 cup butter, cubed

3 garlic cloves, minced

2 cups fresh *or* frozen
    corn, thawed

4 medium roma tomatoes,
    chopped

1 cup vegetable broth

2 tablespoons minced fresh thyme *or* 2 teaspoons dried thyme

1 teaspoon chili powder

1/2 teaspoon salt

1/2 teaspoon pepper

1/4 to 1/2 teaspoon cayenne pepper

1 pound uncooked medium shrimp, peeled and deveined

1 cup heavy whipping cream

In a large skillet, saute the first six ingredients in butter until vegetables are tender. Add garlic; cook 1 minute longer. Add the corn, tomatoes, broth, thyme, chili powder, salt, pepper and cayenne. Bring to a boil. Reduce heat; simmer, uncovered, for 10 minutes.

Stir in shrimp and cream. Bring to a gentle boil. Simmer, uncovered, for 8-10 minutes or until shrimp turn pink.

EDITOR'S NOTE: Wear disposable gloves when cutting hot peppers; the oils can burn skin. Avoid touching your face.

LIMA BEAN OKRA SOUP

PREP: 20 min. | **COOK:** 15 min.
YIELD: 7 servings.

The unique flavor in this soup comes from the combination of vegetables with sweet spices.
CLARA COULSON MINNEY WASHINGTON COURT HOUSE, OHIO

- 1 medium green pepper, chopped
- 1 medium onion, chopped
- 1/4 teaspoon whole cloves
- 1 tablespoon butter
- 3 cups vegetable broth
- 3 cups chopped tomatoes
- 2-1/2 cups sliced fresh *or* frozen okra, thawed
- 1 cup frozen lima beans, thawed
- 1/2 cup fresh *or* frozen corn, thawed
- 1/2 to 1 teaspoon salt
- 1/4 to 1/2 teaspoon ground allspice
- 1/4 teaspoon pepper
- 1/8 teaspoon cayenne pepper

In a large saucepan, saute the green pepper, onion and cloves in butter until vegetables are tender. Discard cloves.

Stir in the remaining ingredients. Bring to a boil. Reduce heat; cover and simmer for 15-20 minutes or until beans are tender.

OKRA AND BUTTER BEAN STEW

PREP: 25 min. | **COOK:** 45 min. | **YIELD:** 12 servings (1 cup each).

I adapted this stew from my mom's down-home Louisiana recipe. It turns okra-haters into okra-lovers—guaranteed!
KAYA MACK WICHITA FALLS, TEXAS

- 7 bacon strips, chopped
- 1 pound smoked sausage, halved and thinly sliced
- 1 large onion, chopped
- 2 small green peppers, chopped
- 3 cups water
- 2 cans (16 ounces *each*) butter beans, rinsed and drained
- 1 can (14-1/2 ounces) diced tomatoes, undrained
- 1 can (12 ounces) tomato paste
- 1 teaspoon pepper
- 1/4 teaspoon salt
- 1 package (16 ounces) frozen sliced okra

Hot cooked rice, optional

In a Dutch oven, cook bacon and sausage over medium heat until bacon is crisp. Remove to paper towels; drain, reserving 2 tablespoons drippings.

Cook onion and green peppers in the drippings until tender. Stir in the water, beans, tomatoes, tomato paste, pepper and salt. Bring to a boil. Reduce heat; simmer, uncovered, for 10 minutes. Add bacon and sausage; cook 10 minutes.

Stir in okra. Cover and cook for 8-10 minutes or until okra is tender. Serve with rice if desired.

OUT OF OKRA?

Okra is a popular vegetable in the South, where it is often added to soups and stews. When okra is sliced, it releases a substance that naturally thickens any liquid it is cooked in. Although the taste and texture of okra are unique, some folks think its mild flavor resembles that of green beans or eggplant. Those two vegetables may be substituted for okra in many soups and stews. However, without okra's thickening properties, cornstarch or flour may have to be added.
TASTE OF HOME TEST KITCHEN

EASY CHICKEN AND DUMPLINGS

PREP/TOTAL TIME: 30 min. | YIELD: 6 servings.

Perfect for autumn nights, this main course soup is speedy, comforting and a delicious one-dish meal.

NANCY TUCK ELK FALLS, KANSAS

- 3 celery ribs, chopped
- 1 cup sliced fresh carrots
- 3 cans (14-1/2 ounces *each*) reduced-sodium chicken broth
- 1/2 teaspoon poultry seasoning
- 1/8 teaspoon pepper
- 3 cups cubed cooked chicken breast
- 1-2/3 cups reduced-fat biscuit/baking mix
- 2/3 cup fat-free milk

In a Dutch oven coated with cooking spray, saute celery and carrots for 5 minutes. Stir in the broth, poultry seasoning and pepper. Bring to a boil. Reduce heat; simmer, uncovered. Add chicken.

For dumplings, combine biscuit mix and milk. Drop by tablespoonfuls onto simmering broth. Cover and simmer for 10-15 minutes or until a toothpick inserted into a dumpling comes out clean (do not lift cover while simmering).

WATERMELON GAZPACHO

PREP/TOTAL TIME: 25 min. | YIELD: 4 servings.

Serve this delightfully simple soup as a first course or with pita and hummus for a complete meal.

NICOLE DEELAH NASHVILLE, TENNESSEE

- 4 cups cubed watermelon, seeded, *divided*
- 2 tablespoons lime juice
- 1 tablespoon grated lime peel
- 1 teaspoon minced fresh gingerroot
- 1 teaspoon salt
- 1 cup chopped tomato
- 1/2 cup chopped cucumber
- 1/2 cup chopped green pepper
- 1/4 cup minced fresh cilantro
- 2 tablespoons chopped green onion
- 1 tablespoon finely chopped seeded jalapeno pepper

Puree 3 cups watermelon in a blender. Cut the remaining watermelon into 1/2-inch pieces; set aside.

In a large bowl, combine the watermelon puree, lime juice, lime peel, ginger and salt. Stir in the tomato, cucumber, green pepper, cilantro, onion, jalapeno and cubed watermelon. Chill until serving.

EDITOR'S NOTE: Wear disposable gloves when cutting hot peppers; the oils can burn skin. Avoid touching your face.

VEGETABLE BEEF SOUP

CRAB CORN CHOWDER

PREP/TOTAL TIME: 25 min. | **YIELD:** 8 servings.

No time to make a homemade soup? Think again! You'll be ladling out steamy bowls of this satisfying chowder in no time. Canned corn and crab blend beautifully in the creamy, colorful soup. It's one of the best I've ever tasted.
SARAH MCCLANAHAN RALEIGH, NORTH CAROLINA

- 3 teaspoons chicken bouillon granules
- 2 cups boiling water
- 6 bacon strips, diced
- 1/3 cup *each* diced sweet red, yellow and orange peppers
- 1/2 cup chopped onion
- 1/4 cup all-purpose flour
- 3 cups half-and-half cream
- 2 cans (14-3/4 ounces *each*) cream-style corn
- 1-1/2 teaspoons seasoned salt
- 1/2 teaspoon dried basil
- 1/4 to 1/2 teaspoon cayenne pepper
- 2 cans (6 ounces *each*) crabmeat, drained, flaked and cartilage removed *or* 2 cups imitation crabmeat, flaked
- 1/2 cup minced chives

Dissolve bouillon in water; set aside. In a Dutch oven, cook bacon over medium heat until crisp. Remove bacon to paper towels to drain, reserving drippings.

In the same pan, saute peppers and onion in drippings until tender. Stir in flour. Gradually stir in bouillon. Bring to a boil; cook and stir for 2 minutes or until thickened.

Reduce heat; gradually stir in cream and corn. Add the seasoned salt, basil and cayenne. Cook for 8-10 minutes or until heated through, stirring occasionally (do not boil). Stir in the crab. Garnish each bowl with bacon and chives.

VEGETABLE BEEF SOUP

PREP/TOTAL TIME: 30 min. | **YIELD:** 14 servings (3-1/2 quarts).

Brimming with veggies, my hearty soup will warm family and friends right to their toes! It's especially good served with corn bread, and even better the second day. **MARIE CARLISLE** SUMRALL, MISSISSIPPI

- 4 cups cubed peeled potatoes
- 6 cups water
- 1 pound ground beef
- 5 teaspoons beef bouillon granules
- 1 can (10-3/4 ounces) condensed tomato soup, undiluted
- 2 cups frozen corn, thawed
- 2 cups frozen sliced carrots, thawed
- 2 cups frozen cut green beans, thawed
- 2 cups frozen sliced okra, thawed
- 3 tablespoons dried minced onion

In a Dutch oven, bring potatoes and water to a boil. Cover and cook for 10-15 minutes or until tender. Meanwhile, in a large skillet, cook beef over medium heat until no longer pink; drain.

Add the bouillon, soup, vegetables, dried minced onion and beef to the undrained potatoes. Bring to a boil. Reduce heat; simmer, uncovered, for 8-10 minutes or until heated through, stirring occasionally.

APPLES...NOT JUST FOR EATING
To keep potatoes from sprouting before I can use them, I put an apple in the bag with the spuds.
REVENA K. PRAIRIE VILLAGE, KANSAS

OYSTER STEW

PREP: 15 min. | **COOK:** 30 min. | **YIELD:** 12 servings.

A Southern favorite, oyster stew is a simple pleasure I enjoy as often as I can. The broth's buttery richness complements the oysters' briny flavor.

CHRISTA SCOTT SANTA FE, NEW MEXICO

- 3 medium leeks (white portion only), chopped
- 1/4 cup butter, cubed
- 2 medium potatoes, peeled and diced
- 2 cups hot water
- 3 teaspoons chicken bouillon granules
- 2 cups milk
- 2 cups half-and-half cream
- 4 cans (16 ounces *each*) oysters, drained
- 1/4 teaspoon cayenne pepper

Salt and pepper to taste

Minced fresh parsley

In a Dutch oven, saute leeks in butter for 10 minutes or until tender. Add the potatoes, water and bouillon; cover and simmer 20 minutes or until potatoes are tender. Cool.

Transfer to a blender. Cover and process until blended. Return to the pan; stir in the milk, cream, oysters, cayenne, salt and pepper. Cook on low until heated through (do not boil). Garnish with parsley.

SHRIMP AND BLACK BEAN SOUP

PREP: 20 min. | **COOK:** 40 min.
YIELD: 8 servings (3 quarts).

Packed with tomatoes, chilies, black beans, corn and, of course, shrimp, this is a bold and spicy medley. My family thinks it's especially good in cold weather.

ELIZABETH LEWIS HAYDEN, ALABAMA

- 1 large onion, chopped
- 1 tablespoon olive oil
- 2 cans (14-1/2 ounces *each*) reduced-sodium chicken broth
- 2 cans (10 ounces *each*) diced tomatoes and green chilies, undrained
- 2 cups frozen corn
- 1 can (15 ounces) black beans, rinsed and drained
- 1 can (14-1/2 ounces) diced tomatoes, undrained
- 4-1/2 teaspoons chili powder
- 1 teaspoon sugar
- 1/2 teaspoon salt
- 1 pound uncooked medium shrimp, peeled and deveined
- 1/4 cup minced fresh parsley

In a Dutch oven, saute onion in oil for 3-4 minutes or until tender. Add the broth, tomatoes and green chilies, corn, black beans, tomatoes, chili powder, sugar and salt. Bring to a boil, stirring occasionally. Reduce heat; cover and simmer for 20 minutes.

Stir in shrimp; cook 5-6 minutes longer or until shrimp turn pink. Stir in parsley.

TOMATO GARLIC SOUP

PREP: 70 min. | **COOK:** 1 hour | **YIELD:** 18-20 servings (4-1/2 quarts).

Unlike canned tomato soup, this homemade version is thick and features a more robust flavor. I like to make this soup when I'm expecting a lot of people for dinner. **LYNN THOMPSON** RESTON, VIRGINIA

10 whole garlic bulbs

1/2 cup olive oil

4 cans (one 14-1/2 ounces, three 28 ounces) diced tomatoes, undrained

1 medium onion, diced

3 cans (14-1/2 ounces *each*) stewed tomatoes

2/3 cup heavy whipping cream

1 to 3 tablespoons chopped pickled jalapeno peppers

2 teaspoons garlic pepper blend

2 teaspoons sugar

1-1/2 teaspoons salt

Croutons and shredded Parmesan cheese, optional

Remove papery outer skin from garlic (do not peel or separate cloves). Cut top off of garlic bulb. Drizzle with oil. Wrap each bulb in heavy-duty foil. Bake at 425° for 30-35 minutes or until softened. Cool for 10-15 minutes. Squeeze softened garlic into a blender. Add the 14-1/2-oz. can of diced tomatoes; cover and process until smooth. Set aside.

Transfer 1/4 cup oil from the foil to a Dutch oven or soup kettle (discard the remaining oil). Saute onion in oil over medium heat until tender.

Stir in the stewed tomatoes, cream, jalapenos, garlic pepper, sugar, salt, pureed tomato mixture and remaining diced tomatoes. Bring to a boil. Reduce heat; cover and simmer for 1 hour. Garnish with croutons and cheese if desired.

CRAWFISH ETOUFFEE

PREP: 15 min. | **COOK:** 50 min. | **YIELD:** 6-8 servings.

Etouffee is typically served with shellfish over rice and is similar to gumbo. This dish has its roots in New Orleans and the bayou country of Louisiana. I like to serve this Cajun sensation when I entertain.

TAMRA DUNCAN LINCOLN, ARKANSAS

1/2 cup butter, cubed

1/2 cup plus 2 tablespoons
   all-purpose flour

1-1/4 cups chopped celery

1 cup chopped green pepper

1/2 cup chopped green onions

1 can (14-1/2 ounces)
   chicken broth

1 cup water

1/4 cup minced fresh parsley

1 tablespoon tomato paste

1 bay leaf

1/2 teaspoon salt

1/4 teaspoon pepper

1/4 teaspoon cayenne pepper

2 pounds frozen cooked crawfish tail meat, thawed

Hot cooked rice

In a large heavy skillet, melt butter; stir in flour. Cook and stir over low heat for about 20 minutes until mixture is a caramel-colored paste. Add the celery, pepper and onions; stir until coated. Add the broth, water, parsley, tomato paste, bay leaf, salt, pepper and cayenne pepper. Bring to a boil.

Reduce heat; cover and simmer for 30 minutes, stirring occasionally. Discard bay leaf. Add crawfish and heat through. Serve with rice.

HAM AND BEAN SOUP

PREP: 30 min. + soaking | **COOK:** 1-1/2 hours
YIELD: 15 servings (3-3/4 quarts).

The name of this soup sounds simple, but the flavor is wonderfully rich. **AMANDA REED** MILFORD, DELAWARE

- 1 pound dried navy beans
- 2 medium onions, chopped
- 2 teaspoons canola oil
- 2 celery ribs, chopped
- 10 cups water
- 4 cups cubed fully cooked ham
- 1 cup mashed potatoes (without added milk and butter)
- 1/2 cup shredded carrot
- 2 tablespoons Worcestershire sauce
- 1 teaspoon salt
- 1/2 teaspoon dried thyme
- 1/2 teaspoon pepper
- 2 bay leaves
- 1 meaty ham bone *or* 2 smoked ham hocks
- 1/4 cup minced fresh parsley

Place beans in a Dutch oven; add water to cover by 2 in. Bring to a boil; boil for 2 minutes. Remove from the heat; cover and let stand for 1 to 4 hours or until beans are softened. Drain and rinse beans, discarding liquid.

In the same pan, saute onions in oil for 2 minutes. Add celery; cook until tender. Stir in the beans, water, ham, potatoes, carrot, Worcestershire sauce, salt, thyme, pepper and bay leaves. Add ham bone. Bring to a boil. Reduce heat; cover and simmer for 1-1/4 to 1-1/2 hours or until beans are tender.

Discard bay leaves. Remove ham bone; set aside until cool. Remove ham from bone and cut into cubes. Discard bone. Return ham to soup; heat through. Garnish with parsley.

BRUNSWICK STEW

PREP: 1 hour + cooling | **COOK:** 45 min.
YIELD: 6 servings.

For a hearty meal, try this thick stew filled to the brim with potatoes, lima beans, corn and tomatoes. Authentic versions call for rabbit or squirrel, but I think you will love my recipe calling for tender chunks of chicken. **MILDRED SHERRER** FORT WORTH, TEXAS

- 1 broiler/fryer chicken (3-1/2 to 4 pounds), cut up
- 2 cups water
- 4 medium potatoes, peeled and cubed
- 2 medium onions, sliced
- 1 can (15-1/4 ounces) lima beans, rinsed and drained
- 1 teaspoon salt
- 1/2 teaspoon pepper

Dash cayenne pepper

- 1 can (15-1/4 ounces) corn, drained
- 1 can (14-1/2 ounces) diced tomatoes, undrained
- 1/4 cup butter
- 1/2 cup dry bread crumbs

In a Dutch oven, slowly bring the chicken and water to a boil. Cover and simmer for 45-60 minutes or until chicken is tender, skimming the surface as foam rises.

Remove chicken and set aside until cool enough to handle. Remove and discard skin and bones. Cube chicken and return to broth.

Add the potatoes, onions, beans and seasonings. Bring to a boil. Reduce heat; simmer, uncovered, for 30 minutes or until potatoes are tender. Stir in remaining ingredients. Simmer, uncovered, for 10 minutes or until slightly thickened.

SOUTHERN OKRA BEAN STEW

PREP/TOTAL TIME: 30 min. | **YIELD:** 11 servings.

When this spicy stew's simmering on the stove, my family has a hard time waiting for dinner. It's much like a thick tomato-based soup with a hearty mix of okra, brown rice and beans. **BEVERLY MCDOWELL** ATHENS, GEORGIA

4 cups water

1 can (28 ounces) diced
   tomatoes, undrained

1-1/2 cups chopped green peppers

1 large onion, chopped

3 garlic cloves, minced

1 teaspoon Italian seasoning

1 teaspoon chili powder

1/2 to 1 teaspoon hot
   pepper sauce

3/4 teaspoon salt

1 bay leaf

4 cups cooked brown rice

2 cans (16 ounces *each*) kidney beans, rinsed and drained

3 cans (8 ounces *each*) tomato sauce

1 package (16 ounces) frozen sliced okra

In a large Dutch oven or soup kettle, combine the first 10 ingredients. Bring to a boil. Reduce heat; simmer, uncovered, for 5 minutes.

Add the rice, beans, tomato sauce and okra. Simmer, uncovered, for 8-10 minutes or until the vegetables are tender. Discard bay leaf.

NEW ORLEANS GUMBO

PREP: 25 min. | **COOK:** 20 min. | **YIELD:** 8 servings.

This hearty gumbo is a nice taste of the French Quarter made right in your own kitchen.
DOLORES BRIDGES DANVILLE, KENTUCKY

2 cups chicken broth

1 cup uncooked converted rice

2 celery ribs, chopped

1 medium onion, chopped

2 garlic cloves, minced

1 can (28 ounces) diced
   tomatoes, undrained

1 pound boneless skinless
   chicken breasts, cut into
   1/2-inch cubes

1/2 pound smoked kielbasa *or*
   Polish sausage, cut into
   1/2-inch slices

1 teaspoon dried thyme

1 teaspoon pepper

2 bay leaves

1/4 teaspoon cayenne pepper

3 tablespoons all-purpose flour

1/4 cup cold water

1 pound uncooked medium shrimp, peeled and deveined

1 large green pepper, chopped

1/4 cup minced fresh parsley

In a large saucepan, bring broth to a boil. Stir in the rice, celery, onion and garlic. Reduce heat; cover and simmer for 20 minutes.

Meanwhile, in a Dutch oven, combine the tomatoes, chicken, kielbasa, thyme, pepper, bay leaves and cayenne. Bring to a boil. Reduce heat; cover and simmer for 10 minutes.

Combine flour and water until smooth; gradually stir into chicken mixture. Stir in shrimp and green pepper. Cook, uncovered, over medium heat for 4-6 minutes or until shrimp turn pink and gumbo is thickened. Discard bay leaves.

Remove rice from the heat and let stand for 5 minutes; stir in parsley. Serve with gumbo.

NEW ORLEANS GUMBO

SALMON WITH CARIBBEAN SALSA, PG. 90

SEAFOOD

Sample some of the freshest catches in the South. You will love the vibrant flavors of succulent shrimp, tender fillets, perfectly seasoned crabcakes, crawfish and more.

FISH TACOS WITH
AVOCADO SAUCE, PG. 88

CAJUN SHRIMP LASAGNA ROLL-UPS

PREP: 30 min. | **BAKE:** 25 min. + standing | **YIELD:** 6 servings.

If you enjoy Creole and Cajun dishes, you'll devour this one. The seasoning and andouille sausage give it a nice kick, and seafood fans will appreciate the shrimp. **MARY BETH HARRIS-MURPHREE** TYLER, TEXAS

1-1/4 pounds uncooked medium shrimp, peeled and deveined

1 medium onion, chopped

2 tablespoons olive oil

4 medium tomatoes, seeded and chopped

2 tablespoons Cajun seasoning

3 garlic cloves, minced

1/4 cup butter, cubed

1/4 cup all-purpose flour

2 cups milk

1-1/2 cups (6 ounces) shredded cheddar cheese

1 cup diced fully cooked andouille sausage

12 lasagna noodles, cooked and drained

4 ounces pepper jack cheese, shredded

1 teaspoon paprika

In a large skillet, saute shrimp and onion in oil until shrimp turn pink. Stir in tomatoes and Cajun seasoning; set aside.

In a large saucepan, saute garlic in butter for 1 minute. Stir in flour until blended. Gradually add milk. Bring to a boil over medium heat; cook and stir for 2 minutes or until thickened. Remove from the heat; stir in cheddar cheese until smooth. Add sausage; set aside.

Spread 1/3 cup shrimp mixture over each noodle. Carefully roll up; place seam side down in a greased 13-in. x 9-in. baking dish. Top with cheese sauce. Sprinkle with pepper jack cheese and paprika.

Cover and bake at 350° for 15 minutes. Uncover; bake 10-15 minutes longer or until bubbly. Let stand 15 minutes before serving.

CATFISH SPREAD

PREP: 20 min. + chilling | **YIELD:** 5 cups.

Whenever we have a fish fry, we begin the meal with this dip. My children and grandchildren love it, and it gets rave reviews at picnics and potlucks. Someone always requests the recipe.
EDNA CARTER WEST POINT, VIRGINIA

- 1 pound catfish fillets
- 2 teaspoons water
- 2 packages (8 ounces *each*) cream cheese, softened
- 2 packages (5.2 ounces *each*) garlic-herb cheese spread
- 4 green onions, thinly sliced
- 1/2 cup minced fresh parsley
- 1 tablespoon lemon juice
- 2 teaspoons Worcestershire sauce
- 1/8 teaspoon garlic powder
- 1/8 teaspoon cayenne pepper

Dash paprika

- 1 can (6 ounces) crabmeat, drained, flaked and cartilage removed
- 1 can (6 ounces) small shrimp, rinsed and drained

Assorted fresh vegetables

Place catfish in a 2-qt. microwave-safe dish; drizzle with water. Cover and microwave on high for 4-6 minutes or until fish flakes easily with a fork. Drain and discard cooking liquid. Using a fork, flake fish into small pieces; set aside.

In a large bowl, beat cream cheese and cheese spread until smooth. Add the onions, parsley, lemon juice, Worcestershire sauce and seasonings and mix well. Stir in the crab, shrimp and catfish. Cover and refrigerate for at least 2 hours. Serve with vegetables.

EDITOR'S NOTE: This recipe was tested in a 1,100-watt microwave.

CITRUS BAKED FISH

PREP: 5 min. + marinating
BAKE: 15 min. | **YIELD:** 4 servings.

My recipe combines two of Florida's best: fish and citrus.
PHYLLIS ALLEN VERO BEACH, FLORIDA

- 1/4 cup thawed orange juice concentrate
- 1 tablespoon canola oil
- 1 teaspoon snipped fresh dill *or* 1/4 teaspoon dill weed
- 4 red snapper *or* tilapia fillets (6 ounces *each*)
- 2 orange slices, halved

Paprika

In a resealable plastic bag, combine the orange juice concentrate, oil and dill; add fish. Seal bag and turn to coat; refrigerate for at least 15 minutes.

Drain and discard marinade. Place the fillets in a greased 15-in. x 10-in. x 1-in. baking pan. Cover and bake at 350° for 15-20 minutes or until fish flakes easily with a fork.

Dip cut edges of orange slices in paprika; serve with fish.

CREAMY SHRIMP NOODLE SKILLET

PREP: 15 min. | **COOK:** 20 min. | **YIELD:** 6-8 servings.

The half-and-half cream gives a delightful richness to this flavorful seafood dish, which draws compliments each time I serve it to family and friends.

CORA ROBIN ST. BERNARD, LOUISIANA

- 1 package (16 ounces) medium egg noodles
- 2 medium onions, chopped
- 1 medium green pepper, chopped
- 2 celery ribs, chopped
- 3 garlic cloves, minced
- 3/4 cup butter
- 1 tablespoon all-purpose flour
- 3 cups half-and-half cream
- 1-1/2 pounds uncooked medium shrimp, peeled and deveined
- 1 jalapeno pepper, seeded and chopped
- 2 tablespoons minced fresh parsley
- 8 ounces process cheese (Velveeta), cubed

Cook noodles according to package directions; drain and set aside.

In a large saucepan or Dutch oven, saute the onions, green pepper, celery and garlic in butter until tender. Stir in flour until blended. Gradually stir in cream, Bring to a boil; cook and stir for 2 minutes or until thickened.

Reduce heat; add the shrimp, jalapeno pepper and parsley. Simmer, uncovered, for 3 minutes. Stir in cheese; cook 3 minutes longer or until cheese is melted. Stir in noodles; heat through.

EDITOR'S NOTE: Wear disposable gloves when cutting hot peppers; the oils can burn skin. Avoid touching your face.

TILAPIA WITH JASMINE RICE

PREP/TOTAL TIME: 30 min. | **YIELD:** 2 servings.

I think you'll agree: This recipe for tender, full-flavored tilapia is to die for. Fragrant jasmine rice brings a special touch to this mouthwatering entree.

SHIRL PARSONS CAPE CARTERET, NORTH CAROLINA

- 3/4 cup water
- 1/2 cup uncooked jasmine rice
- 1-1/2 teaspoons butter
- 1/4 teaspoon ground cumin
- 1/4 teaspoon seafood seasoning
- 1/4 teaspoon pepper
- 1/8 teaspoon salt
- 2 tilapia fillets (6 ounces *each*)
- 1/4 cup fat-free Italian salad dressing

In a large saucepan, bring the water, rice and butter to a boil. Reduce heat; cover and simmer for 15-20 minutes or until liquid is absorbed and rice is tender.

Combine the seasonings; sprinkle over fillets. Place salad dressing in a large skillet; cook over medium heat until heated through. Add fish; cook for 3-4 minutes on each side or until fish flakes easily with a fork. Serve with rice.

CILANTRO-LIME SALMON

PREP/TOTAL TIME: 20 min. | **YIELD:** 2 servings.

Fresh lime brightens the taste of this microwave-fast salmon that is sized just right for a pair.

LILY JULOW GAINESVILLE, FLORIDA

2 tablespoons sour cream

1 green onion, chopped

1 tablespoon minced
   fresh cilantro

1 garlic clove, minced

1/4 teaspoon minced
   fresh gingerroot

1/4 teaspoon grated lime peel

1/8 teaspoon salt

Dash ground cumin

Dash pepper

Dash crushed red pepper flakes

   2 salmon fillets (6 ounces *each*)

Lime wedges

In a small bowl, combine the first 10 ingredients. Place fillets skin side down in a greased 1-1/2-qt. microwave-safe dish; top with sour cream mixture.

   Cover and microwave on high for 4-6 minutes or until fish flakes easily with a fork. Serve with lime wedges.

   EDITOR'S NOTE: This recipe was tested in a 1,100-watt microwave.

CATFISH PARMESAN

PREP: 15 min. | **BAKE:** 20 min.
YIELD: 6 servings.

Mississippi is the nation's largest producer of farm-raised catfish. My family loves this dish, which shows off our state's pride and joy.
MRS. W. D. BAKER STARKVILLE, MISSISSIPPI

- 3/4 cup dry bread crumbs
- 3 tablespoons grated Parmesan cheese
- 2 tablespoons chopped fresh parsley
- 1/2 teaspoon salt
- 1/4 teaspoon paprika
- 1/8 teaspoon *each* pepper, dried oregano and basil
- 6 fresh *or* frozen catfish fillets (3 to 5 ounces *each*)
- 1/2 cup butter, melted

In a shallow bowl, combine the bread crumbs, Parmesan cheese, parsley and seasonings. Dip catfish in butter, then in crumb mixture. Arrange in a greased 13-in. x 9-in. baking dish.

Bake, uncovered, at 375° for 20-25 minutes or until fish flakes easily with a fork.

FISH TACOS WITH AVOCADO SAUCE

PREP: 30 min. + marinating | **BROIL:** 10 min. | **YIELD:** 4 servings.

A good friend, who normally doesn't eat fish, went back for fourth helpings of these flavorful tacos. I bet you will, too.
CORTNEY CLAESON SPOKANE, WASHINGTON

- 1/4 cup lemon juice
- 1 tablespoon olive oil
- 3 garlic cloves, minced
- 1 pound halibut *or* tilapia fillets

SAUCE:
- 2 medium ripe avocados, *divided*
- 1/4 cup fat-free sour cream
- 1/4 cup reduced-fat mayonnaise
- 1 tablespoon lime juice
- 1 garlic clove, minced
- 1 teaspoon dill weed
- 1/4 teaspoon *each* ground cumin, dried oregano and dried parsley flakes

Dash cayenne pepper

SALSA:
- 1 medium tomato, seeded and chopped
- 1 small red onion, chopped
- 4-1/2 teaspoons chopped seeded jalapeno pepper
- 1 tablespoon minced fresh cilantro
- 1-1/2 teaspoons lime juice
- 1 garlic clove, minced
- 1/8 teaspoon salt

TACOS:
- 8 flour tortillas (6 inches)
- 2 cups shredded cabbage

In a large resealable plastic bag, combine the lemon juice, oil and garlic. Add the halibut; seal bag and turn to coat. Refrigerate for 30 minutes.

For sauce and salsa, peel and cube avocados. In a small bowl, mash 1/4 cup avocado. Stir in the remaining sauce ingredients. Place remaining avocado in a small bowl; stir in the remaining salsa ingredients. Refrigerate sauce and salsa until serving.

Drain fish and discard marinade. Broil halibut 4-6 in. from the heat for 8-10 minutes or until fish flakes easily with a fork. Place fish on the center of each tortilla. Top each with 1/4 cup cabbage, about 1 tablespoon sauce and 1/4 cup salsa.

EDITOR'S NOTE: Wear disposable gloves when cutting hot peppers; the oils can burn skin. Avoid touching your face.

LOUISIANA SHRIMP ❧

PREP: 40 min. | **BAKE:** 20 min. | **YIELD:** 10 servings.

This is a Lenten favorite at our home. I serve it right out of the roaster with corn on the cob and boiled potatoes. **SUNDRA HAUCK** BOGALUSA, LOUISIANA

- 1 pound butter, cubed
- 3 medium lemons, sliced
- 2 tablespoons plus 1-1/2 teaspoons coarsely ground pepper
- 2 tablespoons Worcestershire sauce
- 2 garlic cloves, minced
- 1/2 teaspoon salt
- 1/2 teaspoon hot pepper sauce
- 2-1/2 pounds uncooked shell-on medium shrimp

In a large saucepan, combine the first seven ingredients. Bring to a boil. Reduce heat; cover and simmer for 30 minutes, stirring occasionally.

Place shrimp in a large roasting pan; pour butter mixture over top. Bake, uncovered, at 375° for 20-25 minutes or until shrimp turn pink. Serve warm with a slotted spoon.

SALMON CROQUETTES ❧

PREP/TOTAL TIME: 30 min. | **YIELD:** 4-6 servings.

Mom frequently served salmon when I was a girl. Learning the ropes in the kitchen as I grew up,

I got the chore of deboning the salmon. I didn't mind, because these light crisp croquettes are the delicious result. **MARY MCGUIRE** GRAHAM, NORTH CAROLINA

- 1 can (14-3/4 ounces) pink salmon, drained, deboned and flaked
- 1 cup evaporated milk, *divided*
- 1-1/2 cups cornflake crumbs, *divided*
- 1/4 cup dill pickle relish
- 1/4 cup finely chopped celery
- 2 tablespoons finely chopped onion

Oil for deep-fat frying

TARTAR SAUCE:

- 2/3 cup evaporated milk
- 1/4 cup mayonnaise
- 2 tablespoons dill pickle relish
- 1 tablespoon finely chopped onion

In a large bowl, combine the salmon, 1/2 cup milk, 1/2 cup crumbs, relish, celery and onion. With wet hands, shape 1/4 cupfuls into cones. Dip into remaining milk, then into remaining crumbs. Heat oil in a deep-fat fryer to 365°. Fry croquettes, a few at a time, for 2 to 2-1/2 minutes or until golden brown. Drain on paper towels; keep warm.

In a small saucepan, combine tartar sauce ingredients; cook over medium-low heat until heated through and slightly thickened. Serve warm with croquettes.

SALMON WITH CARIBBEAN SALSA

PREP: 25 min. + chilling | **BAKE:** 25 min. | **YIELD:** 8 servings (5 cups salsa).

Salmon fillets smothered in tropical fruit salsa make an elegant main dish recipe. The cinnamon-spiced seasoning is a wonderful complement to grilled chicken, too. **MARY JONES** WILLIAMSTOWN, WEST VIRGINIA

SEASONING:

- 1 tablespoon salt
- 1 tablespoon ground nutmeg
- 1 tablespoon pepper
- 1-1/2 teaspoons *each* ground ginger, cinnamon and allspice
- 1-1/2 teaspoons brown sugar

SALMON:

- 1 salmon fillet (3 pounds)
- 4-1/2 teaspoons olive oil

SALSA:

- 1 medium mango
- 1 medium papaya
- 1 medium green pepper
- 1 medium sweet red pepper
- 1 cup finely chopped fresh pineapple
- 1/4 cup finely chopped red onion
- 3 tablespoons minced fresh cilantro
- 2 tablespoons lime juice
- 1 tablespoon olive oil
- 1/2 teaspoon salt

Combine the seasoning ingredients. Place fillet in a greased 15-in. x 10-in. x 1-in. baking pan; sprinkle with 1 tablespoon seasoning. (Save remaining seasoning for another use.) Drizzle salmon with oil. Cover and refrigerate for at least 2 hours.

Peel and finely chop mango and papaya; place in a large bowl. Finely chop the peppers; add to bowl. Add the remaining salsa ingredients and gently stir until blended. Cover and refrigerate for at least 2 hours.

Bake salmon at 350° for 25-30 minutes or until fish flakes. Serve with salsa.

HERBED CORNMEAL CRABCAKES

PREP/TOTAL TIME: 30 min. | **YIELD:** 2 servings.

I created these crispy crabcakes to include some of the fresh herbs from my garden. My husband loves them and requests them quite often. The corn bread coating is a little something special. **AUDREY COLLINS** COLUMBUS, GEORGIA

- 2 tablespoons cornmeal
- 2 tablespoons dry bread crumbs
- 1 tablespoon all-purpose flour
- 1/4 teaspoon garlic powder
- 1/8 teaspoon onion powder
- 1/8 teaspoon salt

CRABCAKES:

- 1 egg, beaten
- 1/4 cup dry bread crumbs
- 2 tablespoons minced chives
- 1 tablespoon minced fresh parsley
- 1-1/2 teaspoons minced fresh thyme
- 1 tablespoon mayonnaise
- 1 tablespoon tartar sauce
- 2 teaspoons spicy brown mustard
- 1/2 teaspoon lemon juice
- 1/2 teaspoon Worcestershire sauce
- 1/4 teaspoon celery salt
- 1 can (6 ounces) crabmeat, drained, flaked and cartilage removed
- 2 tablespoons canola oil

In a shallow bowl, combine the first six ingredients; set aside.

In a bowl, combine the egg, bread crumbs, chives, parsley, thyme, mayonnaise, tartar sauce, mustard, lemon juice, Worcestershire sauce and celery salt. Fold in crab. Shape into four patties; coat with cornmeal mixture.

In a large skillet over medium heat, cook crabcakes in oil for 3-4 minutes on each side or until golden brown.

HERBED CORNMEAL CRABCAKES

TILAPIA WITH CORN SALSA

PREP/TOTAL TIME: 10 min. | **YIELD:** 4 servings.

My family loves fish, and this super-fast and delicious dish is very popular at my house. Though it tastes like it takes a long time, it cooks in minutes under the broiler. Garnish it with lemon wedges and serve it with couscous.

BRENDA COFFEY SINGER ISLAND, FLORIDA

4 tilapia fillets (6 ounces *each*)

1 tablespoon olive oil

1/4 teaspoon salt

1/4 teaspoon pepper

1 can (15 ounces) black beans, rinsed and drained

1 can (11 ounces) whole kernel corn, drained

3/4 cup Italian salad dressing

2 tablespoons chopped green onion

2 tablespoons chopped sweet red pepper

Drizzle both sides of fillets with oil; sprinkle with salt and pepper.

Broil 4-6 in. from the heat for 5-7 minutes or until fish flakes easily with a fork.

Meanwhile, in a small bowl, combine the remaining ingredients. Serve with fish.

CITRUS TUNA STEAKS

PREP: 10 min. + marinating | **GRILL:** 20 min. | **YIELD:** 4 servings.

This grilled fish is a summertime favorite my family requests often. I adapted it from a traditional Jamaican jerk recipe.

SHANNON EDWARDS ARLINGTON, TEXAS

- 1 medium pink grapefruit
- 1/4 cup lemon juice
- 1/4 cup lime juice
- 2 tablespoons honey
- 1 tablespoon snipped fresh dill *or* 1 teaspoon dill weed
- 1 teaspoon crushed red pepper flakes
- 2 teaspoons minced fresh gingerroot
- 4 tuna steak *or* fillets (6 ounces ea*ch*)

Peel and section grapefruit over a bowl, reserving juice. Refrigerate half of the grapefruit sections. Add remaining grapefruit to the reserved grapefruit juice. Add the lemon juice, lime juice, honey, dill, red pepper flakes and ginger. Remove 1/4 cup for basting; cover and refrigerate. Pour remaining marinade into a large resealable plastic bag; add the tuna steaks. Seal bag and turn to coat; refrigerate for 30 minutes, turning once.

Drain and discard marinade. Using long-handled tongs, moisten a paper towel with cooking oil and lightly coat the grill rack. Grill tuna, uncovered, over medium heat or broil 4 in. from the heat for 6-7 minutes on each side, basting frequently with reserved marinade.

Top tuna steaks with reserved grapefruit sections. Cover and cook 5 minutes longer for medium-rare or until slightly pink in the center.

TROUT MEUNIERE

PREP/TOTAL TIME: 15 min.
YIELD: 4 servings.

Meuniere is a French term that refers to a simple cooking method of sauteeing lightly coated food, usually fish, in butter. It is quick and great for a weekend meal.

NANCY KELLEY NASHVILLE, TENNESSEE

- 4 trout fillets (6 ounces *each*)
- 1-1/3 cups crushed saltines
- 4 tablespoons butter, *divided*
- 1 package (2-1/4 ounces) sliced almonds
- 2 tablespoons lemon juice

Coat both sides of fillets with crushed saltines. In a skillet, melt 3 tablespoons butter over medium-high heat. Cook fillets for 3-5 minutes on each side or until fish flakes easily with a fork. Remove and keep warm.

In the same skillet, cook and stir the almonds in remaining butter until lightly toasted. Stir in the lemon juice. Serve with trout.

SEASONED CRABCAKES

PREP: 20 min. + chilling | **COOK:** 10 min.
YIELD: 8 crabcakes.

These scrumptious crabcakes won First Place at the National Hard Crab Derby in Crisfield, Maryland. I entered them on a whim after trying many crabcake recipes for my family.

BETSY HEDEMAN TIMONIUM, MARYLAND

- 3 cans (6 ounces *each*) crabmeat, drained, flaked and cartilage removed
- 1 cup cubed bread
- 2 eggs
- 3 tablespoons mayonnaise
- 3 tablespoons half-and-half cream
- 1 tablespoon lemon juice
- 1 tablespoon butter, melted
- 1-1/2 teaspoons seafood seasoning
- 1 teaspoon Worcestershire sauce
- 1 teaspoon salt
- 1/2 cup dry bread crumbs
- 1/2 cup canola oil

In a large bowl, combine crab and bread cubes. In another bowl, whisk the eggs, mayonnaise, cream, lemon juice, butter, seafood seasoning, Worcestershire sauce and salt. Add to crab mixture and mix gently (mixture will be moist).

Place bread crumbs in a dish. Drop crab mixture by 1/3 cupfuls into crumbs; shape each into a 3/4-in.-thick patty. Carefully turn to coat. Cover and refrigerate for at least 2 hours.

In a skillet, cook crabcakes in oil for 4-5 minutes on each side or until golden brown and crispy.

TRUE SHRIMP CREOLE

PREP: 20 min. | **COOK:** 50 min. | **YIELD:** 4-5 servings.

This dish is even better if refrigerated overnight to allow all the flavors to blend.

JOHNNIE MCLEOD BASTROP, LOUISIANA

- 1/4 cup all-purpose flour
- 1/2 cup canola oil
- 1 medium onion, chopped
- 1 medium green pepper, chopped
- 1 celery rib, chopped
- 1 garlic clove, minced
- 1 can (14-1/2 ounces) stewed tomatoes
- 1 can (6 ounces) tomato paste
- 4 bay leaves
- 1 tablespoon Worcestershire sauce
- 1/2 teaspoon hot pepper sauce

Salt and pepper to taste

- 2 pounds fresh *or* frozen uncooked medium shrimp, peeled and deveined

Hot cooked rice

In a large heavy skillet, combine the flour and oil until smooth. Cook and stir over medium heat until flour is a rich deep brown. Add the onion, green pepper and celery; cook for 5-6 minutes or until vegetables are tender. Add garlic; cook 1 minute longer. Stir in the tomatoes, tomato paste, bay leaves, Worcestershire sauce, hot pepper sauce, salt and pepper. Cover and simmer for 45-50 minutes or until heated through.

Add shrimp. Simmer, uncovered, for 5-6 minutes or until shrimp turn pink. Discard bay leaves. Serve with rice.

SIMPLE MARINATED SHRIMP

PREP: 10 min. + marinating | **YIELD:** 14 servings.

Seafood is a staple here in Florida. This recipe is quick and easy to make and can be prepared well in advance.
I always get a lot of requests for the recipe when I make it for a party or special occasion.

MARGARET DELONG LAKE BUTLER, FLORIDA

2 pounds cooked medium
  shrimp, peeled and deveined

1 medium red onion, sliced
  and separated into rings

2 medium lemons, cut
  into slices

1 cup pitted ripe olives, drained

1/2 cup olive oil

1/3 cup minced fresh parsley

3 tablespoons lemon juice

3 tablespoons red wine vinegar

1 garlic clove, minced

1 bay leaf

1 tablespoon minced fresh basil *or* 1 teaspoon dried basil

1 teaspoon salt

1 teaspoon ground mustard

1/4 teaspoon pepper

In a 3-qt. glass serving bowl, combine the shrimp, onion, lemons and olives. In a jar with a tight-fitting lid, combine the remaining ingredients; shake well. Pour over shrimp mixture and stir gently to coat.

Cover and refrigerate for 24 hours, stirring occasionally. Discard bay leaf before serving.

GARLIC-LIME SEA BASS

PREP: 45 min. | **BAKE:** 30 min. | **YIELD:** 4 servings.

I was a chef on a dive boat, and this was one of my favorite ways to serve our fresh catch.
PEG NELSON ISLAMORADA, FLORIDA

1 whole garlic bulb

1 teaspoon olive oil

1/4 cup butter, cubed

1 large onion, chopped

2 to 3 tablespoons lime juice

1 tablespoon spicy brown mustard

1/4 teaspoon salt

1/4 teaspoon pepper

4 sea bass *or* grouper fillets (8 ounces *each*)

Remove papery outer skin from garlic (do not peel or separate cloves). Cut top off of bulb. Brush with oil. Wrap in heavy-duty foil. Bake at 425° for 30-35 minutes or until softened. Cool for 10-15 minutes.

Reduce heat to 350°. In a small saucepan, melt butter. Squeeze softened garlic into pan. Stir in the onion, lime juice, mustard, salt and pepper. Cook and stir over medium heat until onion is tender.

Arrange the fillets in an ungreased 11-in. x 7-in. baking dish; top with onion mixture. Bake, uncovered, for 30-35 minutes or until fish flakes easily with a fork.

SHRIMP-STUFFED SOLE

PREP/TOTAL TIME: 15 min. | **YIELD:** 4 servings.

If you like stuffed fish, this recipe is the way to go. It's so easy to assemble and cooks in just a few minutes in the microwave. Try it with chicken instead of sole, if you prefer, for a meal that's equally good.
ROBERT BISHOP LEXINGTON, KENTUCKY

4 sole fillets, halved lengthwise

1 tablespoon lemon juice

1/8 teaspoon onion salt *or* onion powder

1/4 cup butter, melted, *divided*

1 can (6 ounces) small shrimp, rinsed and drained

1/3 cup milk

1/4 cup finely chopped celery

2 teaspoons minced fresh parsley

1 cup cubed bread, toasted

Dash paprika

Sprinkle fillets with lemon juice and onion salt; set aside. Pour 2 tablespoons butter into an 8-in. square microwave-safe dish. Add the shrimp, milk, celery and parsley. Cover and microwave on high for 1 to 1-1/2 minutes or until celery is tender. Stir in bread cubes.

Spoon shrimp mixture onto fillets. Starting with a short side, roll up each and secure with toothpicks. Place in a greased shallow microwave-safe dish. Brush with remaining butter; sprinkle with paprika.

Cover and microwave on high for 4-6 minutes or until fish flakes easily with a fork. Let stand for 5 minutes before serving. Discard toothpicks.

EDITOR'S NOTE: This recipe was tested in a 1,100-watt microwave.

ELIMINATE "FISHY" FLAVORS
To get rid of "fishy" flavors with just about any type of fish, I cover it with milk. Soak it for 30-90 minutes and cook as directed. It seems to get rid of some of the fishy taste. **SANDY F.** OLIVIA, MINNESOTA

SHRIMP-STUFFED SOLE

CRAWFISH BEIGNETS WITH CAJUN DIPPING SAUCE

PREP: 20 min. | **COOK:** 5 min./batch | **YIELD:** about 2 dozen (3/4 cup sauce).

Get a taste of the Deep South with these slightly spicy beignets. You won't be able to eat just one!

DONNA LANCLOS LAFAYETTE, LOUISIANA

1 egg, beaten

1 pound chopped cooked crawfish tail meat *or* shrimp

4 green onions, chopped

1-1/2 teaspoons butter, melted

1/2 teaspoon salt

1/2 teaspoon cayenne pepper

1/3 cup bread flour

Oil for deep-fat frying

3/4 cup mayonnaise

1/2 cup ketchup

1/4 teaspoon prepared horseradish, optional

1/4 teaspoon hot pepper sauce

In a large bowl, combine the egg, crawfish, onions, butter, salt and cayenne. Stir in flour until blended.

In an electric skillet or deep fryer, heat oil to 375°. Drop tablespoonfuls of batter, a few at a time, into hot oil. Fry until golden brown. Drain on paper towels.

In a small bowl, combine the mayonnaise, ketchup, horseradish if desired and pepper sauce. Serve with beignets.

BARBECUED TROUT

PREP/TOTAL TIME: 20 min. | **YIELD:** 6 servings.

A friend gave me this simple recipe. The sauce really gives the fish a wonderful flavor. Even those who aren't that fond of fish will like it prepared this way. **VIVIAN WOLFRAM** MOUNTAIN HOME, ARKANSAS

- 2/3 cup reduced-sodium soy sauce
- 1/2 cup ketchup
- 2 tablespoons lemon juice
- 2 tablespoons canola oil
- 1 teaspoon dried rosemary, crushed
- 6 pan-dressed trout

Lemon wedges, optional

Combine the soy sauce, ketchup, lemon juice, oil and rosemary; pour two-thirds of marinade into a large resealable plastic bag; add fish. Seal bag and turn to coat; refrigerate bag for 1 hour, turning once. Cover and refrigerate remaining marinade for basting.

Drain and discard marinade. Place fish in a single layer in a well-greased hinged wire grill basket. Grill, covered, over medium heat for 8-10 minutes or until fish is browned on the bottom. Turn and baste with reserved marinade; grill 5-7 minutes longer or until fish flakes easily with a fork. Serve with lemon if desired.

POTATO-CRUSTED SNAPPER

PREP/TOTAL TIME: 30 min.
YIELD: 4 servings.

The crispy potato-crusted fillets are so tender and tasty. They're great with steamed green beans and rice pilaf.
ATHENA RUSSELL
FLORENCE, SOUTH CAROLINA

- 2 eggs, beaten
- 1-1/2 cups mashed potato flakes
- 2 teaspoons dried thyme
- 4 red snapper fillets (6 ounces *each*)
- 1/2 teaspoon salt
- 1/4 teaspoon pepper
- 1/4 cup olive oil

Place eggs in a shallow bowl. In another shallow bowl, combine potato flakes and thyme. Sprinkle fillets with salt and pepper. Dip in eggs and coat with potato mixture.

In a large skillet, cook fillets in oil in batches over medium heat for 4-5 minutes on each side or until fish flakes easily with a fork.

CRAWFISH FETTUCCINE

BROWN SUGAR GLAZED SALMON

PREP: 15 min. | **BAKE:** 20 min. | **YIELD:** 8 servings.

I wasn't a salmon fan until I tried this recipe. The sweet glaze makes it irresistible. **RACHEL GARCIA** ARLINGTON, VIRGINIA

- 1 tablespoon brown sugar
- 2 teaspoons butter
- 1 teaspoon honey
- 1 tablespoon olive oil
- 1 tablespoon Dijon mustard
- 1 tablespoon reduced-sodium soy sauce
- 1/2 to 3/4 teaspoon salt
- 1/4 teaspoon pepper
- 1 salmon fillet (2-1/2 pounds)

In a small saucepan over medium heat, cook and stir the brown sugar, butter and honey until melted. Remove from the heat; whisk in the oil, mustard, soy sauce, salt and pepper. Cool for 5 minutes.

Place salmon in a large foil-lined baking pan; spoon brown sugar mixture over salmon. Bake, uncovered, at 350° for 20-25 minutes or until fish flakes easily with a fork.

CRAWFISH FETTUCCINE

PREP: 30 min. | **COOK:** 30 min. | **YIELD:** 8 servings.

I have lived in this close-knit community all my life and enjoy cooking Cajun dishes, especially those with seafood. Along with a green salad and garlic bread, this dish is great for family gatherings. The recipe can easily be doubled to serve a larger group. **CAROLYN LEJEUNE** WELSH, LOUISIANA

- 1 large onion, chopped
- 1 medium sweet red pepper, chopped
- 2/3 cup sliced green onions
- 1 celery rib, chopped
- 1-1/4 cups butter, cubed
- 1 garlic clove, minced
- 1/4 cup all-purpose flour
- 8 ounces process cheese (Velveeta), cubed
- 1 cup half-and-half cream
- 1 tablespoon chopped jalapeno pepper
- 1/2 teaspoon salt
- 8 ounces uncooked fettuccine
- 1-1/2 pounds frozen cooked crawfish tails, thawed, *or* cooked medium shrimp, peeled and deveined

In a Dutch oven, saute the onion, red pepper, green onions and celery in butter for 5 minutes or until vegetables are crisp-tender. Add garlic; cook 1 minute longer. Stir in flour until blended; cook and stir for 2 minutes. Add the cheese, cream, jalapeno and salt; cook and stir for 10 minutes or until mixture is thickened and cheese is melted.

Meanwhile, cook fettuccine according to package directions; drain. Stir fettuccine and crawfish into the vegetable mixture. Cook, uncovered, over medium heat for 10 minutes or until heated through, stirring occasionally.

EDITOR'S NOTE: Wear disposable gloves when cutting hot peppers; the oils can burn skin. Avoid touching your face.

CHANGE IT UP WITH CRAWFISH

Crawfish, also referred to as crayfish or crawdad, are freshwater crustaceans that resemble small lobsters, to which they are closely related. Cooking with tail meat is quick and easy. In fact, most of your favorite recipes that call for shrimp, crab or lobster can be modified to use crawfish. Use the tail meat as a topping on meat entrees and pizzas, or use it as a filling or stuffing for other meats, pasta dishes or crepes. **TASTE OF HOME TEST KITCHEN**

CREOLE BAKED TILAPIA

PREP/TOTAL TIME: 25 min.
YIELD: 4 servings.

Since I'm originally from Louisiana, I love Creole cooking. This is quick and easy as well as healthy. It's great served with your favorite rice dish.

CAROLYN COLLINS FREEPORT, TEXAS

- 4 tilapia fillets (6 ounces *each*)
- 1 can (8 ounces) tomato sauce
- 1 small green pepper, thinly sliced
- 1/2 cup chopped red onion
- 1 teaspoon Creole seasoning

Place tilapia in an ungreased 13-in. x 9-in. baking dish. In a bowl, combine the tomato sauce, green pepper, onion and Creole seasoning; pour over the fillets.

Bake, uncovered, at 350° for 20-25 minutes or until fish flakes easily with a fork.

EDITOR'S NOTE: The following spices may be substituted for 1 teaspoon Creole seasoning: 1/4 teaspoon of dried thyme, ground cumin and cayenne pepper.

GROUPER WITH CRABMEAT SAUCE

PREP: 25 min. | **BROIL:** 15 min. | **YIELD:** 8 servings.

A creamy seafood sauce drapes over mild-flavored grouper for an elegant entree. Whether served to my family or to hundreds of people at an event, it's always a winner. **VIRGINIA ANTHONY** JACKSONVILLE, FLORIDA

- 8 grouper *or* red snapper fillets (8 ounces *each*), skin removed
- 1/4 cup lemon juice
- 2 tablespoons marinade for chicken
- 1 tablespoon seafood seasoning
- 1 tablespoon olive oil

SAUCE:

- 2 large onions, chopped
- 1 large sweet red pepper, chopped
- 8 green onions, chopped
- 2 garlic cloves, minced
- 1/4 cup butter, cubed
- 3 tablespoons all-purpose flour
- 2 teaspoons seafood seasoning
- 2-1/2 cups half-and-half cream
- 2 cups fresh crabmeat
- 1/4 cup minced fresh parsley

Place fillets on a foil-lined 15-in. x 10-in. x 1-in. baking pan.

In a small bowl, combine the lemon juice, marinade for chicken, seafood seasoning and oil; brush over fillets. Broil 4 in. from the heat for 6-7 minutes on each side or until fish flakes easily with a fork.

Meanwhile, for sauce, in a large skillet, saute the onions, red pepper, green onions and garlic in butter until tender. Stir in flour and seafood seasoning until blended; gradually add cream. Bring to a boil; cook and stir for 2 minutes or until thickened. Gently stir in crabmeat; heat through. Serve with fish. Sprinkle with parsley.

EDITOR'S NOTE: This recipe was tested with Lea & Perrins Marinade for Chicken.

DELICIOUS SERVING OPTIONS

Grouper with Crabmeat Sauce is great served with a spinach pasta. Just cook enough for 8 side servings and toss with a little olive oil, minced garlic and shredded Romano. **TASTE OF HOME TEST KITCHEN**

SOUTHERN PECAN CATFISH

PREP/TOTAL TIME: 30 min. | **YIELD:** 4 servings.

For this super-fast recipe, I coat catfish in pecans, then top it with a thick, rich cream sauce. It looks like you spent all day on it, but it's actually very speedy to prepare. Garnish it with lemon wedges, parsley or more chopped pecans. **MARY ANN GRIFFIN** BOWLING GREEN, KENTUCKY

1 cup finely chopped
   pecans, *divided*

1/2 cup cornmeal

1 teaspoon salt, *divided*

1 teaspoon pepper, *divided*

4 catfish fillets (6 ounces *each*)

1/2 cup butter, *divided*

1/2 cup heavy whipping cream

2 tablespoons lemon juice

1 to 2 tablespoons minced
   fresh parsley

In a shallow bowl, combine 1/2 cup pecans, cornmeal, 1/2 teaspoon salt and 1/2 teaspoon pepper. Coat catfish with pecan mixture.

In a large skillet, melt 1/4 cup butter over medium-high heat; fry fillets for 6-7 minutes on each side or until fish flakes easily with a fork. Remove and keep warm.

In the same skillet, melt remaining butter over medium heat. Add remaining pecans; cook and stir for 1 minute. Add the cream, lemon juice and remaining salt and pepper; cook and stir for 1 minute. Stir in parsley. Serve with catfish.

CREOLE CHICKEN, PG. 128

POULTRY

Fry it to crisp perfection, slather it in barbecue sauce or bake it in a savory potpie. Whatever method you choose, poultry's versatility makes it almost too easy to put a family-pleasing meal on the table.

CHICKEN POTPIE, PG. 108

MASCARPONE-PESTO CHICKEN ROLLS

PREP: 20 min. | **BAKE:** 35 min. | **YIELD:** 4 servings.

Who could resist the great flavor of these golden-brown roll-ups spiraled with rich mascarpone cheese and prepared pesto? What's more, they're easy to make. **SHERYL LITTLE** SHERWOOD, ARKANSAS

- **4** boneless skinless chicken breast halves (6 ounces *each*)
- **3/4** teaspoon garlic salt
- **1/2** cup mascarpone cheese
- **1/4** cup prepared pesto
- **1** egg
- **2** teaspoons water
- **1** cup seasoned bread crumbs
- **8** teaspoons butter, melted, *divided*
- **8** ounces uncooked fettuccine

Fresh basil leaves, optional

Flatten chicken breasts to 1/4-in. thickness; sprinkle with garlic salt. Combine cheese and pesto; spread over chicken. Roll up each from a short side and secure with toothpicks.

In a bowl, whisk egg and water. Place bread crumbs in a separate shallow bowl. Dip chicken in egg mixture, then coat with crumbs. Place seam side down in a greased 11-in. x 7-in. baking dish. Drizzle with 4 teaspoons butter. Bake, uncovered, at 350° for 35-40 minutes or until a meat thermometer reads 170°. Discard toothpicks.

Meanwhile, cook fettuccine according to package directions. Drain fettuccine; toss with remaining butter. Serve with chicken. Garnish with basil if desired.

PECAN-CRUSTED TURKEY CUTLETS

PREP/TOTAL TIME: 25 min. | **YIELD:** 4 servings.

As this dish proves, turkey isn't just for the holidays. In fact, this turkey favorite is good any night of the week. Finished in 25 minutes, these cutlets are moist and tender. Pecans make this entree extra-crisp and delightful. **LISA VARNER** EL PASO, TEXAS

1/3 cup all-purpose flour
2 egg whites
1 egg
3 tablespoons honey Dijon mustard
1/2 teaspoon cayenne pepper
1/4 teaspoon salt
2/3 cup dry bread crumbs
2/3 cup ground pecans
1 package (17.6 ounces) turkey breast cutlets
1/4 cup canola oil

Place flour in a shallow bowl. In another shallow bowl, whisk the egg whites, egg, mustard, cayenne and salt. In another shallow bowl, combine bread crumbs and pecans. Coat cutlets with flour, then dip in egg mixture and coat with bread crumb mixture.

In a large skillet, cook turkey in oil in batches over medium heat for 2-3 minutes on each side or until juices run clear.

DIJON CHICKEN

PREP: 15 min. | **BAKE:** 1 hour
YIELD: 4-6 servings.

I want to share one of the easiest recipes I have ever made! The Dijon mustard adds so much flavor and the dish comes together so quickly.

CAROL ROBERTS DUMAS, TEXAS

1/2 cup Dijon mustard
1/2 cup water
1 broiler/fryer chicken
  (3 to 4 pounds), cut up
1 package (8 ounces) herb-
  seasoned stuffing, crushed

In a shallow bowl, combine mustard and water; dip the chicken pieces, then roll in stuffing. Place in a greased 13-in. x 9-in. baking pan. Sprinkle with the remaining stuffing.

Bake, uncovered, at 350° for 1 hour or until juices run clear.

CHICKEN POTPIE

PREP: 30 min. | **BAKE:** 25 min. | **YIELD:** 4 servings.

Few dishes are as comforting as the popular potpie. This satisfying version is loaded with veggies and chunks of chicken. **LUCILLE TERRY** FRANKFORT, KENTUCKY

- 3 medium carrots, sliced
- 2 medium red potatoes, cut into 1/2-inch pieces
- 1 medium turnip, peeled and cut into 1/2-inch pieces
- 1/4 cup butter, cubed
- 1/4 cup all-purpose flour
- 2 cups chicken broth
- 1 teaspoon dried thyme
- 1/2 teaspoon salt
- 1/2 teaspoon pepper
- 2 cups cubed cooked chicken
- 1 cup frozen peas, thawed
- 1 jar (4-1/2 ounces) sliced mushrooms, drained
- 4 green onions, sliced

Pastry for single-crust pie (9 inches)

Place the carrots, potatoes and turnip in a large saucepan; cover with water. Bring to a boil. Reduce heat; cover and cook for 10-15 minutes or until vegetables are tender.

Meanwhile, in a saucepan, melt butter over medium heat. Stir in flour until smooth. Gradually add the broth, thyme, salt and pepper. Bring to a boil; cook and stir for 2 minutes or until slightly thickened.

Drain vegetables and place in a large bowl; stir in the white sauce, chicken, peas, mushrooms and onions. Transfer to a greased 2-qt. round baking dish.

Place pastry over filling; trim, seal and flute edges. Cut slits in top. Bake at 375° for 25-30 minutes or until crust is golden brown and filling is bubbly.

BASIC CHICKEN BARBECUE

PREP: 10 min. + marinating | **GRILL:** 35 min. **YIELD:** 4 servings.

As far as I'm concerned, there's no better way to spend a summer night than sitting outdoors with the family and enjoying a hot-off-the-grill meal like this.
SHERRY SCHMIDT FRANKLIN, VIRGINIA

- 1 cup white vinegar
- 3 tablespoons sugar
- 2 tablespoons salt
- 1 cup water
- 1/2 cup canola oil
- 1 tablespoon poultry seasoning
- 1 tablespoon pepper
- 1 broiler/fryer chicken (3 to 3-1/2 pounds), cut up

In a small bowl, whisk the vinegar, sugar and salt. Whisk in the water, oil, poultry seasoning and pepper. Reserve 1/2 cup for basting; cover and refrigerate. Pour remaining marinade into a large resealable plastic bag; add the chicken. Seal bag and turn to coat. Refrigerate for 2-4 hours.

Drain and discard marinade from chicken. Grill, covered, over medium heat for 35-45 minutes or until juices run clear, turning and basting occasionally with reserved marinade.

GRILLED CORNISH HENS

PREP: 15 min. | **GRILL:** 50 min. | **YIELD:** 4 servings.

I like experimenting with different foods and adapting them to my own tastes. These hens are one of my specialties, an entree I concocted by combining a few different recipes. The moist meat has a pleasant grilled flavor that's accented with garlic and ginger. **DAVID BARUCH** WESTON, FLORIDA

1/4 cup butter, softened

2 green onions, finely chopped

2 tablespoons minced fresh parsley

2 tablespoons grated fresh gingerroot

3 garlic cloves, minced

1 teaspoon salt, *divided*

1/2 teaspoon pepper, *divided*

4 Cornish game hens (20 to 24 ounces *each*)

In a small bowl, combine the butter, onions, parsley, ginger, garlic, 1/2 teaspoon salt and 1/4 teaspoon pepper.

Rub mixture under the skin and over the top of each game hen. Sprinkle remaining salt and pepper inside the hen cavities.

Using long-handled tongs, moisten a paper towel with cooking oil and lightly coat the grill rack. Prepare grill for indirect heat, using a drip pan.

Place hens breast side up over drip pan and grill, covered, over indirect medium heat for 45-60 minutes or until a meat thermometer reads 180° and the meat juices run clear.

LEMON THYME CHICKEN

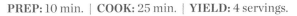

PREP: 10 min. | **COOK:** 25 min. | **YIELD:** 4 servings.

Buttered onions are a great addition to the lemon sauce of this easy supper. Best of all, it takes only a few minutes to brown the lightly breaded chicken on the stove top. **KAY SHIMONEK** CORSICANA, TEXAS

- 3 tablespoons all-purpose flour
- 1/2 teaspoon salt
- 1/4 teaspoon pepper
- 4 boneless skinless chicken breast halves (4 ounces *each*)
- 2 teaspoons olive oil
- 1 medium onion, chopped
- 1 tablespoon butter
- 1/2 teaspoon dried thyme
- 1 cup chicken broth
- 3 tablespoons lemon juice
- 2 tablespoons minced fresh parsley

In a small bowl, combine the flour, salt and pepper. Set aside 4-1/2 teaspoons for sauce. Sprinkle the remaining flour mixture over both sides of chicken.

In a nonstick skillet coated with cooking spray, cook chicken in oil over medium heat for 7-9 minutes on each side or until juices run clear. Remove and keep warm.

In the same pan, saute onion in butter until tender. Add thyme and reserved flour mixture; stir until blended. Gradually stir in the broth and lemon juice, scraping up any browned bits from bottom of pan. Bring to a boil; cook and stir for 2 minutes or until thickened. Serve over chicken. Sprinkle with parsley.

CHICKEN WITH COUNTRY GRAVY

PREP: 15 min. | **BAKE:** 50 min. | **YIELD:** 2 servings.

My mother, grandson and I worked together to create our signature oven-fried chicken. We tweaked the ingredients and seasonings each time, until we made this cherished recipe.
LINDA FOREMAN LOCUST GROVE, OKLAHOMA

- 2 tablespoons butter
- 2 tablespoons canola oil
- 1/4 cup all-purpose flour
- 1/4 teaspoon paprika
- Dash *each* seasoned salt, garlic powder, salt and pepper
- 2 chicken leg quarters

GRAVY:
- 1 tablespoon all-purpose flour
- 2/3 cup milk
- 1/8 teaspoon salt
- 1/4 teaspoon pepper

Place butter and oil in a large ovenproof skillet. Place in a 425° oven for 5 minutes. Meanwhile, in a large resealable plastic bag, combine flour and seasonings; add the chicken, one piece at a time. Seal bag and toss to coat.

Carefully place chicken, skin side down, in hot skillet. Bake, uncovered, for 15-20 minutes on each side or until a meat thermometer reads 180°. Remove from oven and keep warm.

Transfer 1 tablespoon of drippings from the skillet to a small saucepan; stir in flour until smooth. Gradually stir in the milk, salt and pepper. Bring to a boil; cook and stir for 2 minutes or until thickened. Serve with chicken.

ROSEMARY TURKEY BREAST

PREP: 10 min. | **BAKE:** 1-1/2 hours + standing
YIELD: 11 servings.

I season turkey with a blend of rosemary, garlic and paprika. Because I rub that mixture directly on the meat under the skin, I can remove the skin before serving and not lose any of the flavor.
DOROTHY PRITCHETT WILLS POINT, TEXAS

- 2 tablespoons olive oil
- 8 to 10 garlic cloves
- 3 tablespoons chopped fresh rosemary
  or 3 teaspoons dried rosemary, crushed
- 1 teaspoon salt
- 1 teaspoon paprika
- 1/2 teaspoon coarsely ground pepper
- 1 bone-in turkey breast (4 pounds)

In a food processor, combine the oil, garlic, rosemary, salt, paprika and pepper; cover and process until garlic is coarsely chopped.

With your fingers, carefully loosen the skin from both sides of turkey breast. Spread half of the garlic mixture over the meat under the skin. Smooth skin over meat and secure to underside of breast with toothpicks. Spread remaining garlic mixture over turkey skin.

Place turkey breast on a rack in a shallow roasting pan. Bake, uncovered, at 325° for 1-1/2 to 2 hours or until a thermometer reads 170°. Let stand for 15 minutes before slicing. Discard toothpicks.

ORANGE-PECAN HOT WINGS

PREP: 25 min. | **BAKE:** 55 min. | **YIELD:** 8-10 servings.

We like to use our own Florida oranges and orange juice in lots of different ways. Here's one of our favorite ways to enjoy it. **JUNE JONES** HUDSON, FLORIDA

- 3 pounds whole chicken wings
- 3 eggs
- 1 can (6 ounces) frozen orange juice
  concentrate, thawed
- 2 tablespoons water
- 1 cup all-purpose flour
- 1/2 cup finely chopped pecans
- 1/2 cup butter, melted

RED HOT SAUCE:

- 2 cups ketchup
- 3/4 cup packed brown sugar
- 2 to 3 tablespoons hot pepper sauce

Cut chicken wings into three pieces; discard wing tips.

In a bowl, whisk eggs, orange juice concentrate and water. In another bowl or a resealable plastic bag, combine flour and pecans. Dip wings in egg mixture, then roll or toss in flour mixture.

Pour butter into a 15-in. x 10-in. x 1-in. baking pan. Arrange wings in a single layer in pan. Bake, uncovered, at 375° for 25 minutes. Meanwhile, combine sauce ingredients. Spoon half over the wings; turn. Top with remaining sauce. Bake 30 minutes longer or until meat juices run clear.

EDITOR'S NOTE: Uncooked chicken wing sections (wingettes) may be substituted for whole chicken wings.

HOT CHICKEN SALAD

PREP: 10 min. | **BAKE:** 30 min. | **YIELD:** 4 servings.

I know you'll enjoy this rich and creamy chicken dish. Topped with crunchy potato chips and almonds, the delicious casserole is a fabulous way to use up leftover chicken. **DORIS HEATH** FRANKLIN, NORTH CAROLINA

2 cups diced cooked chicken

1 can (10-3/4 ounces) condensed cream of chicken soup, undiluted

2 celery ribs, finely chopped

1/2 cup mayonnaise

1 can (4 ounces) mushroom stems and pieces, drained

2 tablespoons finely chopped onion

1/2 cup crushed butter-flavored crackers (about 12 crackers)

1/2 cup crushed potato chips

1/2 cup sliced almonds, toasted

In a large bowl, combine the chicken, soup, celery, mayonnaise, mushrooms and onion. Stir in cracker crumbs. Spoon into a greased 1-1/2-qt. baking dish.

Bake, uncovered, at 375° for 15 minutes. Sprinkle with potato chips and almonds. Bake 15 minutes longer or until bubbly and lightly browned.

CHORIZO-STUFFED TURKEY BREAST WITH MEXICAN GRITS

PREP: 30 min. | **BAKE:** 1-1/4 hours + standing | **YIELD:** 6 servings.

This recipe features a wonderful combination of well-seasoned ingredients. Unique and impressive, it's just perfect for company. **VERONICA GANTLEY** NORFOLK, VIRGINIA

1 boneless skinless turkey breast half (2 pounds)

1/2 pound uncooked chorizo, crumbled

2 tablespoons olive oil

1 teaspoon salt, *divided*

1 teaspoon pepper, *divided*

2 cups water

1 cup milk

1 cup quick-cooking grits

1 can (4 ounces) chopped green chilies

1/2 cup shredded Mexican cheese blend

Minced fresh parsley, optional

Cover turkey with plastic wrap; flatten to 1/2-in. thickness. Remove plastic. Spread chorizo over turkey to within 1 in. of edges. Roll up jelly-roll style, starting with a short side; tie with kitchen string.

Rub with oil. Sprinkle with 1/2 teaspoon salt and 1/2 teaspoon pepper. In a large ovenproof skillet, brown turkey on all sides. Bake at 350° for 1-1/4 to 1-1/2 hours or until a meat thermometer reads 170°. Cover and let stand for 10 minutes before slicing.

In a large saucepan, bring the water, milk and remaining salt to a boil. Slowly stir in grits. Reduce heat; cook and stir for 5-7 minutes or until thickened. Stir in the chilies, cheese and remaining pepper. Serve grits with turkey. Sprinkle with parsley if desired.

COOKING WITH CHORIZO

Chorizo is a coarsely ground fresh or smoked pork sausage that has Mexican, Spanish and Portuguese origins and is traditionally flavored with paprika or chili powder. **TASTE OF HOME TEST KITCHEN**

CHORIZO-STUFFED TURKEY BREAST WITH MEXICAN GRITS

CHICKEN 'N' DRESSING CASSEROLE

PREP: 1 hour | **BAKE:** 35 min. | **YIELD:** 8 servings.

This casserole is a real favorite in our area and in my family, too. It's a great way to use leftover chicken or turkey, and so easy that even beginner cooks will have success making it. **BILLIE BLANTON** KINGSPORT, TENNESSEE

4 cups cubed cooked chicken

2 tablespoons all-purpose flour

1/2 cup chicken broth

1/2 cup milk

Salt and pepper to taste

DRESSING:

2 celery ribs, chopped

1 small onion, finely chopped

1 tablespoon butter

1 teaspoon rubbed sage

1/2 teaspoon poultry seasoning

1/4 teaspoon salt

1/8 teaspoon pepper

2 cups unseasoned stuffing cubes, crushed

2 cups coarsely crumbled corn bread

1/2 cup chicken broth

1 egg, beaten

GRAVY:

1/4 cup butter

6 tablespoons all-purpose flour

2 cups chicken broth

1/2 cup milk

Place chicken in a greased 2-qt. baking dish; set aside. In a small saucepan, combine the flour, broth and milk until smooth. Bring to a boil; cook and stir for 2 minutes. Season with salt and pepper. Spoon over chicken.

In a skillet, saute celery and onion in butter until tender. Stir in seasonings. Remove from the heat; add the stuffing cubes, corn bread, broth and egg. Mix well. Spoon over chicken mixture. Cover and bake at 350° for 35-40 minutes or until a thermometer inserted near the center reads 160°.

For gravy, melt butter in a small saucepan. Stir in flour until smooth; gradually add broth and milk. Bring to a boil; cook and stir for 2 minutes or until thickened. Serve with chicken and dressing.

HONEY ROSEMARY CHICKEN

PREP: 5 min. + marinating | **BAKE:** 55 min.
YIELD: 6 servings.

I never get tired of finding new ways to cook with herbs. A rosemary marinade sweetened with honey gives this moist chicken wonderful flavor and a pretty golden sheen. **ELSIE BARTON** HOOVER, ALABAMA

- 1/4 cup honey
- 1/4 cup balsamic vinegar
- 1/4 cup minced fresh rosemary
- 2 tablespoons olive oil
- 6 bone-in skinless chicken breast halves (7 ounces *each*)
- 1 teaspoon salt
- 1/4 teaspoon pepper

In a small bowl, combine the honey, vinegar, rosemary and oil. Pour half of the marinade into a large resealable plastic bag; add the chicken. Seal bag and turn to coat; refrigerate for 2 hours. Cover and refrigerate remaining marinade.

Drain and discard marinade from chicken. Place chicken bone side down in a 13-in. x 9-in. baking pan. Sprinkle with salt and pepper.

Bake, uncovered, at 350° for 55-65 minutes or until a thermometer reaches 170°, basting occasionally with the reserved marinade.

SHREDDED BARBECUE CHICKEN OVER GRITS

PREP: 20 min. | **COOK:** 25 min. | **YIELD:** 6 servings.

There's nothing like juicy meat over steaming grits. And the pumpkin in these grits makes them taste like a spicy, comforting bowl of fall flavors.

ERIN RENOUF MYLROIE SANTA CLARA, UTAH

- 1 pound boneless skinless chicken breasts
- 1/4 teaspoon pepper
- 1 can (14-1/2 ounces) reduced-sodium chicken broth, *divided*
- 1 cup hickory smoke-flavored barbecue sauce
- 1/4 cup molasses
- 1 tablespoon ground ancho chili pepper
- 1/2 teaspoon ground cinnamon
- 2-1/4 cups water
- 1 cup quick-cooking grits
- 1 cup canned pumpkin
- 3/4 cup shredded pepper jack cheese
- 1 medium tomato, seeded and chopped
- 6 tablespoons reduced-fat sour cream
- 2 green onions, chopped
- 2 tablespoons minced fresh cilantro

Sprinkle chicken with pepper; place in a large nonstick skillet coated with cooking spray.

In a large bowl, combine 1 cup broth, barbecue sauce, molasses, chili pepper and cinnamon; pour over chicken. Bring to a boil. Reduce heat; cover and simmer for 20-25 minutes or until a thermometer reads 170°. Shred chicken with two forks and return to the skillet.

Meanwhile, in a saucepan, bring water and remaining broth to a boil. Slowly stir in grits and pumpkin. Reduce heat; cook and stir for 5-7 minutes or until thickened. Stir in cheese until melted.

Divide grits among six serving bowls; top each with 1/2 cup chicken mixture. Serve with tomato, sour cream, green onions and cilantro.

BAYOU BURGERS WITH SPICY REMOULADE

PREP/TOTAL TIME: 30 min. | **YIELD:** 4 servings.

I like to serve these Southern, slightly spicy and flavorful burgers with sweet potato fries.
MICHELE CLAYBROOK-LUCAS MEDIA, PENNSYLVANIA

- 1 small onion, chopped
- 2 tablespoons olive oil
- 1/4 pound fully cooked andouille sausage link, casing removed, finely chopped
- 1 teaspoon Creole seasoning
- 3/4 teaspoon garlic powder, *divided*
- 1/4 teaspoon salt
- 1/4 teaspoon pepper
- 1 pound ground turkey
- 1/4 pound Italian turkey sausage link, casing removed
- 4 slices cheddar cheese
- 1/2 cup Miracle Whip
- 2 tablespoons lemon juice
- 1 tablespoon hot pepper sauce
- 2 teaspoons sweet pickle relish
- 1 teaspoon capers, drained
- 4 kaiser rolls, split
- 1 tablespoon butter

In a large skillet, saute onion in oil until tender. Add andouille sausage; cook 1 minute longer. Transfer to a large bowl. Stir in the Creole seasoning, 1/4 teaspoon garlic powder, salt and pepper. Crumble turkey and turkey sausage over mixture and mix well. Shape into four patties.

In a large skillet over medium heat, cook burgers for 5-7 minutes on each side or until a thermometer reads 165° and juices run clear. Top with cheese; cover and cook for 1-2 minutes or until cheese is melted.

For remoulade, in a small bowl, combine the Miracle Whip, lemon juice, pepper sauce, relish and capers. Spread rolls with butter and sprinkle with remaining garlic powder. Broil 4 in. from the heat for 2-3 minutes or until lightly browned. Serve burgers on rolls with remoulade.

EDITOR'S NOTE: The following spices may be substituted for 1 teaspoon Creole seasoning: 1/4 teaspoon each of dried thyme, ground cumin and cayenne pepper.

HONEY BALSAMIC CHICKEN

PREP/TOTAL TIME: 20 min. | **YIELD:** 2 servings.

This is a recipe I adapted from a cookbook that featured quick and easy recipes. I adjusted the seasonings somewhat and added a bit more honey to better suit my taste. LISA VARNER EL PASO, TEXAS

- 2 boneless skinless chicken breast halves (5 ounces *each*)
- 1/2 teaspoon garlic salt
- 1/8 teaspoon coarsely ground pepper
- 2 teaspoons canola oil
- 1 tablespoon balsamic vinegar
- 1 tablespoon honey
- 1/2 teaspoon dried basil

Sprinkle chicken with garlic salt and pepper. In a large skillet over medium heat, cook chicken in oil for 4-7 minutes on each side or until juices run clear. Remove and keep warm.

Add the vinegar, honey and basil to the same skillet; cook and stir for 1 minute. Return chicken to the pan; heat through, turning to coat with glaze.

CHICKEN ARTICHOKE PASTA

PREP/TOTAL TIME: 30 min. | **YIELD:** 4 servings.

Here's a colorful, delicious chicken dish that's easy enough for weeknights but special enough for guests. Oregano, garlic and a light wine sauce add lovely flavor. **CATHY DICK** ROANOKE, VIRGINIA

2-1/4 cups uncooked ziti *or*
  6 ounces uncooked fettuccine

1 pound boneless skinless
 chicken breasts, cut into
 thin strips

3 teaspoons olive oil, *divided*

1/2 cup fresh broccoli florets

1/2 cup sliced fresh mushrooms

1/2 cup cherry tomatoes, halved

2 garlic cloves, minced

1 can (14 ounces) water-packed
 artichoke hearts, rinsed,
 drained and halved

1/2 teaspoon salt

1/2 teaspoon dried oregano

2 teaspoons all-purpose flour

1/4 cup reduced-sodium chicken broth

1/3 cup white wine *or* additional reduced-sodium chicken broth

1 tablespoon minced fresh parsley

1 tablespoon shredded Parmesan cheese

Cook ziti according to package directions. Meanwhile, in a large nonstick skillet coated with cooking spray, cook chicken in 2 teaspoons oil over medium heat until no longer pink. Remove and keep warm.

In the same skillet, cook and stir broccoli in remaining oil for 2 minutes. Stir in the mushrooms, tomatoes and garlic; cook 2 minutes longer. Add the artichokes, salt and oregano; heat through.

Combine the flour with broth and wine or additional broth until smooth; stir into the pan. Bring to a boil; cook and stir for 1-2 minutes or until thickened. Add parsley and reserved chicken.

Drain ziti; add to chicken mixture and toss to coat. Sprinkle with cheese.

CHICKEN AND OKRA GUMBO

PREP: 40 min. | **COOK:** 2 hours | **YIELD:** 8-10 servings.

We used to live in New Orleans, but our stomachs don't know we moved yet. I still make many Creole dishes, and gumbo is one of our favorites. **CATHERINE BOUIS** PALM HARBOR, FLORIDA

- 1 broiler/fryer chicken (2-1/2 to 3 pounds), cut up
- 2 quarts water
- 1/4 cup canola oil *or* bacon drippings
- 2 tablespoons all-purpose flour
- 2 medium onions, chopped
- 2 celery ribs, chopped
- 1 medium green pepper, chopped
- 3 garlic cloves, minced
- 1 can (28 ounces) tomatoes, drained
- 2 cups fresh *or* frozen sliced okra
- 2 bay leaves
- 1 teaspoon dried basil
- 1 teaspoon salt
- 1/2 teaspoon pepper
- 1 to 2 teaspoons hot pepper sauce
- 2 tablespoons sliced green onions

Minced fresh parsley

Hot cooked rice

Place chicken and water in a large kettle. Cover and bring to a boil. Reduce heat; cover and simmer for 30-45 minutes or until chicken is tender.

Remove chicken; reserve broth. Set chicken aside until cool enough to handle. Remove chicken from bones; discard bones and cut chicken into cubes; set aside.

In a soup kettle, combine oil or drippings and flour until smooth. Cook over medium-high heat for 5 minutes, stirring constantly. Reduce heat to medium. Cook and stir about 5 minutes more or until mixture is reddish-brown (the color of a penny). Turn the heat to high. Stir in 2 cups reserved broth. Bring to a boil; cook and stir for 2 minutes or until thickened.

Add the onions, celery, green pepper and garlic; cook and stir for 5 minutes. Add the chicken, tomatoes, okra, bay leaves, basil, salt, pepper and pepper sauce. Cover and simmer for 1-1/2 to 2 hours.

Discard bay leaves. Garnish with green onions and parsley. Serve with rice.

GOLDEN APRICOT-GLAZED TURKEY BREAST

PREP: 10 min. | **BAKE:** 1-1/2 hours + standing | **YIELD:** 15 servings.

Basted with a simple glaze, this wonderfully moist and tender turkey bakes to a lovely golden brown. Make it the centerpiece of your holiday table; guests will be glad you did. **GREG FONTENOT** THE WOODLANDS, TEXAS

- 1/2 cup apricot preserves
- 1/4 cup balsamic vinegar
- 1/4 teaspoon pepper

Dash salt

- 1 bone-in turkey breast (5 pounds)

Combine the preserves, vinegar, pepper and salt. Place turkey breast on a rack in a large shallow roasting pan.

Bake, uncovered, at 325° for 1-1/2 to 2 hours or until a thermometer reads 170°, basting every 30 minutes with apricot mixture. (Cover loosely with foil if turkey browns too quickly.) Cover and let stand for 15 minutes before slicing.

GOLDEN APRICOT-GLAZED TURKEY BREAST

NUTTY OVEN-FRIED CHICKEN

PREP: 10 min. | **COOK:** 1 hour | **YIELD:** 6-8 servings.

The pecans that give this dish its unique nutty flavor are plentiful in the South, and so is chicken. I love to prepare and serve this easy dish because the chicken comes out moist, tasty and crispy. **DIANE HIXON** NICEVILLE, FLORIDA

- 1/2 cup evaporated milk
- 1 cup biscuit/baking mix
- 1/3 cup finely chopped pecans
- 2 teaspoons paprika
- 1/2 teaspoon salt
- 1/2 teaspoon poultry seasoning
- 1/2 teaspoon rubbed sage
- 1 broiler/fryer chicken
  (3 to 4 pounds), cut up
- 1/3 cup butter, melted

Place milk in a shallow bowl. In another shallow bowl, combine the baking mix, pecans and seasonings. Dip chicken pieces in milk, then coat generously with pecan mixture.

Place in a lightly greased 13-in. x 9-in. baking dish. Drizzle with butter. Bake, uncovered, at 350° for 1 hour or until chicken is golden brown and crispy and juices run clear.

SAUSAGE & RICE STEW

PREP: 20 min. | **COOK:** 30 min. | **YIELD:** 6 servings.

My husband loves sausage, so I find ways to serve it with healthy ingredients, like beans and spinach. This hearty recipe will have your taste buds begging for more. **KELLY YOUNG** COCOA, FLORIDA

- 1 package (14 ounces) smoked turkey kielbasa, halved lengthwise and sliced
- 1 large sweet onion, chopped
- 2 shallots, chopped
- 1 tablespoon chopped pickled jalapeno slices
- 3 garlic cloves, minced
- 1 tablespoon canola oil
- 2 cups water
- 1 can (14-1/2 ounces) reduced-sodium chicken broth
- 2 cans (15 ounces *each*) white kidney *or* cannellini beans, rinsed and drained
- 1 cup uncooked long grain rice
- 1 teaspoon dried oregano
- 1 teaspoon dried thyme
- 1/2 teaspoon pepper
- 2 cups fresh baby spinach

In a Dutch oven, saute the kielbasa, onion, shallots, jalapeno and garlic in oil until onion is tender. Add the water, broth, beans, rice and seasonings. Bring to a boil.

Reduce heat; cover and simmer for 15-20 minutes or until rice is tender. Stir in spinach. Cook 5 minutes longer or until spinach is wilted.

TURKEY BARBECUE

PREP: 15 min. | **COOK:** 25 min. | **YIELD:** 8 servings.

I got this recipe from my daughter-in-law, but added my own touches to give the chunky sandwiches some zip.
ARLENE ANDERSON SAN ANTONIO, TEXAS

- 1 celery rib, chopped
- 1 medium onion, chopped
- 1/4 cup chopped green pepper
- 1 tablespoon canola oil
- 1/4 cup packed brown sugar
- 1/4 cup ketchup
- 1/4 cup picante sauce
- 2 tablespoons Worcestershire sauce
- 1-1/2 teaspoons chili powder
- 1 teaspoon salt
- 1/8 teaspon pepper
- Dash hot pepper sauce
- 4 cups cubed cooked turkey
- 8 whole wheat hamburger buns, split

In a large nonstick skillet, saute the celery, onion and green pepper in oil for 3-4 minutes or until tender. Stir in the brown sugar, ketchup, picante sauce, Worcestershire sauce, chili powder, salt, pepper and pepper sauce; bring to a boil.

Reduce heat; simmer, uncovered, for 3-4 minutes. Add turkey; simmer 10 minutes longer or until heated through. Serve turkey in buns.

BISCUIT-TOPPED LEMON CHICKEN

PEANUTTY CHICKEN

PREP: 10 min. | **COOK:** 45 min. | **YIELD:** 4 servings.

We use peanuts in a variety of dishes. This tender chicken, covered in a tasty gravy and sprinkled with peanuts, has a zip that perks up taste buds. **MARY KAY DIXSON** DECATUR, ALABAMA

1 teaspoon chili powder

1 teaspoon salt

1/4 teaspoon pepper

1 broiler/fryer chicken (3-1/2 to 4 pounds), cut up

5 tablespoons butter

1 cup orange juice

2/3 to 1 cup salted peanuts

Orange slices *or* minced fresh cilantro, optional

In a small bowl, combine the chili powder, salt and pepper; rub over chicken. In a large skillet, saute chicken in butter until golden brown. Reduce heat; cover and cook for 30 minutes or until juices run clear.

Transfer chicken to a serving platter and keep warm. Add orange juice to skillet, stirring to loosen browned bits from pan; simmer for 5 minutes. Pour over chicken. Sprinkle with peanuts. Garnish with orange slices and cilantro if desired.

BISCUIT-TOPPED LEMON CHICKEN

PREP: 40 min. | **BAKE:** 35 min. | **YIELD:** 15 servings (30 biscuits).

This homey recipe combines two of my favorite things: hot, crusty biscuits and a flavorful lemon-pepper sauce. I've served it with potatoes and carrots baked alongside. **PATTIE ISHEE** STRINGER, MISSISSIPPI

2 large onions, finely chopped

4 celery ribs, finely chopped

1 cup butter, cubed

2 garlic cloves, minced

8 green onions, thinly sliced

2/3 cup all-purpose flour

8 cups 2% milk

12 cups cubed cooked chicken

2 cans (10-3/4 ounces *each*) condensed cream of chicken soup, undiluted

1/2 cup lemon juice

2 tablespoons grated lemon peel

2 teaspoons pepper

1 teaspoon salt

CHEDDAR BISCUITS:

5 cups self-rising flour

2 cups 2% milk

2 cups (8 ounces) shredded cheddar cheese

1/4 cup butter, melted

In a Dutch oven, saute onions and celery in butter. Add garlic; cook 1 minute longer. Add green onions. Stir in flour until blended; gradually add milk. Bring to a boil; cook and stir for 2 minutes or until thickened.

Stir in the chicken, soup, lemon juice and peel, pepper and salt; heat through. Pour into two greased 13-in. x 9-in. baking dishes; set aside.

In a large bowl, combine the biscuit ingredients just until moistened. Turn onto a lightly floured surface; knead 8-10 times. Pat or roll out to 3/4-in. thickness. With a floured 2-1/2-in. biscuit cutter, cut out 30 biscuits.

Place over chicken mixture. Bake, uncovered, at 350° for 35-40 minutes or until golden brown.

EDITOR'S NOTE: As a substitute for a cup of self-rising flour, place 1-1/2 teaspoons baking powder and 1/2 teaspoon salt in a measuring cup. Add all-purpose flour to measure 1 cup.

KENTUCKY GRILLED CHICKEN

PREP: 5 min. + marinating | **GRILL:** 40 min.
YIELD: 10 servings.

This chicken is perfect for an outdoor summer meal, and my family thinks it's fantastic. It takes about an hour on the grill but is worth the wait. I use a new paintbrush to "mop" on the basting sauce.

JILL EVELY WILMORE, KENTUCKY

    1 **cup cider vinegar**

1/2 **cup canola oil**

    5 **teaspoons Worcestershire sauce**

    4 **teaspoons hot pepper sauce**

    2 **teaspoons salt**

 10 **bone-in chicken breast halves (10 ounces *each*)**

In a small bowl, combine the first five ingredients. Pour 1 cup marinade into a large resealable plastic bag; add the chicken. Seal bag and turn to coat; refrigerate for at least 4 hours. Cover and refrigerate the remaining marinade for basting.

    Drain and discard marinade from chicken. Using long-handled tongs, moisten a paper towel with cooking oil and lightly coat the grill rack. Prepare grill for indirect heat, using a drip pan.

    Place chicken breast bone side down and grill, covered, over indirect medium heat for 20 minutes on each side or until a thermometer reads 170°, basting occasionally with reserved marinade.

RABBIT GUMBO

PREP: 20 min. | **COOK:** 2 hours | **YIELD:** 4-6 servings.

My husband's family has enjoyed this satisfying gumbo for many years. Bold seasonings and savory sausage slices enhance the mild meat. We especially like this Cajun dish on cool evenings.

MARIE REINE ST. AMANT, LOUISIANA

    1 **small onion, chopped**

    1 **small green pepper, chopped**

1/4 **cup canola oil**

    1 **dressed rabbit (about 3 pounds), cut into pieces**

1/2 **pound smoked sausage, halved and cut into 1/4-inch slices**

    1 **teaspoon salt**

1/2 **teaspoon dried thyme**

1/4 **teaspoon pepper**

1/4 **teaspoon cayenne pepper**

1/2 **cup sliced okra**

Hot cooked rice

In a Dutch oven, saute onion and green pepper in oil until tender. Add rabbit and enough water to cover. Cover and simmer for 1-1/2 to 2 hours or until meat is very tender.

    Add the sausage, salt, thyme, pepper and cayenne. Simmer, uncovered, for 15-20 minutes. Remove rabbit. When cool enough to handle, remove meat from bones; discard bones. Cut meat into bite-size pieces; return to pan. Stir in okra; bring to a boil. Serve in bowls over rice.

HERBED ROAST CHICKEN

PREP: 15 min. + marinating | **BAKE:** 2-1/4 hours + standing | **YIELD:** 8 servings.

I've been using this easy recipe for years. Marinating the chicken before roasting gives it a mild citrus tang and a lovely appearance. **SAMUEL ONIZUK** ELKTON, MARYLAND

One 2-gallon resealable plastic bag

    1/2 cup orange juice

    1/3 cup olive oil

    2 tablespoons butter, melted

    1 tablespoon balsamic vinegar

    1 tablespoon Worcestershire sauce

    6 garlic cloves, minced

    1 tablespoon minced chives

    1 tablespoon dried parsley flakes

    1 tablespoon dried basil

    1 teaspoon salt

    1 teaspoon pepper

    1/2 teaspoon dried marjoram

    1/2 teaspoon dried rosemary, crushed

    1/4 teaspoon dried tarragon

    1 roasting chicken (6 to 7 pounds)

In the 2-gallon resealable plastic bag, combine the orange juice, oil, butter, vinegar, Worcestershire sauce, garlic, chives and seasonings. Add the chicken; seal bag and turn to coat. Refrigerate for 8 hours or overnight, turning occasionally.

    Drain and discard marinade. Place chicken on a rack in a shallow roasting pan. Bake, uncovered, at 350° for 2-1/4 to 2-3/4 hours or until a thermometer reads 180°. Cover loosely with foil if chicken browns too quickly. Cover and let stand for 15 minutes before carving.

MARINATED TURKEY TENDERLOINS

CHEDDAR CHICKEN SPAGHETTI

PREP: 15 min. | **BAKE:** 20 min. | **YIELD:** 6-8 servings.

My son Charlie was a picky eater when he was young, so I put together some of the things he likes. To this day, he says it's his favorite dish! Children will be proud helping mix up this family favorite.

ANN ROBINSON DAUPHIN ISLAND, ALABAMA

- 1 package (7 ounces) spaghetti, broken
- 2 cups cubed cooked chicken
- 2 cups (8 ounces) shredded cheddar cheese, *divided*
- 1 can (10-3/4 ounces) condensed cream of chicken soup, undiluted
- 1 cup milk
- 1 tablespoon diced pimientos, optional
- 1/4 teaspoon salt
- 1/4 teaspoon pepper

Cook spaghetti according to package directions. Meanwhile, in a large bowl, combine the chicken, 1 cup cheese, soup, milk, pimientos if desired, salt and pepper. Drain spaghetti; add to the chicken mixture and toss to coat.

Transfer to a greased 13-in. x 9-in. baking dish. Sprinkle with the remaining cheese. Bake, uncovered, at 350° for 20-25 minutes or until heated through.

MARINATED TURKEY TENDERLOINS

PREP: 10 min. + marinating | **GRILL:** 15 min. | **YIELD:** 8 servings.

A savory-sweet teriyaki and soy sauce mixture make these grilled tenderloins incredibly flavorful, yet simple.

LINDA GREGG SPARTANBURG, SOUTH CAROLINA

- 1/4 cup canola oil
- 1/4 cup reduced-sodium soy sauce
- 1/4 cup reduced-sodium teriyaki sauce
- 2 tablespoons red wine vinegar
- 1 tablespoon lime juice
- 1 tablespoon Dijon mustard
- 2 garlic cloves, minced
- 2 teaspoons coarsely ground pepper
- 1-1/2 teaspoons dried parsley flakes
- 1-1/2 teaspoons dried basil
- 1/2 teaspoon onion powder
- 2 pounds turkey breast tenderloins

In a 2-cup measuring cup, combine the first 11 ingredients. Pour 2/3 cup into a large resealable plastic bag; add turkey. Seal bag and turn to coat; refrigerate for 8 hours or overnight. Cover and refrigerate remaining marinade.

Drain and discard marinade from turkey. Using long-handled tongs, moisten a paper towel with cooking oil and lightly coat the grill rack.

Grill, covered, over medium heat or broil 4 in. from the heat for 7-9 minutes on each side or until a thermometer reads 170°, basting frequently with the reserved marinade.

MARINATED MEATS AT THE READY

I freeze uncooked chicken and meats in different marinades. I transfer the meat to the refrigerator a day or two before cooking to let it absorb the marinade as it thaws. **CHRISTI G.,** TULSA, OKLAHOMA

CARIBBEAN CHICKEN TENDERLOINS

PREP/TOTAL TIME: 20 min. | **YIELD:** 4 servings.

This recipe is so fast and tasty. The light and sweet sauce perfectly offsets the bold jerk seasoning.

LAURA McALLISTER MORGANTON, NORTH CAROLINA

- 1 pound chicken tenderloins
- 2 teaspoons Caribbean jerk seasoning
- 3 teaspoons olive oil, *divided*
- 2-1/2 cups cut fresh asparagus (2-inch pieces)
- 1 cup pineapple tidbits, drained
- 4 green onions, chopped
- 2 teaspoons cornstarch
- 1 cup unsweetened pineapple juice
- 1 tablespoon spicy brown mustard
- 2 cups hot cooked rice

Rub chicken with jerk seasoning. In a large skillet coated with cooking spray, cook chicken in 1 teaspoon oil over medium heat for 3-4 minutes on each side or until juices run clear. Remove and keep warm.

In the same skillet, saute the asparagus, pineapple and onions in remaining oil for 2-3 minutes or until tender.

Combine the cornstarch, pineapple juice and mustard until smooth; gradually stir into the pan. Bring to a boil; cook and stir for 2 minutes or until thickened. Serve with chicken and rice.

CREOLE CHICKEN

PREP: 15 min. | **COOK:** 25 min. | **YIELD:** 2 servings.

Chili powder lends just a hint of heat to this full-flavored and oh-so-easy chicken entree.

SUSAN SHIELDS ENGLEWOOD, FLORIDA

- 2 boneless skinless chicken breast halves (4 ounces *each*)
- 1 teaspoon canola oil
- 1 can (14-1/2 ounces) stewed tomatoes, cut up
- 1/3 cup julienned green pepper
- 1/4 cup chopped celery
- 1/4 cup sliced onion
- 1/2 to 1 teaspoon chili powder
- 1/2 teaspoon dried thyme
- 1/8 teaspoon pepper
- 1 cup hot cooked rice

In a small nonstick skillet coated with cooking spray, cook chicken in oil over medium heat for 5-6 minutes on each side or until a thermometer reads 170°. Remove and keep warm.

In the same skillet, combine the tomatoes, green pepper, celery, onion, chili powder, thyme and pepper. Bring to a boil. Reduce heat; cover and simmer for 10 minutes or until vegetables are crisp-tender. Return chicken to pan; heat through. Serve with rice.

CITRUS GRILLED TURKEY CUTLETS

PREP: 15 min. + marinating | **GRILL:** 5 min. | **YIELD:** 4 servings.

My family enjoys this turkey recipe year-round, but it's especially nice in summer as an alternative to grilled chicken. Add a green salad, grilled veggies and some crusty bread for a great dinner.

JANICE MENTZER SHARPSBURG, MARYLAND

2 tablespoons *each* lemon, lime and orange juices

1 tablespoon minced fresh cilantro

1 tablespoon canola oil

1 tablespoon honey

1 small garlic clove, minced

1/2 teaspoon salt

1/2 teaspoon chili powder

1/4 teaspoon ground cumin

1/4 teaspoon pepper

1 package (17.6 ounces) turkey breast cutlets

In a large resealable plastic bag, combine the juices, cilantro, oil, honey, garlic and seasonings; add turkey. Seal bag and turn to coat; refrigerate for 2 hours.

Drain and discard marinade. Using long-handled tongs, moisten a paper towel with cooking oil and lightly coat the grill rack.

Grill turkey, covered, over medium heat or broil 4 in. from the heat for 2-4 minutes on each side or until no longer pink.

TURKEY A LA KING

FAVORITE BARBECUED CHICKEN

PREP: 15 min. | **GRILL:** 35 min. | **YIELD:** 6 servings.

What could be a more enjoyable dinner than barbecued chicken? This recipe comes from my father-in-law, and is one we've served at many family reunions. The homemade sauce beats any store-bought variety.
BOBBIE MORGAN WOODSTOCK, GEORGIA

1 broiler/fryer chicken
   (3 pounds), cut up
Salt and pepper to taste

BARBECUE SAUCE:

1 small onion, finely chopped
1 tablespoon canola oil
1 cup ketchup
2 tablespoons lemon juice
1 tablespoon brown sugar
1 tablespoon water
1/2 teaspoon ground mustard
1/4 teaspoon garlic powder

1/8 teaspoon pepper
Dash salt
Dash hot pepper sauce

Sprinkle chicken with salt and pepper. Grill chicken, skin side down, uncovered, over medium heat for 20 minutes.

Meanwhile, in a small saucepan, saute the onion in oil until tender. Stir in the remaining sauce ingredients. Bring to a boil. Reduce heat; simmer, uncovered, for 10 minutes.

Turn chicken; grill 15-25 minutes longer or until juices run clear, brushing often with barbecue sauce.

TURKEY A LA KING

PREP/TOTAL TIME: 20 min. | **YIELD:** 5 servings.

My friend made me this creamy casserole when I brought my twins home from the hospital. It's quick to make, but special enough to serve to guests. **VALERIE GEE** WEST SENECA, NEW YORK

1 tube (6 ounces) refrigerated
   buttermilk biscuits
1/4 cup butter, cubed
1/2 cup all-purpose flour
1 can (14-1/2 ounces)
   chicken broth
1 cup milk
2 cups cubed cooked turkey
1 cup sliced cooked carrots

1 cup cut fresh green beans
1/2 teaspoon salt
1/4 teaspoon pepper

Bake biscuits according to package directions. Meanwhile, in a large saucepan, melt butter. Stir in flour until smooth; gradually add broth and milk. Bring to a boil; cook and stir for 1-2 minutes or until thickened.

Stir in the turkey, carrots, green beans, salt and pepper; heat through. Serve with biscuits.

LEFTOVER MAKEOVERS!
Looking for another way to use up leftover turkey? Try this simple, quick-to-fix potpie. In a prepared pie crust, layer leftover mashed potatoes, chopped turkey and vegetables, then pour on the gravy. Put on the top crust and bake until the crust is golden. **TAMMI S.,** UTICA, NEW YORK

CREOLE PORK CHOPS, PG. 140

PORK

If plain ol' chicken has you yawning, give pork a try. These mouthwatering selections show you how to bake it, grill it, shred it, marinate it and more in true Southern style.

CRAWFISH-STUFFED
PORK TENDERLOINS, PG. 152

SODA POP CHOPS WITH SMASHED POTATOES

PREP: 25 min. | **COOK:** 15 min. | **YIELD:** 4 servings.

Root beer gives this family-friendly recipe a tangy taste kids will love. Served alongside the smashed potatoes, these chops make a scrumptious stick-to-the-ribs meal any weeknight. **TASTE OF HOME TEST KITCHEN**

1-1/2 pounds small red
　　potatoes, halved
　1 cup root beer
　1 cup ketchup
　1 tablespoon brown sugar
　2 teaspoons chili powder
　2 teaspoons Worcestershire
　　sauce
1/4 teaspoon garlic powder
　2 tablespoons all-purpose flour
3/4 teaspoon pepper, *divided*
1/2 teaspoon salt, *divided*
　4 bone-in pork loin chops
　　(7 ounces *each*)
　2 tablespoons olive oil
　2 tablespoons butter
1/4 teaspoon garlic powder

Place potatoes in a large saucepan and cover with water. Bring to a boil. Reduce heat; cover and cook for 15-20 minutes or until tender.

Meanwhile, in a small bowl, combine the root beer, ketchup, brown sugar, chili powder, Worcestershire sauce and garlic powder; set aside. In a large resealable plastic bag, combine the flour, 1/2 teaspoon pepper and 1/4 teaspoon salt. Add pork chops, one at a time, and shake to coat.

In a large skillet, cook chops in oil over medium heat for 2-3 minutes on each side or until chops are lightly browned; drain. Add root beer mixture. Bring to a boil. Reduce heat; cover and simmer for 6-8 minutes or until a thermometer reads 145°. Remove pork and keep warm. Let stand for 5 minutes before serving.

Bring sauce to a boil; cook until liquid is reduced by half. Meanwhile, drain potatoes; mash with butter, garlic powder and remaining salt and pepper. Serve with pork chops and sauce.

PORK CHOPS WITH MUSHROOM GRAVY

PREP: 25 min. | **COOK:** 1-3/4 hours | **YIELD:** 4 servings.

This dish, based on the "moist meat" method of preparation my grandmother used, gets passed around the table a second time. I serve it with mashed potatoes, peas and cranberry sauce. **NANCY SCHILLING** BERKELEY SPRINGS, WEST VIRGINIA

1/2 cup all-purpose flour, *divided*
1/2 cup seasoned bread
　　crumbs, *divided*
　4 pork chops (1/2 inch thick)
　2 tablespoons canola oil
　1 medium onion, sliced
　2 garlic cloves, minced
1/4 teaspoon pepper
　3 cups water
　2 tablespoons beef bouillon
　　granules
　1 teaspoon browning
　　sauce, optional

　2 bay leaves
　1 jar (4-1/2 ounces) sliced mushrooms, drained
1/2 cup cold water

In a large resealable plastic bag, combine half of the flour and bread crumbs; add pork chops, a few at a time. Seal bag and toss to coat.

In a large skillet, cook chops in oil over medium heat for 2-3 minutes on each side or until lightly browned; drain. Add the onion, garlic, pepper and water. Stir in the bouillon, browning sauce if desired and bay leaves; bring to a boil. Reduce heat; cover and simmer for 4-6 minutes or until a thermometer reads 145°.

Discard bay leaves. Remove pork to serving platter and keep warm. Let stand for 5 minutes before serving. Add mushrooms to skillet. Combine cold water and remaining flour until smooth; stir into pan juices. Bring to a boil, stirring constantly until thickened and bubbly. Stir in the remaining bread crumbs. Serve with pork chops.

SODA POP CHOPS WITH SMASHED POTATOES

GRANDMA EDNA'S CAJUN PORK

PREP: 35 min. | **COOK:** 6 hours + standing | **YIELD:** 12 servings (2-1/4 cups sauce).

My grandma Edna Mills used to make this every year as part of our Christmas dinner. She's been gone for a few years, but we still carry on her delicious tradition. TONYA CLINE GREENVILLE, OHIO

1 small onion

1 celery rib

1 small green pepper

3 tablespoons butter

3 garlic cloves, minced

2 teaspoons dried thyme

1 teaspoon paprika

1/2 teaspoon *each* salt, white pepper and pepper

1/2 teaspoon ground mustard

1/2 teaspoon hot pepper sauce

1 boneless whole pork loin roast (4 pounds)

2 tablespoons cornstarch

2 tablespoons cold water

Finely chop vegetables. In a large skillet, saute vegetables in butter until tender. Add garlic; cook 1 minute longer. Stir in seasonings and pepper sauce.

Cut roast in half. Cut several slits in roast to within 1/2 in. of bottom. Place in a 4-qt. slow cooker. Spoon onion mixture between slits and over the top of meat. Cover and cook on low for 6-8 hours or until pork is tender.

Transfer roast to a serving platter; keep warm. Let stand for 10 minutes before slicing. Pour cooking juices into a small saucepan. Combine cornstarch and water until smooth; stir into the pan. Bring to a boil; cook and stir for 2 minutes or until thickened. Serve with roast.

HAM WITH SPICED-CHERRY SAUCE

PREP: 15 min. | **BAKE:** 2 hours 20 min. + standing | **YIELD:** 18 servings.

This showstopping entree will have everyone coming back for more. It's a simple treatment that lends an appealing sweet-tart flavor to tender ham. **SHERRY THOMPSON** SENECA, SOUTH CAROLINA

- 1 boneless fully cooked ham (6 pounds)
- 2 jars (12 ounces *each*) cherry preserves
- 1/2 cup cider vinegar
- 1/4 cup packed brown sugar
- 1/4 cup water
- 1/2 teaspoon *each* ground cinnamon, nutmeg and allspice

Place ham on a rack in a shallow roasting pan. Score the surface of the ham, making diamond shapes 1/2 in. deep. Bake, uncovered, at 325° for 2 hours.

Meanwhile, in a small saucepan, combine the preserves, vinegar, brown sugar, water and spices. Bring to a boil. Reduce heat; cover and simmer for 3-4 minutes or until sugar is dissolved.

Pour 3/4 cup sauce mixture over the ham. Bake 20-30 minutes longer or until a thermometer reads 140°. Serve with remaining sauce.

CHILI-APRICOT PORK CHOPS

PREP/TOTAL TIME: 20 min.
YIELD: 4 servings.

With a slightly spicy-sweet glaze created with just four ingredients, these chops are not only tasty, they're super-easy, too.
LILY JULOW GAINESVILLE, FLORIDA

- 1/4 cup apricot preserves
- 1/4 cup chili sauce
- 1 tablespoon spicy brown mustard
- 1 tablespoon water
- 4 bone-in pork loin chops (7 ounces *each*)
- 1/4 teaspoon salt
- 1/4 teaspoon pepper

In a small bowl, combine the preserves, chili sauce, mustard and water. Sprinkle pork chops with salt and pepper. Spoon glaze over both sides of pork.

Broil 4-5 in. from the heat for 4-5 minutes on each side or until a thermometer reads 145°. Let stand for 5 minutes before serving.

LIMA BEANS WITH PORK SAUSAGE

PREP: 5 min. + standing | **COOK:** 50 min.
YIELD: 8-10 servings.

This is a delicious dish to bring to a potluck or church supper. It is so easy to put together and you will be returning home with an empty dish.

RUBY WOOD SUGAR LAND, TEXAS

- 1 pound dried lima beans
- 6 cups water
- 1/2 teaspoon salt
- 1 pound bulk pork sausage
- 2-1/2 cups tomato juice
- 1/2 teaspoon chili powder
- 1/8 teaspoon pepper
- 1 teaspoon dried basil

In a Dutch oven, bring beans, water and salt to a boil. Remove from the heat; cover and let stand for 1 hour (or soak beans overnight). Do not drain. Bring beans to a boil. Reduce heat; cover and simmer for 45 minutes or until tender.

Meanwhile, shape sausage into 3/4-in. balls; brown in a large skillet until a thermometer reads 160°. Drain fat. Stir in the tomato juice, chili powder, pepper and basil.

Drain beans; add sausage mixture. Simmer for 10 minutes or until heated through, stirring occasionally.

BOURBON BAKED HAM

PREP: 15 min. | **BAKE:** 2 hours 20 min.
YIELD: 15 servings.

Because of its simple ingredient list, easy preparation and unbeatable flavor, this baked ham recipe is one you'll rely on often. The honey-bourbon glaze not only looks lovely, but also helps to seal in the meat's juices.
JEAN ADAMS WAYCROSS, GEORGIA

- 1 bone-in fully cooked spiral-sliced ham (7 to 9 pounds)
- 1 cup honey
- 1/2 cup bourbon
- 1/2 cup molasses
- 1/4 cup orange juice
- 2 tablespoons Dijon mustard

Place ham on a rack in a shallow roasting pan. Score the surface of the ham, making diamond shapes 1/2-in. deep. Bake at 325° for 2 hours.

In a small saucepan, combine the remaining ingredients; cook and stir until smooth.

Brush ham with some of the glaze; bake 20-25 minutes longer or until a meat thermometer reads 140°, brushing occasionally with remaining glaze.

SMOTHERED PORK CHOPS

PREP/TOTAL TIME: 20 min. | **YIELD:** 4 servings.

These pork chops can be prepared in a flash using convenient stuffing mix, but they boast a delicious from-scratch flavor. You'll love the mouthwatering aroma of simmering apples, cinnamon and brown sugar. It's a dish my mom used to make when I was still living at home. The sweetness of the apple mixture makes such a nice complement to the savory stuffing and chops. **SIMONE GREENE** WINCHESTER, VIRGINIA

- 1 package (6 ounces) chicken stuffing mix
- 4 boneless pork loin chops (6 ounces *each*)
- 1 tablespoon butter
- 4 medium apples, peeled and cut into wedges
- 1/2 cup packed brown sugar
- 1/4 cup water
- 1/4 teaspoon salt
- 1/4 teaspoon ground cinnamon

Prepare stuffing mix according to package directions. Meanwhile, in a large skillet, cook pork chops in butter over medium heat for 2-3 minutes on each side or until lightly browned.

Stir in the apples, brown sugar, water and salt. Top the meat with stuffing; sprinkle with cinnamon. Bring to a boil. Reduce heat; cover and simmer for 4-6 minutes or until a thermometer inserted in the meat reads 145°. Let stand for 5 minutes before serving.

CREOLE PORK CHOPS

PREP/TOTAL TIME: 30 min. | **YIELD:** 4 servings.

I've had this recipe for more than 20 years and love it. Since the children are grown, I now cook just half the recipe. And it's so easy! You'll be in and out of the kitchen in no time.

ANN ROGERS OCALA, FLORIDA

- 1/2 teaspoon salt
- 1/2 teaspoon dried basil
- 1/2 teaspoon paprika
- 1/2 teaspoon pepper
- 1/4 teaspoon ground cumin
- 1/8 to 1/4 teaspoon cayenne pepper
- 4 boneless pork loin chops (4 ounces *each*)
- 2 tablespoons canola oil
- 1 can (8 ounces) tomato sauce
- 1/2 cup chopped onion
- 1/2 cup chopped green pepper
- 1/4 cup chopped celery
- 1 tablespoon Worcestershire sauce
- 1/2 teaspoon minced garlic

In a small bowl, combine the first six ingredients; rub over both sides of pork.

In a large skillet, cook chops in oil over medium heat for 2-3 minutes on each side or until chops are lightly browned; drain. Add the remaining ingredients. Cover and cook 4-6 minutes longer or until a thermometer reads 145°. Let stand for 5 minutes.

Serve immediately if desired, or cool before placing in a freezer container. Cover and freeze for up to 3 months.

TO USE FROZEN PORK CHOPS: Thaw in the refrigerator overnight. Cover and microwave on high for 8-10 minutes or until heated through, stirring once.

APRICOT-GLAZED HAM STEAK

PREP/TOTAL TIME: 15 min.
YIELD: 2 servings.

Want to prepare a small Easter meal? I suggest this savory-sweet entree. Glazing ham with apricot gives it an attractive look and delicious flavor.

GALELAH DOWELL FAIRLAND, OKLAHOMA

- 1 boneless fully cooked ham steak (6 ounces)
- 1 tablespoon brown sugar
- 1 tablespoon apricot preserves
- 3/4 teaspoon ground mustard

Dash ground cloves

Place ham steak in a baking dish coated with cooking spray. Combine the remaining ingredients; spoon over the ham.

Bake, uncovered, at 350° for 10-15 minutes or until heated through. Cut in half to serve.

PORK CHOPS WITH DIJON SAUCE

PREP/TOTAL TIME: 30 min. | **YIELD:** 4 servings.

Here's a main course that tastes rich but isn't high in saturated fat. It's easy for weeknights and the creamy sauce makes it special enough for weekends.

BONNIE BROWN-WATSON HOUSTON, TEXAS

- 4 boneless pork loin chops (3/4-inch thick and 6 ounces *each*)
- 1/4 teaspoon salt
- 1/4 teaspoon pepper
- 2 teaspoons canola oil
- 1/3 cup reduced-sodium chicken broth
- 2 tablespoons Dijon mustard
- 1/3 cup fat-free half-and-half

Sprinkle pork chops with salt and pepper. In a nonstick skillet coated with cooking spray, brown chops in oil for 4-5 minutes on each side or until a thermometer reads 145°. Remove and keep warm. Let meat stand for 5 minutes before serving.

Stir broth into skillet, scraping up any browned bits. Stir in the mustard until blended. Stir in the half-and-half. Bring to a boil. Reduce heat; simmer, uncovered, for 5-6 minutes or until thickened, stirring occasionally. Serve with pork chops.

GRILLED PORK TENDERLOINS

PREP: 10 min. + marinating | **GRILL:** 20 min.
YIELD: 8-10 servings.

We do a lot of grilling during the summer months, and this recipe is one my entire family loves.

BETSY CARRINGTON LAWRENCEBURG, TENNESSEE

- 1/3 cup honey
- 1/3 cup reduced-sodium soy sauce
- 1/3 cup teriyaki sauce
- 3 tablespoons brown sugar
- 1 tablespoon minced fresh gingerroot
- 3 garlic cloves, minced
- 4 teaspoons ketchup
- 1/2 teaspoon onion powder
- 1/2 teaspoon ground cinnamon
- 1/4 teaspoon cayenne pepper
- 2 pork tenderloins (about 1 pound *each*)

Hot cooked rice

In a bowl, combine the first 10 ingredients. Pour half of the marinade into a large resealable plastic bag; add tenderloins. Seal bag and turn to coat; refrigerate for 8 hours, turning occasionally. Cover and refrigerate remaining marinade.

Drain and discard marinade from meat. Grill, covered, over indirect medium-hot heat for 10-12 minutes on each side or until a thermometer reads 145°, basting with reserved marinade. Let stand for 5 minutes before slicing. Serve with rice.

ANDOUILLE-STUFFED PORK LOIN

PREP: 30 min. | **BAKE:** 40 min. | **YIELD:** 12 servings.

This andouille-stuffed and bacon-wrapped pork loin is full of bold flavors and simple to prepare. It is a faculty potluck favorite. This recipe may be prepared ahead, covered, refrigerated and baked before a potluck to provide a wonderful, warm entree. **JUDY ARMSTRONG** PRAIRIEVILLE, LOUISIANA

1/4 cup Dijon mustard

2 tablespoons apricot preserves

1 tablespoon minced fresh rosemary *or* 1 teaspoon dried rosemary, crushed

1 tablespoon minced fresh thyme *or* 1 teaspoon dried thyme

3 garlic cloves, minced

2 boneless pork loin roasts (2 pounds *each*)

1 teaspoon salt

1 teaspoon pepper

4 fully cooked andouille sausage links (about 1 pound)

12 bacon strips

1/2 cup chicken broth

1/2 cup white wine *or* additional chicken broth

In a small bowl, combine the first five ingredients. Set aside.

Make a lengthwise slit down the center of each roast to within 1/2 in. of bottom. Open roast so it lies flat; cover with plastic wrap. Flatten slightly. Remove plastic wrap. Season with salt and pepper.

Arrange two sausage links in center of each roast. Close roasts; brush with mustard mixture. Wrap each roast with bacon. Tie several times with kitchen string; secure ends with toothpicks. Place on a rack in a shallow roasting pan. Pour broth and wine into roasting pan.

Bake, uncovered, at 400° for 40-50 minutes or until a thermometer inserted into the pork loin reads 145 °. Let stand 5 minutes before slicing. Discard string and toothpicks.

MUSTARD BOURBON KABOBS

PREP/COOK TIME: 20 min. | **YIELD:** 4 servings.

You'll love the tangy and subtly sweet blend of mustard and bourbon in these tasty, no-fuss kabobs. Make a little extra marinade and serve the kabobs with a side of brown rice. **BARBARA WHITE** KATY, TEXAS

- **6 tablespoons brown sugar**
- **6 tablespoons Dijon mustard**
- **3 tablespoons bourbon** *or* **apple cider**
- **3 tablespoons reduced-sodium soy sauce**
- **1 pork tenderloin (1 pound), cut into 3/4-inch cubes**

In a small bowl, combine the brown sugar, mustard, bourbon and soy sauce. Pour 3/4 cup marinade into a large resealable plastic bag; add pork. Seal bag and turn to coat; refrigerate for 8 hours or overnight. Cover and refrigerate remaining marinade.

Drain and discard marinade from pork. Thread pork onto four metal or soaked wooden skewers. Using long-handled tongs, moisten a paper towel with cooking oil and lightly coat the grill rack.

Grill, covered, over medium heat or broil 4 in. from the heat for 10-15 minutes or until tender, turning and basting occasionally with reserved marinade.

A VERSATILE CUT

Since pork tenderloin takes only minutes to cook—30 minutes to roast whole—it's ideal for weeknight meals. It's mighty versatile too: Tenderloin is great cut into cubes for kabobs, medallions for sauteing and strips for stir-frying.
TASTE OF HOME TEST KITCHEN

LEMON-PECAN PORK CHOPS

PREP/TOTAL TIME: 15 min.
YIELD: 4 servings.

Here is a delicious dish that's quick to make and unforgettable to taste. I serve the chops with garlic mashed potatoes and sweet peas or a colorful mix of vegetables.
KATIE SLOAN CHARLOTTE, NORTH CAROLINA

- **4 boneless pork loin chops (7 ounces each)**
- **1 teaspoon lemon-pepper seasoning**
- **1/2 teaspoon garlic salt**
- **1 tablespoon butter**
- **1 cup chopped pecans**
- **1/4 cup lemon juice**

Sprinkle pork chops with lemon pepper and garlic salt. In a large skillet over medium heat, cook chops in butter for 4-5 minutes on each side or until a thermometer reads 145°. Remove and keep warm. Let stand 5 minutes before serving.

Add the pecans and lemon juice to the skillet; cook and stir for 1 minute or until heated through. Spoon over pork chops.

CUBAN PORK ROAST

PREP: 10 min. + marinating | **BAKE:** 1 hour + standing | **YIELD:** 12 servings.

A citrus and spice marinade seasons this moist, tender roast. The pork is flavorful but mild, so everyone likes it. You can serve it Cuban-style with black beans and rice, or make a traditional Cuban sandwich of pork, ham, Swiss cheese, tomatoes, lettuce, mustard, mayonnaise and dill pickle. **VIRGINIA CRONK** LITTLE TORCH KEY, FLORIDA

- 1 cup lime juice
- 1 cup orange juice
- 10 garlic cloves, minced
- 4 teaspoons ground cumin
- 2 tablespoons minced fresh thyme *or* 2 teaspoons dried thyme
- 2 tablespoons minced fresh cilantro
- 4 bay leaves
- 1 boneless pork top loin roast (3 pounds)
- 1/2 teaspoon salt
- 1/4 teaspoon pepper

In a large bowl, combine the first seven ingredients. Pour half of the marinade into a large resealable plastic bag; add the pork roast. Seal bag and turn to coat; refrigerate for 2 hours. Refrigerate remaining marinade.

Drain and discard marinade from pork. Place roast in an ungreased 13-in. x 9-in. baking dish. Pour reserved marinade over the roast. Sprinkle with salt and pepper.

Cover and bake at 350° for 45 minutes. Uncover; baste with pan drippings. Bake 15 minutes longer or until a thermometer reads 145°. Discard bay leaves. Let roast stand for 10 minutes before slicing.

PULLED PORK TATERS

PREP: 15 min. | **COOK:** 6 hours | **YIELD:** 6 servings.

If you want something a little out of the ordinary—but a hit every time—to top your baked potatoes, this is it. The savory pork, cheddar cheese and dollop of sour cream make it a complete meal. **SHANNON HARRIS** TYLER, TEXAS

- 1 boneless pork loin roast (2 to 3 pounds)
- 1 medium onion, chopped
- 1 cup ketchup
- 1 cup root beer
- 1/4 cup cider vinegar
- 2 tablespoons Worcestershire sauce
- 1 tablespoon Louisiana-style hot sauce
- 2 teaspoons salt
- 2 teaspoons pepper
- 1 teaspoon ground mustard
- 6 large potatoes
- 1 tablespoon cornstarch
- 1 tablespoon cold water
- 6 tablespoons butter
- 1-1/2 cups (6 ounces) shredded cheddar cheese
- 6 tablespoons sour cream

Place roast in a 5-qt. slow cooker. Top with onion. Combine the ketchup, root beer, vinegar, Worcestershire, hot sauce, salt, pepper and mustard; pour over top. Cover and cook on low for 6 to 8 hours or until meat is tender.

Meanwhile, scrub and pierce potatoes. Bake at 400° for 50-55 minutes or until tender.

Remove pork; shred meat with two forks. Skim fat from cooking juices; transfer to a large saucepan. Bring liquid to a boil. Combine cornstarch and water until smooth; gradually stir into the pan. Bring to a boil; cook and stir for 2 minutes or until thickened. Return meat to cooking juices; heat through.

With a sharp knife, cut an "X" in each potato; fluff with a fork. Top each with butter and pork mixture; sprinkle with cheese. Top with sour cream.

PULLED PORK TATERS

SPICED PORK MEDALLIONS WITH BOURBON SAUCE

OVERNIGHT SAUSAGE AND GRITS

PREP: 10 min. + chilling | **BAKE:** 1 hour | **YIELD:** 10-12 servings.

This recipe is so appealing because it can be prepared the night before and then popped into the oven an hour before you want to eat. This hearty dish even works well as a breakfast side dish with pancakes or waffles.
SUSAN HAM CLEVELAND, TENNESSEE

- 3 cups hot cooked grits
- 1 pound bulk pork sausage, cooked and crumbled
- 2-1/2 cups (10 ounces) shredded cheddar cheese
- 3 eggs
- 1-1/2 cups milk
- 3 tablespoons butter, melted
- 1/4 teaspoon garlic powder

In a large bowl, mix the grits, sausage and cheese. Beat the eggs and milk; stir into grits. Add butter and garlic powder. Transfer to a greased 13-in. x 9-in. baking dish. Cover and chill 8 hours or overnight.

Remove from refrigerator 30 minutes before baking. Bake, uncovered, at 350° for 1 hour or until a knife inserted near the center comes out clean. Let stand 5 minutes before cutting.

SPICED PORK MEDALLIONS WITH BOURBON SAUCE

PREP/TOTAL TIME: 25 min. | **YIELD:** 4 servings.

Our tasting panel simply raved over this tender pork with its spicy, sweet sauce. **KATHY KANTRUD** FENTON, MICHIGAN

- 1/2 cup bourbon *or* reduced-sodium chicken broth
- 1/4 cup packed dark brown sugar
- 3 tablespoons white vinegar
- 3 tablespoons reduced-sodium soy sauce
- 2 garlic cloves, minced
- 1/2 teaspoon pepper
- 1/2 teaspoon chili powder
- 1/4 teaspoon ground cinnamon
- 1/8 teaspoon salt
- 1/8 teaspoon ground allspice
- 1 pork tenderloin (1 pound), cut into 12 slices

In a small saucepan, combine the bourbon, brown sugar, vinegar, soy sauce, garlic cloves and pepper. Bring to a boil; cook until liquid is reduced to about 1/2 cup, stirring occasionally.

Meanwhile, combine the chili powder, cinnamon, salt and allspice; rub over pork slices. In a large skillet coated with cooking spray, cook pork over medium heat for 2-4 minutes on each side or until tender. Serve with sauce.

DUAL PURPOSE

A pancake turner works great for stirring puddings or grits because it fits the sides and bottom of the pot well. Everything in the pot is easily mixed and you avoid any lumps. **PHILAMENA P.,** GAINESVILLE, FLORIDA

HONEY BAKED RIBS

PREP: 10 min. + marinating | **BAKE:** 1 hour 30 min. | **YIELD:** 6 servings.

Here's a delicious recipe that's easy to make. All the preparation is done the day before, so it's perfect for those busy days. **MARGE TUBBS** RALEIGH, NORTH CAROLINA

1 can (10-1/2 ounces) beef consomme, undiluted

1/2 cup ketchup

1/2 cup soy sauce

1/2 cup honey

4 garlic cloves, minced

4 pounds bone-in country-style pork ribs, cut into serving-size pieces

Combine the first five ingredients in a bowl. Pour half into a large resealable plastic bag or shallow glass container; add ribs. Cover and refrigerate overnight, turning once. Refrigerate remaining marinade.

Remove ribs to a greased roasting pan; discard marinade. Cover and bake at 425° for 10 minutes. Reduce heat to 325°. Bake 30 minutes longer; drain. Pour reserved marinade over ribs. Bake, uncovered, for 50-70 minutes or until meat is tender, basting frequently.

RATATOUILLE SAUSAGE SAUTE

PREP/TOTAL TIME: 20 min. | **YIELD:** 2 servings.

Trying to get more vegetables into your diet? This skillet dish is a great way. It's also an ideal entree for those on a low-carb diet. **SALLY HOOK** MONTGOMERY, TEXAS

1/2 pound smoked kielbasa *or* Polish sausage, cut into 1/4-inch slices

1/2 cup chopped onion

1 garlic clove, minced

1 small eggplant, peeled and cubed

1 small zucchini, finely chopped

1 small green pepper, finely chopped

1 medium tomato, chopped

1/2 teaspoon salt

1/4 teaspoon dried basil

1/4 teaspoon dried oregano

1/4 teaspoon pepper

2 teaspoons shredded Parmesan cheese

In a large skillet, saute kielbasa and onion until sausage is browned and onion is tender. Add garlic; cook 1 minute longer. Stir in the eggplant, zucchini and green pepper; saute 4-5 minutes or until vegetables are tender.

Stir in the tomato, salt, basil, oregano and pepper; heat through. Sprinkle with cheese.

RATA-WHAT?

Ratatouille is a traditional French Provençal stewed vegetable dish. Traditionally, it is served as a side dish, but also may be served as a meal on its own accompanied by pasta or rice. Tomatoes are a key ingredient, as well as garlic, onions, zucchini, eggplant, bell peppers, marjoram and basil, or bay leaf and thyme, or a mix of green herbs.

TASTE OF HOME TEST KITCHEN

RATATOUILLE SAUSAGE SAUTE

SOUTH CAROLINA-STYLE RIBS

PREP: 15 min. | **BAKE:** 1 hour 30 min. | **YIELD:** 6-8 servings.

This recipe makes some of the best country-style pork ribs you'll ever eat, especially when cooked on a grill. We use the same sauce on barbecued chicken, too. **KAREN CONKLIN** SUPPLY, NORTH CAROLINA

- 4 **pounds pork baby back ribs**
- 1/2 **cup red wine vinegar**
- 1/2 **cup honey**
- 1/2 **cup prepared mustard**
- 2 **tablespoons canola oil**
- 4 **teaspoons Worcestershire sauce**
- 2 **teaspoons butter**
- 2 **teaspoons coarsely ground pepper**
- 1 **teaspoon salt**
- 1 **teaspoon hot pepper sauce**

Cut ribs into serving-size pieces. Place ribs meat side up in a roasting pan. Bake, uncovered, at 350° for 1 hour.

Meanwhile, combine the remaining ingredients in a saucepan. Bring to a boil over medium heat. Reduce heat; simmer, uncovered, for about 30 minutes or until slightly reduced. Remove from the heat; cool at room temperature for 1 hour.

Drain ribs and discard cooking liquid. Bake, uncovered, for 30-60 minutes longer or until ribs are tender, basting occasionally. To grill, moisten a paper towel with cooking oil; using long-handled tongs, lightly coat the grill rack. Brush half of the sauce over ribs. Grill ribs, covered, over medium heat for 15-25 minutes or until browned, turning and basting occasionally with remaining sauce.

CORN-STUFFED CROWN ROAST

PREP: 20 min. | **BAKE:** 3 hours + standing | **YIELD:** 12 servings.

My mother always made this elegant entree for company dinners and special family celebrations. **DOROTHY SWANSON** ST. LOUIS, MISSOURI

- 1 pork crown roast (about 7 pounds and 12 ribs)
- 1/2 teaspoon pepper, *divided*
- 1 cup chopped celery
- 1 cup chopped onion
- 1 cup butter, cubed
- 6 cups crushed corn bread stuffing
- 2 cups frozen corn, thawed
- 2 jars (4-1/2 ounces *each*) sliced mushrooms, undrained
- 1 teaspoon salt
- 1 teaspoon poultry seasoning

Place roast on a rack in a large shallow roasting pan. Sprinkle with 1/4 teaspoon pepper. Cover rib ends with foil. Bake, uncovered, at 350° for 1-1/2 hours.

In a Dutch oven, saute celery and onion in butter until tender. Stir in the stuffing, corn, mushrooms, salt, poultry seasoning and remaining pepper. Carefully spoon 1-3 cups into center of roast. Place remaining stuffing in a greased 2-qt. baking dish. Refrigerate until ready to use.

Bake roast 1 hour longer or until a thermometer reads 165° for stuffing. Cover and bake extra stuffing for 30-40 minutes or until browned. Transfer roast to serving platter; let stand 15 minutes. Remove foil. Cut between ribs to serve.

ORANGE-GLAZED HAM

PREP: 15 min.
BAKE: 1 hour 20 min.
YIELD: 12 servings.

A glaze of brown sugar, orange peel, whiskey and spices makes this holiday ham memorable. If you like, replace the liquor with apple cider.
LAURA MCDOWELL LAKE VILLA, ILLINOIS

- 1 boneless fully cooked ham (4 to 6 pounds)
- 1/3 cup packed brown sugar
- 1/3 cup whiskey *or* apple cider
- 1 tablespoon grated orange peel
- 1/4 teaspoon ground allspice
- 1/8 teaspoon ground cloves

Place ham on a rack in a shallow roasting pan. Cover and bake at 325° for 1 hour.

In a saucepan, combine the brown sugar, whiskey, orange peel, allspice and cloves. Bring to a boil. Reduce heat; simmer, uncovered, for 5-7 minutes or until slightly thickened.

Brush some of the sauce over ham. Bake, uncovered, 20 minutes longer or until a thermometer reads 140°, brushing twice with sauce.

CAROLINA MARINATED PORK TENDERLOIN

PREP: 10 min. + marinating
GRILL: 20 min. | **YIELD:** 4 servings.

You'll need just three ingredients to make a melt-in-your mouth marinade friends and neighbors will rave about.

SHARISSE DUNN
ROCKY POINT, NORTH CAROLINA

1/4 cup molasses
2 tablespoons spicy brown mustard
1 tablespoon cider vinegar
1 pork tenderloin (1 pound)

In a resealable plastic bag, combine the molasses, mustard and vinegar; add pork. Seal bag and turn to coat; refrigerate for 8 hours or overnight.

Prepare grill for indirect heat, using a drip pan. Drain and discard marinade. Moisten a paper towel with cooking oil; using long-handled tongs, lightly coat the grill rack.

Place pork over drip pan and grill, covered, over indirect medium-hot heat for 20-27 minutes or until a thermometer reads 145°, turning occasionally. Let stand for 5 minutes before slicing.

CRAWFISH-STUFFED PORK TENDERLOINS

PREP: 35 min. | **BAKE:** 40 min. | **YIELD:** 8-10 servings.

In Louisiana, crawfish (sometimes called crayfish or crawdads) are popular. Here is a unique way I use them with pork.

KIM BUNTING COLFAX, LOUISIANA

6 green onions, chopped
3/4 cup chopped green pepper
1/4 cup butter
1/2 teaspoon chicken bouillon granules
1/2 cup boiling water
2 cups seasoned stuffing croutons
1 pound cooked crawfish tails *or* cooked medium shrimp, peeled and deveined
4 pork tenderloins (1 pound *each*)
1/2 teaspoon salt
1/4 teaspoon pepper
1/4 cup molasses

GRAVY:

5 teaspoons cornstarch
2 teaspoons beef bouillon granules
1 cup plus 2 tablespoons cold water
1 can (4 ounces) mushroom stems and pieces, undrained
1/4 teaspoon browning sauce, optional

In a large skillet, saute onions and green pepper in butter until tender. Dissolve bouillon in boiling water. Place the croutons in a large bowl; add onion mixture and bouillon mixture. Stir in crawfish tails; set aside.

Cut a lengthwise slit down the center of each tenderloin to within 1/2 in. of bottom. Open tenderloins so they lie flat; cover with plastic wrap. Flatten to 3/4-in. thickness. Remove plastic; sprinkle with salt and pepper. Spoon stuffing over two tenderloins. Top with remaining tenderloins; tie with kitchen string.

Place on a rack in a shallow roasting pan. Cover and bake at 350° for 10 minutes. Brush with half of the molasses. Bake, uncovered, 30-35 minutes longer or until a thermometer inserted into meat reads 145°, brushing once with remaining molasses. Let stand for 5 minutes before slicing.

Meanwhile, in a small saucepan, combine cornstarch, bouillon and water until smooth. Bring to a boil; cook and stir for 2 minutes or until thickened. Add mushrooms and browning sauce if desired. Slice pork; serve with gravy.

PORK ROAST WITH MASHED POTATOES AND GRAVY

PREP: 20 min. | **COOK:** 3 hours + standing | **YIELD:** 4 servings.

This home-style meal can be made ahead of time and reheated. Simply strain and skim the cooking juices and cover and store in the fridge. Finish the gravy in a pan before serving. **LEE BREMSON** KANSAS CITY, MISSOURI

- 1 boneless whole pork loin roast (3 to 4 pounds)
- 1 can (14-1/2 ounces) chicken broth
- 1 cup julienned sweet red pepper
- 1/2 cup chopped onion
- 1/4 cup cider vinegar
- 2 tablespoons Worcestershire sauce
- 1 tablespoon brown sugar
- 2 teaspoons Italian seasoning
- 1 teaspoon salt
- 1 teaspoon pepper
- 2 teaspoons cornstarch
- 2 teaspoons cold water
- 2 cups refrigerated mashed potatoes

Cut roast in half; transfer to a 5-qt. slow cooker. In a small bowl, combine the broth, red pepper, onion, vinegar, Worcestershire sauce, brown sugar and seasonings; pour over pork. Cover and cook on low for 3-4 hours or until meat is tender.

Remove pork; cut some into cubes measuring 2-1/2 cups and refrigerate for another use. Keep remaining pork warm.

For gravy, strain cooking juices and skim fat; pour 1 cup into a small saucepan. Combine cornstarch and water until smooth; stir into cooking juices. Bring to a boil; cook and stir for 2 minutes or until thickened.

Meanwhile, in a small microwave-safe bowl, cook potatoes on high for 2-3 minutes or until heated through. Let meat stand for 10 minutes before slicing; serve with potatoes and gravy.

EDITOR'S NOTE: This recipe was tested in a 1,100-watt microwave.

WHISKEY SIRLOIN STEAK, PG. 169

PEACH-GLAZED BEEF FILETS, PG. 158

BEEF

Hearty and satisfying, beef entrees have a special place at the Southern table. Cajun Corned Beef Hash, Beef Brisket with Mop Sauce and Whiskey Sirloin Steak are just some of the tempting options awaiting your fork and knife.

CREOLE STEAKS

PREP: 15 min. | **COOK:** 35 min. | **YIELD:** 4 servings.

Here's a way to "fancy up" an economical cut of beef. I created the recipe as a Southern variation on Swiss steak, and suggest serving it with rice to catch the flavorful sauce. **NICOLE FILIZETTI** JACKSONVILLE, FLORIDA

1 large onion, chopped

1/4 cup chopped green pepper

1/4 cup chopped celery

4 tablespoons canola oil, *divided*

3 garlic cloves, minced

1 tablespoon all-purpose flour

1/2 teaspoon salt

1/2 teaspoon dried thyme

1/2 teaspoon cayenne pepper

1/2 teaspoon pepper

2 cans (14-1/2 ounces *each*) fire-roasted diced tomatoes, undrained

1/4 teaspoon hot pepper sauce

1 tablespoon lemon juice

4 beef cubed steaks (4 ounces *each*)

Additional salt and pepper

In a large skillet, saute the onion, green pepper and celery in 2 tablespoons oil until crisp-tender. Add garlic; cook 1 minute longer. Stir in the flour, salt, thyme, cayenne and pepper.

Add tomatoes and pepper sauce; bring to a boil. Reduce heat; simmer, uncovered, for 20-25 minutes or until thickened, stirring occasionally. Remove from the heat; stir in lemon juice and keep warm.

Sprinkle steaks with salt and pepper to taste. In another large skillet, cook steaks in remaining oil over medium heat for 3-4 minutes on each side or until no longer pink. Serve with sauce.

BEEF BRISKET WITH MOP SAUCE

PREP: 20 min. | **BAKE:** 2 hours | **YIELD:** 10-12 servings.

When one of our sons lived in the South, I learned that "mop sauce" is traditionally prepared for barbecue cooked in batches so large, the sauce is brushed on the meat with a mop! You won't need a mop for my recipe, but it does have big-time taste. **DARLIS WILFER** WEST BEND, WISCONSIN

- 1/2 cup water
- 1/4 cup cider vinegar
- 1/4 cup Worcestershire sauce
- 1/4 cup ketchup
- 1/4 cup dark corn syrup
- 2 tablespoons canola oil
- 2 tablespoons prepared mustard
- 1 fresh beef brisket (3 pounds)

In a large saucepan, combine the first seven ingredients. Bring to a boil, stirring constantly. Reduce heat; simmer for 5 minutes, stirring occasionally. Remove from the heat.

Place the brisket in a shallow roasting pan; pour sauce over the top. Cover and bake at 350° for 2 to 2-1/2 hours or until meat is tender. Let stand for 5 minutes. Thinly slice meat across the grain.

TANGY BEEF BRISKET: Omit sauce. In a large saucepan, saute 1/2 cup diced onion in 1/4 cup butter until tender. Add 1-3/4 cup ketchup, 3/4 cup packed brown sugar, 1/4 cup Worcestershire sauce, 3 tablespoons lemon juice, 1 tablespoon chili powder, 3/4 teaspoon hot pepper sauce, 1/2 teaspoon each salt and prepared horseradish and 1/4 teaspoon garlic powder. Bring to a boil. Reduce heat; simmer, uncovered, for 30-40 minutes. Proceed as directed in step 2.

EDITOR'S NOTE: This is a fresh beef brisket, not corned beef.

RIBEYES WITH CHILI BUTTER

PREP: 10 min. | **GRILL:** 10 min.
YIELD: 2 servings.

A couple spoonfuls of spicy butter instantly gives steak a slightly zippy slant. Meat lovers will be delighted by the chili and mustard flavors.
ALLAN STACKHOUSE JR.
JENNINGS, LOUISIANA

- 1/4 cup butter, softened
- 1 teaspoon chili powder
- 1/2 teaspoon Dijon mustard
- Dash cayenne pepper
- 2 beef ribeye steaks (8 ounces *each*)
- 1/2 to 1 teaspoon coarsely ground pepper
- 1/4 teaspoon sugar

In a small bowl, beat the butter, chili powder, mustard and cayenne until smooth. Refrigerate until serving.

Rub the steaks with pepper and sugar. Grill, covered, over medium heat for 5-6 minutes on each side or until meat reaches desired doneness (for medium-rare, a thermometer should read 145°; medium, 160°; well-done, 170°). Spoon chili butter over steak.

PEACH-GLAZED BEEF FILETS

PREP/TOTAL TIME: 30 min. | **YIELD:** 2 servings.

I love combining fruits and chilies to make flavorful glazes. This recipe has evolved over the years. It uses ancho chili powder, which lends a nice smoky flavor. I like to serve the flavorful filets over rice, potatoes or cheesy grits. **ANNA GINSBERG** AUSTIN, TEXAS

- 2 beef tenderloin steaks (5 ounces *each*)
- 1/4 teaspoon salt
- 1/8 teaspoon pepper
- 1 teaspoon canola oil
- 1/4 cup peach preserves
- 2 tablespoons chicken broth
- 1 tablespoon balsamic vinegar
- 2 teaspoons minced fresh cilantro
- 3/4 teaspoon ground ancho chili pepper
- 1 garlic clove, minced

Sprinkle beef with salt and pepper. In a skillet, cook steaks in oil over medium heat for 5-8 minutes on each side or until meat reaches desired doneness (for medium-rare, a thermometer should read 145°; medium, 160°; well-done, 170°).

In a small bowl, combine the remaining ingredients; pour over steaks. Cook for 1-2 minutes or until glaze is heated through.

CAJUN PEPPER STEAK

PREP: 20 min. | **COOK:** 1-1/4 hours | **YIELD:** 4 servings.

The seasonings in this recipe turn beef into a zesty dish you'll want to serve again and again.
RONALD TREADWAY ACWORTH, GEORGIA

- 1-1/2 pounds beef top round steak, cubed
- 2 tablespoons butter
- 2 medium onions, halved and sliced
- 2 medium green peppers, julienned
- 1 medium sweet red pepper, julienned
- 1 celery rib, sliced
- 1-1/2 cups water
- 4 teaspoons Worcestershire sauce
- 1 tablespoon chili powder
- 1 tablespoon reduced-sodium soy sauce
- 1/2 to 1 teaspoon Cajun seasoning
- 1/4 teaspoon hot pepper sauce, optional
- 2 tablespoons cornstarch
- 2 tablespoons cold water

Hot cooked egg noodles *or* rice

In a large skillet, brown beef in butter over medium heat; drain. Stir in the onions, peppers and celery; cook and stir for 2 minutes.

Add the water, Worcestershire sauce, chili powder, soy sauce, Cajun seasoning and pepper sauce if desired. Bring to a boil. Reduce heat; cover and simmer for 1 to 1-1/2 hours or until meat is tender.

Combine cornstarch and cold water until smooth; stir into meat mixture. Bring to a boil; cook and stir for 2 minutes or until thickened. Serve with noodles or rice.

SIMPLE MARINATED RIBEYES

PREP: 10 min. + marinating | **GRILL:** 10 min. | **YIELD:** 6 servings.

When spring arrives, out comes the grill! My husband does a great job cooking these steaks to juicy perfection.
They taste so terrific, we enjoy them at least once a week. **SONJA KANE** WENDELL, NORTH CAROLINA

1/2 cup butter, melted
1/4 cup lemon juice
1/4 cup ketchup
2 tablespoons Worcestershire
   sauce
2 tablespoons cider vinegar
2 tablespoons olive oil
4 garlic cloves, minced
1 teaspoon salt

1 teaspoon sugar
1/2 teaspoon hot pepper sauce
Dash cayenne pepper
6 beef ribeye steaks (about 1 inch thick and 12 ounces *each*)

In a large resealable bag, combine the first 11 ingredients. Add the steaks. Seal bag and turn to coat; refrigerate for 6 hours or overnight.

Drain and discard marinade. Grill steaks, uncovered, over medium heat for 5-7 minutes on each side or until the meat reaches desired doneness (for medium-rare, a thermometer should read 145°; medium, 160°; well-done, 170°).

TENDERLOIN FOR TWO WITH CHERRY-BRANDY SAUCE

PREP/TOTAL TIME: 30 min. | **YIELD:** 2 servings.

I'm a stay-at-home mom with an active toddler and busy teenager. An evening alone with my husband is truly a special occasion, so I make this elegant entree for two. **GINA HARDY** LA VERNIA, TEXAS

- 1/4 **cup beef broth**
- 1/4 **cup port wine** *or additional* **beef broth**
- 1 **shallot, thinly sliced**
- 1 **teaspoon tomato paste**
- 1/2 **teaspoon grated horseradish**
- 1/4 **teaspoon whole peppercorns**
- 1 **bay leaf**
- 2 **beef tenderloin steaks (6 ounces** *each***)**
- 1-1/2 **teaspoons olive oil**
- 1 **tablespoon butter,** *divided*
- 1/4 **cup cherry brandy**
- 1-1/2 **teaspoons cherry preserves**

In a saucepan, combine the first seven ingredients. Bring to a boil. Reduce heat; simmer, uncovered, until liquid is slightly thickened and reduced to about 1/3 cup. Strain and discard the shallot, peppercorns and bay leaf; set liquid aside.

In a skillet over medium heat, cook steaks in oil and 1-1/2 teaspoons butter for 5-8 minutes on each side or until meat reaches desired doneness (for medium-rare, a thermometer should read 145°; medium, 160°; well-done, 170°). Remove steaks and keep warm.

Remove pan from the heat; add the reserved broth mixture, then the brandy. Return pan to the heat. Bring to a boil; cook for 5 minutes or until liquid is thickened and reduced to about 1/4 cup. Stir in preserves and remaining butter. Return steaks to the pan; heat through.

CAJUN CORNED BEEF HASH

PREP/TOTAL TIME: 30 min. | **YIELD:** 4 servings.

Neither the taste nor the texture is "mushy" in this tongue-tingling hash. I created the recipe after eating a similar variation while vacationing; it has been an all-time favorite of mine ever since.

DEL MASON MARTENSVILLE, SASKATCHEWAN

- 6 cups frozen shredded hash brown potatoes, thawed
- 1/4 cup butter
- 1/2 cup *each* finely chopped green onions, sweet red pepper and green pepper
- 1 teaspoon seasoned salt
- 3/4 teaspoon Cajun seasoning
- 3/4 teaspoon chili powder
- 1/2 teaspoon pepper
- 1-1/2 cups chopped cooked corned beef
- 1 tablespoon white vinegar
- 8 eggs

Additional Cajun seasoning and hot pepper sauce, optional

In a large skillet, cook hash browns in butter until almost tender. Stir in onions, peppers and seasonings. Cook until hash browns are lightly browned and peppers are tender. Add corned beef; heat through.

Meanwhile, place 2-3 in. of water in a large skillet with high sides; add vinegar. Bring to a boil; reduce heat and simmer gently. Break cold eggs, one at a time, into a custard cup or saucer; holding the cup close to the surface of the water, slip egg into water.

Cook 4 eggs, uncovered, until whites are completely set, about 4 minutes. With a slotted spoon, lift each egg out of the water. Repeat with remaining eggs.

Serve over hash mixture. Sprinkle with additional Cajun seasoning and serve with hot pepper sauce if desired.

CRAB-STUFFED FILET MIGNON

PREP/TOTAL TIME: 30 min. | **YIELD:** 2 servings.

Here's an elegant entree for you and someone special. He or she will be impressed with the flavor; you'll love that it's so fast and easy! **SHANE HARRIS** ABINGDON, VIRGINIA

- 1/2 cup lump crabmeat, drained
- 2 tablespoons shredded Parmesan cheese
- 1 tablespoon chopped green onion
- 1 teaspoon butter, melted
- 2 beef tenderloin steaks (6 ounces *each*)
- 1/4 teaspoon salt
- 1/8 teaspoon pepper

In a small bowl, combine the crabmeat, cheese, onion and butter. Sprinkle steaks with salt and pepper. Cut a horizontal slit through each steak to within 1/2 in. of the opposite side, forming a pocket. Fill with 1/2 cup crab mixture. Secure with kitchen string if necessary.

Broil 4 in. from the heat for 7-9 minutes on each side or until meat reaches desired doneness (for medium-rare, a thermometer should read 145°; medium, 160°; well-done, 170°). Let stand for 5 minutes before serving.

LOADED FLANK STEAK

PREP/TOTAL TIME: 30 min. | **YIELD:** 6 servings.

For a delicious steak dinner, try this recipe. The stuffing makes it elegant enough to serve to guests.
TAMMY THOMAS MUSTANG, OKLAHOMA

- 1/2 cup butter, softened
- 6 bacon strips, cooked and crumbled
- 3 green onions, chopped
- 2 tablespoons ranch salad dressing mix
- 1/2 teaspoon pepper
- 1 beef flank steak (1-1/2 to 2 pounds)

In a small bowl, combine the first five ingredients. Cut a deep slit in steak, forming a pocket. Stuff butter mixture into slit.

Grill steak, covered, over medium heat or broil 4-6 in. from the heat for 6-7 minutes on each side or until meat reaches desired doneness (for medium-rare, a thermometer should read 145°; medium, 160°; well-done, 170°). Let stand 5 minutes before serving. To serve, thinly slice across the grain.

ROASTED GARLIC & HERB PRIME RIB

PREP: 1 hour | **BAKE:** 2-1/2 hours + standing | **YIELD:** 12 servings.

An easy herb rub creates a flavorful crust over an impressive rib roast. The creamy horseradish sauce adds a bit of zest to each tender bite. **MICHELE SOLOMON** CRESTVIEW, FLORIDA

- 1 whole garlic bulb
- 1/4 teaspoon plus 2 tablespoons olive oil, *divided*
- 3 green onions, finely chopped
- 1 tablespoon dried rosemary, crushed
- 1 teaspoon dried thyme
- 1 teaspoon dill weed
- 1 teaspoon onion powder
- 1/2 teaspoon salt
- 1/4 teaspoon pepper
- 1/2 cup dry red wine *or* beef broth
- 1 bone-in beef rib roast (6 to 8 pounds)
- 2 cups beef broth

SAUCE:
- 1 cup (8 ounces) sour cream
- 1 tablespoon prepared horseradish
- 1-1/2 teaspoons dill weed

Remove papery outer skin from garlic (do not peel or separate cloves). Cut top off of garlic bulb. Brush with 1/4 teaspoon oil. Wrap garlic bulb in heavy-duty foil. Bake at 425° for 30-35 minutes or until softened. Cool for 10-15 minutes.

Squeeze softened garlic into a small bowl; stir in the onions, herbs, onion powder, salt and pepper. Add wine and remaining oil. Place roast fat side up in a shallow roasting pan. Cut slits into roast; spoon garlic mixture into slits. Rub remaining garlic mixture over roast. Pour beef broth into bottom of pan.

Bake, uncovered, at 450° for 15 minutes. Reduce heat to 325°; bake 2-1/4 to 2-3/4 hours longer or until meat reaches desired doneness (for medium-rare, a thermometer should read 145°; medium, 160°; well-done, 170°).

Meanwhile, in a small bowl, combine sauce ingredients. Cover and chill until serving. Remove roast to a serving platter and keep warm; let stand for 15 minutes before slicing. Serve with sauce.

ROASTED GARLIC & HERB PRIME RIB

STEAKS WITH CRAB SAUCE

PREP/TOTAL TIME: 25 min. | **YIELD:** 4 servings.

Watch jaws drop when you serve this surf and turf entree that's elegant enough for any occasion. A creamy crab sauce drapes nicely over tender New York strip steaks. **TASTE OF HOME TEST KITCHEN**

- 1 teaspoon dried rosemary, crushed
- 1/2 teaspoon salt
- 1/2 teaspoon pepper
- 4 boneless beef top loin steaks (8 ounces *each*)
- 1 tablespoon canola oil

SAUCE:
- 2 teaspoons cornstarch
- 1/4 cup white wine *or* chicken broth
- 3/4 cup heavy whipping cream
- 1 tablespoon Dijon mustard
- 1/2 teaspoon prepared horseradish
- 1/8 teaspoon salt
- 1/8 teaspoon pepper
- 1 package (8 ounces) imitation crabmeat, coarsely chopped

Combine the rosemary, salt and pepper; rub over steaks. In a large skillet over medium-high heat, cook steaks in oil for 5-8 minutes on each side or until meat reaches desired doneness (for medium-rare, a thermometer should read 145°; medium, 160°; well-done, 170°).

Meanwhile, in a small saucepan, combine the cornstarch and wine or broth until smooth. Stir in the cream, mustard, horseradish, salt and pepper. Bring to a boil; cook and stir for 2 minutes or until thickened. Stir in crab; heat through. Serve over steaks.

EDITOR'S NOTE: Top loin steak may be labeled as strip steak, Kansas City steak, New York strip steak, ambassador steak or boneless club steak in your region.

RED-EYE BEEF ROAST

PREP: 25 min. | **BAKE:** 2 hours + standing
YIELD: 10-12 servings.

Hot sauce adds a touch of zip to this cut of meat. It takes me back to the dinners I enjoyed as a child. I like to use the leftovers in different dishes, including barbecued beef sandwiches. **CAROL STEVENS** BASYE, VIRGINIA

- 1 boneless beef eye of round roast (about 3 pounds)
- 1 tablespoon canola oil
- 2-1/2 cups water, *divided*
- 1 envelope onion soup mix
- 3 tablespoons cider vinegar
- 2 tablespoons Louisiana hot sauce
- 2 tablespoons all-purpose flour

In a Dutch oven, brown roast on all sides in oil over medium-high heat; drain. Combine 3/4 cup water, soup mix, vinegar and hot sauce; pour over roast.

Cover and bake at 325° for 2-3 hours or until tender. Transfer to a serving platter and keep warm. Let stand for 10-15 minutes before slicing.

For gravy, combine flour and remaining water until smooth; stir into meat juices. Bring to a boil; cook and stir for 2 minutes or until thickened. Serve with meat.

CAJUN BEEF TENDERLOIN

PREP: 15 min. | **GRILL:** 50 min. + standing
YIELD: 12 servings.

This spicy entree really warms up a chilly evening. The dry rub keeps the tenderloin nice and moist.
SUZANNE (SUE) DANNAHOWER FORT PIERCE, FLORIDA

- 1 beef tenderloin roast (3 pounds)
- 4 teaspoons salt
- 1 tablespoon paprika
- 2-1/4 teaspoons onion powder
- 1-1/2 teaspoons garlic powder
- 1-1/2 teaspoons white pepper
- 1-1/2 teaspoons pepper
- 1 to 3 teaspoons cayenne pepper
- 1 teaspoon dried basil
- 1/2 teaspoon chili powder
- 1/8 teaspoon dried thyme
- 1/8 teaspoon ground mustard

Dash ground cloves

Tie tenderloin at 2-in. intervals with kitchen string. Combine the seasonings; rub over beef. Using long-handled tongs, moisten a paper towel with cooking oil and lightly coat the grill rack.

Prepare grill for indirect heat using a drip pan. Place tenderloin over drip pan and grill, covered, over indirect medium heat for 50-60 minutes, or until meat reaches desired doneness (for medium-rare, a thermometer should read 145°; medium, 160°; well-done, 170°), turning occasionally. Let stand for 10 minutes before slicing.

To roast the tenderloin, bake on a rack in a roasting pan at 425° for 45-60 minutes or until meat reaches desired doneness.

PEPPERED RIBEYE STEAKS

PREP: 10 min. + chilling | **GRILL:** 25 min.
YIELD: 8 servings.

A true Southerner to the core, I love to cook and this pepper-crusted steak is one of my specialties.
SHARON BICKETT CHESTER, SOUTH CAROLINA

   4 beef ribeye steaks (1-1/2 inches thick)
   1 tablespoon olive oil
   1 tablespoon garlic powder
   1 tablespoon paprika
   2 teaspoons dried ground thyme
   2 teaspoons dried ground oregano
1-1/2 teaspoons pepper
   1 teaspoon salt
   1 teaspoon lemon-pepper seasoning
   1 teaspoon cayenne pepper
   1 teaspoon ground red pepper
Orange slices, optional
Parsley sprigs, optional

Brush steaks with oil. In a bowl, combine seasonings. Sprinkle over steaks and press into both sides. Cover; chill for 1 hour.

Grill steaks, turning once, over medium heat 14-18 minutes for medium-rare; 18-22 minutes for medium; 24-28 minutes for well-done. Place on a warm serving platter; cut across the grain into thick slices. Garnish with orange slices and parsley if desired.

CHIPOTLE BEEF TENDERLOINS

PREP: 40 min. | **GRILL:** 10 min. | **YIELD:** 6 servings.

The subtle smoky heat found in every bite of this juicy beef entree is divine! **GENE PETERS** EDWARDSVILLE, ILLINOIS

3/4 cup chopped sweet onion
3/4 cup chopped green pepper
   1 jalapeno pepper, seeded and minced
   1 chipotle pepper in adobo sauce, minced
   2 tablespoons olive oil
   3 cups seeded chopped tomatoes
   1 tablespoon chipotle hot pepper sauce
   2 teaspoons sugar
   1 teaspoon salt
   1 teaspoon chili powder
1/2 teaspoon ground cumin
   2 tablespoons minced fresh cilantro
   1 teaspoon Liquid Smoke, optional
   6 beef tenderloin steaks (1-1/2 inches thick and 6 ounces *each*)
   2 teaspoons steak seasoning

In a Dutch oven, saute the onion, green pepper, jalapeno and chipotle pepper in oil until tender. Add the next six ingredients. Bring to a boil. Reduce heat; simmer, uncovered, for 30 minutes or until thickened, stirring frequently. Remove from the heat; stir in cilantro and Liquid Smoke if desired.

Meanwhile, sprinkle steaks with steak seasoning. Grill, over medium heat for 7-8 minutes on each side or until meat reaches desired doneness (for medium-rare, a thermometer should read 145°; medium, 160°; well-done, 170°). Serve with sauce.

SOUTHERN BARBECUED BRISKET

PREP: 10 min. | **BAKE:** 3 hours + standing | **YIELD:** 12 servings.

Ever since a former neighbor shared this recipe with me, it has been a family favorite. It serves many people, so it's good for a buffet or a dinner with plenty of guests. The meat gets so tender from baking slowly for several hours.

LORRAINE HODGE MCLEAN, VIRGINIA

1 fresh beef brisket (5 pounds)

1 large onion, chopped

1 cup ketchup

1/4 cup water

3 tablespoons brown sugar

1 tablespoon liquid smoke, optional

2 teaspoons celery seed

1 teaspoon salt

1 teaspoon ground mustard

1/8 teaspoon cayenne pepper

Place brisket on a large sheet of heavy-duty foil; seal tightly. Place in a greased shallow roasting pan. Bake at 325° for 2 to 2-1/2 hours or until meat is tender.

Meanwhile, in a small saucepan, combine the remaining ingredients. Bring to a boil. Reduce heat; cover and simmer for 20 minutes, stirring occasionally. Remove from the heat.

Carefully open foil to allow steam to escape. Remove brisket from foil; let stand for 20 minutes. Thinly slice meat across the grain. Place in an ungreased 13-in. x 9-in. baking dish. Spoon sauce over meat. Cover and bake for 1 hour or until heated through.

EDITOR'S NOTE: This is a fresh beef brisket, not corned beef.

SPICY GRILLED STEAKS

PREP/TOTAL TIME: 20 min. | **YIELD:** 4 servings.

Rubs are a wonderful way to add flavor to meat when you don't have time to marinate. Meat lovers will be in their glory when they see (and smell!) these steaks sizzling on the grill. **TASTE OF HOME TEST KITCHEN**

- 1 tablespoon paprika
- 2 teaspoons dried thyme
- 1 teaspoon onion powder
- 1 teaspoon garlic powder
- 1/2 teaspoon rubbed sage
- 1/2 teaspoon salt
- 1/2 teaspoon pepper
- 1/2 teaspoon cayenne pepper
- 4 boneless beef top loin steaks (12 ounces *each*)

In a small bowl, combine the first eight ingredients. Rub about 1 teaspoon of spice mixture over each side of steaks.

Grill, covered, over medium heat for 6-8 minutes on each side or until meat reaches desired doneness (for medium-rare, a thermometer should read 145°; medium, 160°; well-done, 170°).

EDITOR'S NOTE: Top loin steak may be labeled as strip steak, Kansas City steak, New York strip steak, ambassador steak or boneless club steak in your region.

HERBED STANDING RIB ROAST

PREP: 10 min. | **BAKE:** 2-1/4 hours + standing | **YIELD:** 12 servings.

We're a meat-and-potatoes family, so this roast is right up our alley. It really is the highlight of any dinner—weekday or weekend. Leftovers are great for sandwiches, too. **CAROL STEVENS** BASYE, VIRGINIA

- 3 tablespoons grated onion
- 2 tablespoons olive oil
- 4 garlic cloves, minced
- 2 teaspoons celery seed
- 1 teaspoon coarsely ground pepper
- 1 teaspoon paprika
- 1/4 teaspoon dried thyme
- 1 bone-in beef rib roast (6 to 7 pounds)
- 2 large onions, cut into wedges
- 2 large carrots, cut into 2-inch pieces
- 2 celery ribs, cut into 2-inch pieces
- 1/4 cup red wine *or* beef broth

Assorted herbs and fruit, optional

In a small bowl, combine the first seven ingredients; rub over roast. Place the onions, carrots and celery in a large roasting pan; place roast over vegetables.

Bake, uncovered, at 350° for 2-1/4 to 3 hours or until meat reaches desired doneness (for medium-rare, a thermometer should read 145°; medium, 160°; well-done, 170°).

Remove roast to a serving platter and keep warm; let stand for 15 minutes before slicing.

Meanwhile, for au jus, strain and discard vegetables. Pour drippings into a measuring cup; skim fat. Add wine to roasting pan, stirring to remove any browned bits. Stir in drippings; heat through. Serve with roast. Garnish platter with herbs and fruit if desired.

WHISKEY SIRLOIN STEAK

PREP: 10 min. + marinating
BROIL: 15 min. | **YIELD:** 4 servings.

Moist, tender and slightly sweet from the marinade, this juicy steak boasts wonderful flavor and oh-so-easy preparation. Serve with potatoes and a green vegetable for a complete meal.

TASTE OF HOME TEST KITCHEN

- 1/4 cup whiskey *or* apple cider
- 1/4 cup reduced-sodium soy sauce
- 1 tablespoon sugar
- 1 garlic clove, thinly sliced
- 1/2 teaspoon ground ginger
- 1 beef top sirloin steak (1 inch thick and 1 pound)

In a resealable plastic bag, combine the first five ingredients; add the beef. Seal bag and turn to coat; refrigerate for 8 hours or overnight.

Drain and discard marinade. Place beef on a broiler pan coated with cooking spray. Broil 4-6 in. from the heat for 7-8 minutes on each side or until meat reaches desired doneness (for medium-rare, a thermometer should read 145°; medium, 160°; well-done, 170°).

PEPPER-CRUSTED BEEF TENDERLOIN

PREP: 30 min. + marinating | **BAKE:** 40 min. + standing | **YIELD:** 8 servings.

A coffee-enhanced rub lends robust flavor to juicy beef tenderloin. I often prepare this recipe for my family around the holidays instead of the traditional turkey or ham. The rich mashed potato stuffing adds an extra-special touch.

REBECCA ANDERSON AUSTIN, TEXAS

- 1 cup plus 2 tablespoons dry red wine *or* beef broth, *divided*
- 1 beef tenderloin roast (2 pounds)
- 1 large potato, quartered
- 1/2 cup grated Parmesan cheese
- 3 tablespoons milk
- 4 tablespoons butter, *divided*
- 2 bacon strips, cooked and crumbled
- 1 tablespoon horseradish sauce
- 5 garlic cloves, minced, *divided*
- 1/2 teaspoon garlic salt
- 1 tablespoon minced chives, optional
- 3 tablespoons ground coffee
- 1 tablespoon brown sugar
- 1 tablespoon coarsely ground pepper
- 1-1/4 teaspoons salt, *divided*
- 1 medium onion, halved and sliced
- 1 tablespoon olive oil
- 1 teaspoon lemon juice

Pour 1 cup wine into a large resealable plastic bag; add the beef. Seal bag and turn to coat; refrigerate at least 1 hour.

Place potato in a small saucepan and cover with water. Bring to a boil. Reduce heat; cover and cook for 15-20 minutes or until tender. Drain; mash with cheese, milk, 2 tablespoons butter, bacon, horseradish sauce, 2 garlic cloves, garlic salt and chives if desired; set aside.

Drain and discard marinade. In a small bowl, combine the coffee, brown sugar, pepper and 1 teaspoon salt; rub over beef. Cut a lengthwise slit down the center of the tenderloin to within 3/4 in. of bottom. Open tenderloin so it lies flat; cover with plastic wrap. Flatten to 3/4 in. thickness.

Remove plastic wrap; mound potato mixture over the center. Close tenderloin; tie at 2-in. intervals with kitchen string. Place on a rack in a roasting pan.

Bake, uncovered, at 425° for 40-45 minutes or until meat reaches desired doneness (for medium-rare, a thermometer should read 145°; medium, 160°; well-done, 170°). Remove meat to a serving platter. Cover and let stand for 10 minutes.

Meanwhile, in a small skillet, cook the onion and remaining garlic in oil and remaining butter over medium heat for 15-20 minutes or until onion is golden brown, stirring frequently. Stir in the lemon juice, remaining wine and salt. Slice tenderloin; serve with sauce.

HUSKING GARLIC CLOVES

Fresh garlic cloves add a wonderfully robust flavor to a variety of dishes. Husk a garlic clove in an instant by cutting it in half lengthwise with a sharp knife. If the husk still doesn't come off, quarter the clove. Another trick is to lay the clove on a flat rubber jar opener, fold one side of the opener over and roll the garlic a few times with the palm of your hand. Presto!

TASTE OF HOME TEST KITCHEN

GARLIC POT ROAST

GARLIC POT ROAST

PREP: 20 min. | **BAKE:** 2-1/2 hours | **YIELD:** 8 servings.

My family loves garlic; in their mind, the more the better! So one day, I came up with this recipe. Now my family requests the mouthwatering roast for Sunday dinner every other week. **RHONDA HAMPTON** COOKEVILLE, TENNESSEE

- 1 boneless beef chuck roast (3 pounds)
- 4 garlic cloves, peeled and halved
- 3 teaspoons garlic powder
- 3 teaspoons Italian salad dressing mix
- 1/2 teaspoon pepper
- 1 tablespoon canola oil
- 3 cups water
- 1 envelope onion soup mix
- 1 teaspoon reduced-sodium beef bouillon granules

- 5 medium potatoes, peeled and quartered
- 1 pound fresh baby carrots
- 1 large onion, cut into 1-inch pieces

Using the point of a sharp knife, make eight slits in the roast. Insert garlic into slits. Combine the garlic powder, salad dressing mix and pepper; rub over roast. In a Dutch oven, brown roast in oil on all sides; drain.

Combine the water, onion soup mix and bouillon; pour over roast. Cover and bake at 325° for 1-1/2 hours.

Add the potatoes, carrots and onion. Cover and bake 1 hour longer or until meat and vegetables are tender. Thicken pan juices if desired.

SPICED POT ROAST

PREP: 15 min. | **COOK:** 8 hours | **YIELD:** 6-8 servings.

Just pour these ingredients over your pot roast and let the slow cooker do the work. Herbs and spices give the beef an excellent taste. I often serve this roast over noodles or with mashed potatoes, using the juices as a gravy.
LOREN MARTIN BIG CABIN, OKLAHOMA

- 1 boneless beef chuck roast (2-1/2 pounds)
- 1 medium onion, chopped
- 1 can (14-1/2 ounces) diced tomatoes, undrained
- 1/4 cup white vinegar
- 3 tablespoons tomato puree
- 2 teaspoons Dijon mustard
- 1/2 teaspoon lemon juice
- 4-1/2 teaspoons poppy seeds
- 2 garlic cloves, minced
- 2-1/4 teaspoons sugar
- 1/2 teaspoon ground ginger

- 1/2 teaspoon salt
- 1/2 teaspoon dried rosemary, crushed
- 1/4 teaspoon ground turmeric
- 1/4 teaspoon ground cumin
- 1/4 teaspoon crushed red pepper flakes
- 1/8 teaspoon ground cloves
- 1 bay leaf
  Hot cooked noodles

Place roast in a 3-qt. slow cooker. In a large bowl, combine the onion, tomatoes, vinegar, tomato puree, mustard, lemon juice and seasonings; pour over roast.

Cover and cook on low for 8-9 hours or until meat is tender. Discard bay leaf. Thicken cooking juices if desired. Serve over noodles.

SWEET POTATO MUFFINS, PG. 182

BREADS & BISCUITS

Quite possibly the most quintessential Southern food, biscuits aren't just something to be covered in gravy. They're a revered form of culinary art and a must with every meal. But don't stop with biscuits—enjoy these delicious loaves, rolls and muffins, too!

SAGE CORNMEAL BISCUITS, PG. 177

BANANA NUT BREAD

PREP: 10 min. | **BAKE:** 40 min. + cooling | **YIELD:** 2 loaves (12 slices each).

A yellow cake mix streamlines assembly of this moist golden bread. I searched a long while for a banana bread that was easy to make. This one takes very little time and makes two loaves, so one can be frozen to enjoy later.

MARIE DAVIS PENDLETON, SOUTH CAROLINA

- 1 package (18-1/4 ounces) yellow cake mix
- 1 egg
- 1/2 cup 2% milk
- 1 cup mashed ripe bananas (about 2 medium)
- 1/2 cup chopped pecans

In a large bowl, combine the cake mix, egg and milk. Add bananas; beat on medium speed for 2 minutes. Stir in pecans.

Pour into two greased 8-in. x 4-in. loaf pans. Bake at 350° for 40-45 minutes or until a toothpick inserted near the center comes out clean. Cool for 10 minutes before removing from pans to wire racks to cool completely.

SAGE CORNMEAL BISCUITS

PREP/TOTAL TIME: 30 min. | **YIELD:** 10 biscuits.

My family loves these outstanding savory biscuits with eggs and sausage at breakfast or with meats at dinner. They bake up light and tender and have just the right amount of sage.

MARY KINCAID BOSTIC, NORTH CAROLINA

- 1-1/2 cups all-purpose flour
- 1/2 cup cornmeal
- 3 teaspoons baking powder
- 1/2 to 3/4 teaspoon rubbed sage
- 1/2 teaspoon salt
- 1/3 cup shortening
- 3/4 cup milk

In a large bowl, combine the first five ingredients. Cut in shortening until mixture resembles coarse crumbs. Stir in milk just until moistened.

Turn onto a lightly floured surface. Roll to 3/4-in. thickness; cut with a floured 2-in. biscuit cutter. Place 2 in. apart on an ungreased baking sheet. Bake at 450° for 10-12 minutes or until browned. Serve warm.

QUICK BLUEBERRY MUFFINS

PREP: 15 min. | **BAKE:** 25 min.
YIELD: 6 servings.

Chock-full of blueberries, these yummy muffins are a real hit with my family and friends.

AMY LOU STRICKLAND MARTINEZ, GEORGIA

- 1 cup vanilla ice cream, softened
- 1 cup self-rising flour
- 1 cup fresh blueberries
- 1 tablespoon butter
- 2 tablespoons sugar

In a large bowl, combine ice cream and flour. Fold in blueberries. Spoon into six greased muffin cups.

Bake at 375° for 20-25 minutes or until a toothpick inserted near the center comes out clean. While hot, brush muffin tops with butter and sprinkle with sugar. Serve warm.

BUTTERMILK CORN BREAD

PREP/TOTAL TIME: 30 min. | **YIELD:** 2-4 servings.

My grandmother would refer to this recipe as "comfort food," made from ingredients available on the farm or staples found in her pantry. She always cooked the corn bread in her "seasoned" black skillet, and it turned out slick as butter every time.

ELIZABETH COOPER MADISON, ALABAMA

  1 tablespoon canola oil
  1 cup cornmeal
  1/4 cup all-purpose flour
1-1/2 teaspoons baking powder
  1/2 teaspoon salt
  1/2 teaspoon baking soda
  1 egg
  1 cup buttermilk

Place oil in an 8-in. ovenproof skillet; tilt to coat bottom and sides. Place in a 425° oven for 10 minutes.

In a small bowl, combine cornmeal, flour, baking powder, salt and baking soda. Beat egg and buttermilk; add to dry ingredients just until moistened.

Pour into the hot skillet. Bake for 15 minutes or until golden brown and a toothpick inserted near the center comes out clean.

TANGERINE MUFFINS

PREP/TOTAL TIME: 30 min. | **YIELD:** 1 dozen.

Here's a recipe that represents our state and region. The delicate tangerine flavor gets compliments.

MARGARET YERKES NEW PORT RICHEY, FLORIDA

  2 cups all-purpose flour
1/2 cup sugar
  2 teaspoons baking powder
  1 teaspoon baking soda
1/2 teaspoon salt
  1 cup (8 ounces) vanilla yogurt
  1 egg, lightly beaten
1/4 cup butter, melted
  2 tablespoons milk
  1 cup diced peeled tangerine
  1 tablespoon grated tangerine peel

In a bowl, combine the first five ingredients. In a small bowl, combine the yogurt, egg, butter and milk until smooth; stir into dry ingredients just until moistened. Stir in tangerine and peel.

Fill greased or paper-lined muffin cups two-thirds full. Bake at 400° for 18-20 minutes or until a toothpick comes out clean. Cool for 5 minutes before removing from pan to wire rack.

OVERNIGHT REFRIGERATOR ROLLS

PREP: 25 min. + chilling and rising | **BAKE:** 15 min. | **YIELD:** 1 dozen.

Homemade dinner rolls couldn't be tastier. The buttery flavor of these rolls makes them a heartwarming accompaniment to soups, salads and a variety of entrees. **JENNIFER KAUFFMAN FIGUEROA** GREENVILLE, SOUTH CAROLINA

- 1 package (1/4 ounce) active dry yeast
- 1/2 cup warm water (110° to 115°)
- 1/2 cup warm 2% milk (110° to 115°)
- 1/4 cup butter-flavored shortening
- 1 tablespoon sugar
- 1 teaspoon salt
- 1 egg
- 3 cups all-purpose flour

In a large bowl, dissolve yeast in warm water. Add the milk, shortening, sugar, salt, egg and 2 cups flour. Beat on medium speed for 2 minutes. Stir in enough remaining flour to form a soft dough (do not knead). Place in a greased bowl, turning once to grease the top. Cover and refrigerate overnight.

Punch dough down. Turn onto a lightly floured surface; divide into 12 pieces. Shape each into a ball. Place 2 in. apart on greased baking sheets. Cover and let rise in a warm place until doubled, about 1-1/2 hours.

Bake at 400° for 15-20 minutes or until golden brown. Remove from pans to wire racks.

APPLE PULL-APART BREAD

PREP: 40 min. + rising | **BAKE:** 35 min. + cooling | **YIELD:** 1 loaf.

Drizzled with icing, each piece of this bread is finger-licking good thanks to a yummy filling of apples and pecans. It's well worth the bit of extra effort. **CAROLYN GREGORY** HENDERSONVILLE, TENNESSEE

- 1 package (1/4 ounce) active dry yeast
- 1 cup warm milk
- 1/2 cup butter, melted, *divided*
- 1 egg
- 2/3 cup plus 2 tablespoons sugar, *divided*
- 1 teaspoon salt
- 3 to 3-1/2 cups all-purpose flour
- 1 medium tart apple, peeled and chopped
- 1/2 cup finely chopped pecans
- 1/2 teaspoon ground cinnamon

ICING:
- 1 cup confectioners' sugar
- 3 to 4-1/2 teaspoons hot water
- 1/2 teaspoon vanilla extract

In a large bowl, dissolve yeast in milk. Add 2 tablespoons butter, egg, 2 tablespoons sugar, salt and 3 cups flour; beat until smooth. Add enough remaining flour to form a stiff dough. Turn onto a floured surface; knead until smooth and elastic, 6-8 minutes. Place in a greased bowl, turning once to grease top. Cover and let rise in a warm place until doubled, about 1 hour.

Combine the apple, pecans, cinnamon and remaining sugar; set aside. Punch dough down; divide in half. Cut each half into 16 pieces. On a lightly floured surface, pat or roll out each piece into a 2-1/2-in. circle. Place 1 teaspoon apple mixture in center of circle; pinch edges together and seal, forming a ball. Dip in remaining butter.

In a greased 10-in. tube pan, place 16 balls, seam side down; sprinkle with 1/4 cup apple mixture. Layer remaining balls; sprinkle with remaining apple mixture. Cover and let rise until nearly doubled, about 45 minutes.

Bake at 350° for 35-40 minutes or until golden brown. Cool for 10 minutes; remove from pan to a wire rack. Combine icing ingredients; drizzle over warm bread.

BUTTER-DIPPED BISCUIT SQUARES

PREP/TOTAL TIME: 20 min.
YIELD: 15 biscuits.

These are the easiest and best biscuits I've ever made. They're light and buttery and go well with virtually any meal.
REBEKAH DEWITT STAR CITY, ARKANSAS

- 2 cups self-rising flour
- 2 tablespoons sugar
- 1 cup 2% milk
- All-purpose flour
- 1/2 cup butter, melted

In a large bowl, combine the self-rising flour, sugar and milk. Turn onto a floured surface; sprinkle with all-purpose flour. Pat dough to 1/2-in. thickness. Cut into 3-in. x 2-in. pieces.

Pour butter into an ungreased 13-in. x 9-in. baking pan. Dip one side of each piece into melted butter. Carefully turn to coat. Bake, uncovered, at 450° for 10 minutes or until golden brown.

EDITOR'S NOTE: As a substitute for a cup of self-rising flour, place 1-1/2 teaspoons baking powder and 1/2 teaspoon salt in a measuring cup. Add all-purpose flour to measure 1 cup.

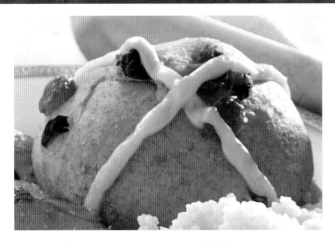

SPICED FRUITED HOT CROSS BUNS

PREP: 40 min. + rising | **BAKE:** 20 min.
YIELD: 2 dozen.

Who says you should only eat Hot Cross Buns in April? The bread machine does all the hard work, so they make an easy and decadent treat anytime that tastes like you put a lot of effort into it. **ALINA NIEMI** HONOLULU, HAWAII

- 1-1/2 cups fat-free milk (70° to 80°)
- 1/4 cup water (70° to 80°)
- 1/4 cup butter, melted
- 1 teaspoon salt
- 2/3 cup sugar
- 2 tablespoons ground flaxseed
- 1 tablespoon grated orange peel
- 2 teaspoons grated lemon peel
- 1/4 teaspoon *each* ground cardamom, cinnamon and nutmeg
- 2-1/4 cups whole wheat flour
- 2 cups all-purpose flour
- 1 package (1/4 ounce) active dry yeast
- 1/2 cup golden raisins
- 1/4 cup dried cranberries
- 1/4 cup chopped crystallized ginger

ICING:
- 3/4 cup confectioners' sugar
- 3/4 teaspoon grated orange peel
- 2 to 3 teaspoons lemon juice

In bread machine pan, place the first 14 ingredients in order suggested by manufacturer. Select dough setting (check dough after 5 minutes of mixing; add 1 to 2 tablespoons of water or flour if needed). Just before the final kneading (your machine may audibly signal this), add the raisins, cranberries and candied ginger.

When cycle is completed, turn dough onto a lightly floured surface. Divide into 24 portions; shape each into a ball. Place 2 in. apart on baking sheets coated with cooking spray. Cover and let rise in a warm place until doubled, about 40 minutes.

Bake at 350° for 20-25 minutes or until golden brown. Remove from pans to wire racks. Combine the icing ingredients; pipe an "X" on each bun.

ENGLISH BATTER BUNS

PREP: 15 min. + rising | **BAKE:** 10 min. | **YIELD:** 1 dozen.

I can't thank my friend enough for passing along this recipe. The simple, tender rolls are a hit at the holidays.
GERALDINE WEST OGDEN, UTAH

- 2 packages (1/4 ounces *each*) active dry yeast
- 1 cup warm milk (110° to 115°)
- 1/2 cup shortening
- 2 tablespoons sugar
- 1 teaspoon salt
- 2 eggs, lightly beaten
- 3-1/2 cups all-purpose flour

Melted butter

In a large bowl, dissolve yeast in warm milk. Add the shortening, sugar, salt, eggs and 2 cups flour; beat on medium speed for 3 minutes. Stir in remaining flour until smooth. Cover and let rise in a warm place until doubled, about 30 minutes.

Stir batter vigorously for 25 strokes (dough will be slightly sticky). Spoon into greased muffin cups. Tap pans to settle the batter. Cover and let rise until batter reaches tops of cups, about 20 minutes.

Bake at 400° for 10-15 minutes or until golden brown. Brush with butter.

TENNESSEE FRY BREAD

PREP/TOTAL TIME: 30 min. | **YIELD:** 8 servings.

You'll need only four ingredients to fix this bread. We like it with scrambled eggs and fried potatoes for breakfast, but you can also dunk it in soup or serve it with coffee. **THRESA SANCHEZ** FRANKLIN, TENNESSEE

3 tablespoons butter

1 cup self-rising flour

1/2 cup buttermilk

All-purpose flour

Place butter in a 12-in. ovenproof skillet; place in a 450° oven for 2-3 minutes or until melted.

In a bowl, combine flour and buttermilk just until moistened. Turn onto a surface dusted with all-purpose flour; knead 4-5 times. Pat dough to 1/4-in. thickness. Cut with a 2-1/2-in. biscuit cutter. Place in a single layer in prepared pan; carefully turn to coat.

Bake at 450° for 12-13 minutes or until golden brown.

EDITOR'S NOTE: As a substitute for 1 cup of self-rising flour, place 1-1/2 teaspoons baking powder and 1/2 teaspoon salt in a measuring cup. Add all-purpose flour to measure 1 cup.

SWEET POTATO MUFFINS

PREP/TOTAL TIME: 25 min. | **YIELD:** 2 dozen.

Sweet potatoes are a popular vegetable here in the South. When I turn them into these freshly baked muffins, they're a popular breakfast item, too! **CHRISTINE JOHNSON** RICETOWN, KENTUCKY

2 cups self-rising flour

2 cups sugar

2 teaspoons ground cinnamon

1 egg

2 cups cold mashed sweet
   potatoes (without added
   butter *or* milk)

1 cup canola oil

GLAZE:

1 cup confectioners' sugar

2 tablespoons plus 1-1/2
   teaspoons 2% milk

1-1/2 teaspoons butter, melted

1 teaspoon vanilla extract

1/2 teaspoon ground cinnamon

In a small bowl, combine the flour, sugar and cinnamon. In another bowl, whisk the egg, sweet potatoes and oil. Stir into dry ingredients just until moistened.

Fill greased muffin cups two-thirds full. Bake at 375° for 15-18 minutes or until a toothpick comes out clean. Cool for 5 minutes before removing from pans to wire racks. In a small bowl, combine glaze ingredients; drizzle over warm muffins.

EDITOR'S NOTE: As a substitute for a cup of self-rising flour, place 1-1/2 teaspoons baking powder and 1/2 teaspoon salt in a measuring cup. Add all-purpose flour to measure 1 cup.

STORING SWEET POTATOES

To keep sweet potatoes fresh, store them in a dry, cool (55-60°) place such a cellar, pantry or garage. Do not store them in the refrigerator, where they will develop a hard core and an "off" taste. If stored properly, sweet potatoes will keep for a month or longer.

TASTE OF HOME TEST KITCHEN

SWEET POTATO MUFFINS

GRANDMA'S ORANGE ROLLS

PREP: 20 min. + rising | **BAKE:** 20 min. | **YIELD:** 2-1/2 dozen.

Our two children and grandchildren love these fine-textured sweet rolls. We have our own orange, lime and grapefruit trees, and it's such a pleasure to go out and pick fruit right off the tree. **NORMA POOLE** AUBURNDALE, FLORIDA

1 package (1/4 ounce)
  active dry yeast

1/4 cup warm water (110° to 115°)

1 cup warm 2% milk
  (110° to 115°)

1/4 cup shortening

1/4 cup sugar

1 teaspoon salt

1 egg, lightly beaten

3-1/2 to 3-3/4 cups all-purpose flour

FILLING:

1 cup sugar

1/2 cup butter, softened

2 tablespoons grated
  orange peel

GLAZE:

1 cup confectioners' sugar

4 teaspoons butter, softened

1/2 teaspoon lemon extract

4 to 5 teaspoons 2% milk

In a large bowl, dissolve yeast in water. Add the milk, shortening, sugar, salt, egg and 3 cups flour. Beat until smooth. Stir in enough remaining flour to form a soft dough.

Knead on a lightly floured surface until smooth and elastic, about 6-8 minutes. Place in a greased bowl, turning once to grease top. Cover and let rise in a warm place until doubled, about 1 hour. Meanwhile, in a small bowl, combine filling ingredients; set aside.

Punch dough down; divide in half. Roll each half into a 15-in. x 10-in. rectangle. Spread half the reserved filling on each rectangle. Roll up, jelly-roll style, starting with a long end. Cut each into 15 rolls.

Place in two greased 11-in. x 7-in. baking pans. Cover and let rise until doubled, about 45 minutes.

Bake at 375° for 20-25 minutes or until lightly browned. In a small bowl, combine the confectioner's sugar, butter, extract and enough milk to achieve desired consistency; spread over warm rolls.

RASPBERRY CRUMBLE COFFEE CAKE

PREP: 20 min. | **BAKE:** 45 min. | **YIELD:** 16-20 servings.

Don't be intimidated by the recipe directions for this coffee cake. It really comes together quite easily. The crumbly topping and sweet, fruity filling are a hit with all who try it. **SHIRLEY BOYKEN** MESA, ARIZONA

FILLING:

- 2/3 cup sugar
- 1/4 cup cornstarch
- 3/4 cup water *or* cranberry-raspberry juice
- 2 cups fresh *or* frozen unsweetened raspberries
- 1 tablespoon lemon juice

COFFEE CAKE:

- 3 cups all-purpose flour
- 1 cup sugar
- 3 teaspoons baking powder
- 1 teaspoon salt
- 1 teaspoon ground cinnamon
- 1/4 teaspoon ground mace
- 1 cup cold butter, cubed
- 2 eggs, lightly beaten
- 1 cup milk
- 1 teaspoon vanilla extract

TOPPING:

- 1/4 cup cold butter, cubed
- 1/2 cup all-purpose flour
- 1/2 cup sugar
- 1/4 cup sliced almonds

For filling, in a large saucepan, combine the sugar, cornstarch and water until smooth. Bring to a boil over medium heat. Cook and stir for 1-2 minutes or until thickened. Add berries and lemon juice. Set aside to cool.

In a large bowl, combine the flour, sugar, baking powder, salt, cinnamon and mace. Cut in butter to form fine crumbs. Stir in the eggs, milk and vanilla until blended. Divide in half.

Spread half of the batter in two greased 8-in. round baking pans. Divide filling and spread evenly over each. Drop remaining batter by small spoonfuls and spread evenly over filling.

For topping, cut butter into flour and sugar; stir in nuts. Sprinkle over tops. Bake at 350° for 40-45 minutes or until lightly brown.

EDITOR'S NOTE: If desired, one coffee cake can be baked in 13-in. x 9-in. baking pan. Bake for 45-50 minutes or until golden brown.

SOUTHERN BUTTERMILK BISCUITS

PREP/TOTAL TIME: 30 min.
YIELD: 9 biscuits.

The recipe for these four-ingredient biscuits has been handed down for many generations.
FRAN THOMPSON
TARBORO, NORTH CAROLINA

- 1/2 cup cold butter, cubed
- 2 cups self-rising flour
- 3/4 cup buttermilk

Melted butter

In a large bowl, cut butter into flour until mixture resembles coarse crumbs. Stir in buttermilk just until moistened. Turn onto a lightly floured surface; knead 3-4 times. Pat or lightly roll to 3/4-in. thickness. Cut with a floured 2-1/2-in. biscuit cutter.

Place on a greased baking sheet. Bake at 425° for 11-13 minutes or until golden brown. Brush tops with butter. Serve warm.

EDITOR'S NOTE: As a substitute for cup of self-rising flour, place 1-1/2 teaspoons baking powder and 1/2 teaspoon salt in a measuring cup. Add all-purpose flour to measure 1 cup.

CHEESY DROP BISCUITS

PREP/TOTAL TIME: 30 min. | **YIELD:** 2 dozen.

It's hard to believe that these buttery bites call for so few items. I keep the ingredients for these family favorites on hand because my sons just love them.
MARLA MILLER ENGLEWOOD, TENNESSEE

- 2 cups self-rising flour
- 1 cup butter, melted
- 1 cup (8 ounces) sour cream
- 1 cup (4 ounces) shredded cheddar cheese

In a large bowl, combine all the ingredients until blended. Drop by rounded tablespoonfuls 2 in. apart onto lightly greased baking sheets.

Bake at 350° for 20-25 minutes or until golden brown. Cool for 5 minutes before removing from pans to wire racks. Serve warm.

EDITOR'S NOTE: As a substitute for a cup of self-rising flour, place 1-1/2 teaspoons baking powder and 1/2 teaspoon salt in a measuring cup. Add all-purpose flour to measure 1 cup.

BUTTERY APPLE BISCUITS

PREP/TOTAL TIME: 30 min. | **YIELD:** 6 biscuits.

What better way to start the day than with warm biscuits filled with apple and the homey sweetness of molasses? Make a double batch and freeze half to enjoy later. **ATHENA RUSSELL** FLORENCE, SOUTH CAROLINA

- 1 cup self-rising flour
- 1-1/2 teaspoons sugar
- Pinch salt
- 3 tablespoons cold butter
- 1 egg, lightly beaten
- 2 tablespoons fat-free milk
- 1 tablespoon molasses
- 1/2 cup chopped peeled tart apple

In a small bowl, combine the flour, sugar and salt. Cut in butter until mixture resembles coarse crumbs. Combine the egg, milk and molasses; stir into flour mixture just until moistened. Stir in apple. Turn onto a lightly floured surface; knead 8-10 times.

Pat or roll out to 1/2-in. thickness; cut with a floured 2-1/2-in. biscuit cutter. Place 2 in. apart on a baking sheet coated with cooking spray. Bake at 425° for 6-8 minutes or until golden brown. Serve warm.

EDITOR'S NOTE: As a substitute for 1 cup of self-rising flour, place 1-1/2 teaspoons baking powder and 1/2 teaspoon salt in a measuring cup. Add all-purpose flour to measure 1 cup.

HAM 'N' CORN FRITTERS

PREP: 20 min. + standing | **COOK:** 15 min. | **YIELD:** 2 dozen.

Here's an old-fashioned recipe that's welcome at any meal. The pretty golden fritters are a perfect addition to a down-home brunch. You'll be amazed at how quickly they disappear. **NELDA CRONBAUGH** BELLE PLAINE, IOWA

2 eggs

1/3 cup milk

1-1/4 cups all-purpose flour

1 tablespoon sugar

2 teaspoons baking powder

1/2 teaspoon salt

Dash pepper

1 cup fresh *or* frozen corn, cooked and drained

1 cup chopped fully cooked ham

Oil for deep-fat frying

Separate eggs; let stand at room temperature for 30 minutes. In a large bowl, beat egg yolks until slightly thickened. Beat in milk. Combine the flour, sugar, baking powder, salt and pepper; add to yolk mixture and mix well. Stir in corn and ham.

In a small bowl, beat egg whites on high speed until stiff peaks form. Fold into the corn mixture.

In an electric skillet or deep-fat fryer, heat oil to 375°. Drop batter by heaping tablespoonfuls, a few at a time, into hot oil. Fry until golden brown, about 1 minute on each side, turning with a slotted spoon. Drain on paper towels.

DOWN HOME HUSH PUPPIES

PREP: 15 min. + standing | **COOK:** 20 min. | **YIELD:** 2-1/2 dozen.

Hush puppies are a classic side served at many get-togethers in the South. The sweet and spicy flavor has delighted friends and family for decades. **GENE PITTS** WILSONVILLE, ALABAMA

- 1 cup cornmeal
- 1 cup self-rising flour
- 1-1/2 teaspoons baking powder
- 1/2 teaspoon salt
- 1 large onion, chopped
- 2 jalapeno peppers, seeded and diced
- 1/4 cup sugar
- 1 egg
- 1 cup buttermilk

Canola oil

In a large bowl, combine first seven ingredients. Add egg and buttermilk; stir until dry ingredients are moistened. Set aside at room temperature for 30 minutes. Do not stir again.

In an electric skillet or deep fryer, heat 2-3 in. of oil to 375°. Drop batter by rounded tablespoonfuls, a few at a time, into hot oil. Fry until golden brown, about 1-1/2 minutes on each side. Drain on paper towels.

EDITOR'S NOTE: As a substitute for 1 cup of self-rising flour, place 1-1/2 teaspoons baking powder and 1/2 teaspoon salt in a measuring cup. Add all-purpose flour to measure 1 cup.

PECAN STICKY BUNS

PREP: 45 min. + rising | **BAKE:** 20 min. | **YIELD:** 1 dozen.

These homemade caramel rolls have the old-fashioned goodness my family craves. Tender and nutty, the buns disappear fast on Christmas morning—or any other time I serve them. **JULIA SPENCE** NEW BRAUNFELS, TEXAS

- 4 to 4-1/2 cups all-purpose flour, *divided*
- 1/3 cup sugar
- 1 package (1/4 ounce) active dry yeast
- 1/2 teaspoon salt
- 1 cup 2% milk
- 1/4 cup butter, cubed
- 2 eggs

TOPPING:

- 1/3 cup butter, cubed
- 2/3 cup packed brown sugar
- 2 tablespoons light corn syrup
- 1 cup chopped pecans

FILLING:

- 3 tablespoons butter, melted
- 1/2 cup packed brown sugar
- 1/3 cup sugar
- 2 tablespoons ground cinnamon

In a large bowl, combine 2 cups flour, sugar, yeast and salt. In a small saucepan, heat milk and butter to 120°-130°. Add to dry ingredients; beat just until moistened. Add eggs; beat until smooth. Stir in enough remaining flour to form a soft dough (dough will be sticky).

Turn onto a floured surface; knead until smooth and elastic, about 6-8 minutes. Place in a greased bowl, turning once to grease top. Cover and let rise in a warm place until doubled, about 1 hour.

In a small saucepan, melt butter over medium heat. Stir in brown sugar and corn syrup until combined. Pour into a well-greased 13-in. x 9-in. baking dish. Sprinkle with pecans.

Punch dough down. Turn onto a floured surface. Roll into a 12-in. x 8-in. rectangle; brush with melted butter. Combine sugars and cinnamon; sprinkle over dough to within 1/2 in. of edges and press into dough. Roll up jelly-roll style, starting with a long side; pinch seam to seal.

Cut into 12 slices. Place cut side down in prepared baking dish. Cover and let rise until doubled, about 30 minutes.

Bake at 375° for 20-25 minutes or until golden brown. Immediately invert onto a serving platter. Serve warm.

PECAN STICKY BUNS

OLD-FASHIONED MACARONI AND CHEESE, PG. 218

ASPARAGUS AND
SUN-DRIED TOMATOES, PG. 202

SIDES

"Would you please pass the..." You won't be able to make up your mind which home-style side dish to try first! From ooey-gooey mac and cheese to comforting grits, this chapter offers a whole gang of sidekicks to accompany your Southern-style meals.

TOMATO 'N' CORN RISOTTO

PREP: 15 min. | **COOK:** 35 min. | **YIELD:** 5 servings.

I enjoy making this recipe because it uses items from my garden. Milk and Parmesan cheese give this side dish a creaminess everyone's sure to enjoy. **ANGELA LIVELY** BAXTER, TENNESSEE

2-1/2 cups water
2 cups whole milk
3 tablespoons chicken broth
1 large onion, finely chopped
2 tablespoons butter
1 garlic clove, minced
3/4 cup uncooked arborio rice
1-1/3 cups fresh corn (about 5 ears of corn)
1 medium tomato, peeled, seeded and chopped
1/2 cup grated Parmesan cheese
1/2 cup fresh basil leaves, thinly sliced
1/2 teaspoon salt
Pepper to taste

In a large saucepan, heat the water, milk and broth; keep warm.

In a large skillet, saute onion in butter until tender. Add garlic; cook 1 minute longer. Add rice; cook and stir for 2-3 minutes. Stir in 1 cup hot water mixture. Cook and stir until all liquid is absorbed.

Add remaining water mixture, 1/2 cup at a time, stirring constantly. Allow the liquid to absorb between additions. Cook until risotto is creamy and rice is almost tender. (Cooking time is about 20 minutes.) Stir in the remaining ingredients; heat through.

WHITE 'N' SWEET MASHED POTATOES

PREP/TOTAL TIME: 30 min. | **YIELD:** 8 servings.

Sweet potatoes are a staple of Southern cooking here in North Carolina. This recipe combines them with russet potatoes, making simple mashed potatoes a very special treat. **GAIL DREWS** FLAT ROCK, NORTH CAROLINA

- 1-1/2 pounds russet potatoes (about 4 medium), peeled and cubed
- 1-1/2 pounds sweet potatoes (about 4 medium), peeled and cubed
- 1 cup milk, warmed
- 1/4 cup butter, cubed
- 1 teaspoon salt
- 1/2 teaspoon ground cinnamon
- 1/4 teaspoon ground nutmeg

Place russet potatoes and sweet potatoes in a large saucepan and cover with water. Bring to a boil. Reduce heat; cover and simmer for 15-20 minutes or until tender. Drain.

In a large bowl, mash the potatoes with the milk, butter, salt, cinnamon and nutmeg until the potatoes reach desired consistency.

CARROTS AND PINEAPPLE

PREP/TOTAL TIME: 20 min.
YIELD: 4 servings.

An irresistible glaze has kept this side dish on my family's most requested list for years.
CORA CHRISTIAN CHURCH HILL, TENNESSEE

- 2 cups baby carrots
- 1 can (20 ounces) pineapple chunks, undrained
- 4 teaspoons cornstarch
- 1/2 teaspoon ground cinnamon
- 1/2 cup packed brown sugar
- 1 tablespoon butter

In a saucepan, bring 1 in. of water to a boil; place carrots in a steamer basket over water. Cover; steam for 8-10 minutes or until crisp-tender. Drain pineapple, reserving juice; set pineapple aside.

In a saucepan, combine cornstarch and cinnamon. Add the brown sugar, butter and reserved juice. Bring to a boil; cook and stir for 2 minutes or until thickened. Stir in the carrots and pineapple; heat through.

SMOKY BEANS

PREP: 20 min. | **BAKE:** 45 min.
YIELD: 90-95 servings.

These beans are a perfect side dish to almost any meal. Try serving them with your favorite grilled meat!

PAT TURNER SENECA, SOUTH CAROLINA

- 3 **pounds sliced bacon, diced**
- 3 **medium sweet onions, chopped**
- 6 **cans (28 ounces *each*) baked beans, undrained**
- 6 **cans (16 ounces *each*) kidney beans, rinsed and drained**
- 6 **cans (16 ounces *each*) butter beans, rinsed and drained**
- 4 **packages (12 ounces *each*) miniature smoked sausages, cut in thirds**
- 3 **cups packed brown sugar**
- 1-1/2 **cups ketchup**
- 1-1/2 **cups cider vinegar**
- 1 **tablespoon garlic powder**
- 1 **tablespoon ground mustard**

In a Dutch oven, cook bacon over medium heat until crisp. Using a slotted spoon, remove to paper towels; drain drippings, reserving 3 tablespoons. Saute onions in reserved drippings until tender.

In a very large bowl, combine the beans, sausage, bacon and onions. Combine the remaining ingredients; stir into bean mixture.

Pour the mixture into four greased 13-in. x 9-in. baking dishes. Bake, uncovered, at 350° for 45-55 minutes or until heated through.

PLANTAIN FRITTERS

PREP/TOTAL TIME: 20 min. | **YIELD:** 28 fritters.

These golden brown fritters are a favorite recipe of my aunt's. If you don't have plantains on hand, you can substitute bananas instead.

HEATHER EWALD BOTHELL, WASHINGTON

- 2 **large ripe plantains *or* bananas, peeled**
- 1 **cup self-rising flour**
- 1 **small onion, cut into wedges**
- 1/4 **teaspoon salt**

Dash pepper

Oil for deep-fat frying

Place the peeled plantains in a food processor. Cover and process until smooth. Add the self-rising flour, onion, salt and pepper; cover and process until blended (batter will be moist).

In an electric skillet or deep-fat fryer, heat 1/4 in. of oil to 375°. Drop tablespoonfuls of batter, a few at a time, into hot oil. Cook for 1 minute on each side or until golden brown. Drain on paper towels.

EDITOR'S NOTE: As a substitute for 1 cup of self-rising flour, place 1-1/2 teaspoons baking powder and 1/2 teaspoon salt in a measuring cup. Add all-purpose flour to measure 1 cup.

VIDALIA ONION BAKE

PREP: 25 min. | **BAKE:** 20 min. | **YIELD:** 8 servings.

The mild taste of Vidalias makes this bake appealing to onion lovers and nonlovers alike. It's an excellent accompaniment to beef, pork or chicken. **KATRINA STITT** ZEPHYRHILLS, FLORIDA

- **6 large sweet onions, sliced (about 12 cups)**
- **1/2 cup butter, cubed**
- **2 cups crushed butter-flavored crackers**
- **1 cup shredded Parmesan cheese**
- **1/2 cup shredded cheddar cheese**
- **1/4 cup shredded Romano cheese**

In a large skillet, saute onions in butter until tender and liquid has evaporated. Place half of the onions in a greased 2-qt. baking dish; sprinkle with half of the cracker crumbs and cheeses. Repeat layers.

Bake, uncovered, at 325° for 20-25 minutes or until golden brown.

WHITE CHEDDAR SCALLOPED POTATOES

PREP: 40 min. | **BAKE:** 70 min. | **YIELD:** 8 servings.

This recipe has evolved over the past several years. After I added the thyme, ham and sour cream, my husband declared, "This is it!" You can even serve it as an entree with a salad and homemade French bread.

HOPE TOOLE MUSCLE SHOALS, ALABAMA

- 1 medium onion, finely chopped
- 1/4 cup butter, cubed
- 1/4 cup all-purpose flour
- 1 teaspoon dried parsley flakes
- 1 teaspoon salt
- 1/2 teaspoon pepper
- 1/2 teaspoon dried thyme
- 3 cups 2% milk
- 1 can (10-3/4 ounces) condensed cream of mushroom soup, undiluted
- 1 cup (8 ounces) sour cream
- 8 cups thinly sliced peeled potatoes
- 3-1/2 cups cubed fully cooked ham
- 2 cups (8 ounces) shredded white cheddar cheese

In a large saucepan, saute onion in butter until tender. Stir in the flour, parsley, salt, pepper and thyme until blended. Gradually add milk. Bring to a boil; cook and stir for 2 minutes or until thickened. Stir in soup. Remove from the heat; stir in sour cream until blended.

In a large bowl, combine potatoes and ham. In a greased 13-in. x 9-in. baking dish, layer with half of the potato mixture, white cheddar cheese and white sauce. Repeat layers.

Cover and bake at 375° for 30 minutes. Uncover; bake 40-50 minutes longer or until potatoes are tender.

CHEESY CREAMED CORN

PREP: 5 min. | **COOK:** 4 hours
YIELD: 12 servings.

Even those who usually don't eat much corn will ask for a second helping of this creamy, cheesy side dish. Folks love the flavor, but I love how easy it is to make with ingredients I usually have on hand.

MARY ANN TRUITT WICHITA, KANSAS

- 3 packages (16 ounces *each*) frozen corn
- 2 packages (one 8 ounces, one 3 ounces) cream cheese, cubed
- 1/4 cup butter, cubed
- 3 tablespoons water
- 3 tablespoons milk
- 2 tablespoons sugar
- 6 slices process American cheese, cut into small pieces

In a 3-qt. slow cooker, combine all the ingredients. Cover and cook on low for 4 hours or until heated through and the cheeses are melted. Stir well before serving.

MEXICORN GRITS

PREP: 20 min. | **BAKE:** 35 min. | **YIELD:** 10 servings.

I grew up on grits and have fixed them in various ways. I decided to put a new twist on them with this recipe, and my husband says it's a keeper. Even the leftovers are good. **BARBARA MOORHEAD** GAFFNEY, SOUTH CAROLINA

- 4 cups 2% milk
- 1/2 cup plus 1/3 cup butter, *divided*
- 1 cup quick-cooking grits
- 2 eggs
- 1 can (11 ounces) Mexicorn, drained
- 1 can (4 ounces) chopped green chilies
- 1 cup (4 ounces) shredded Mexican cheese blend
- 1 teaspoon salt
- 1/4 teaspoon white pepper
- 1 cup shredded Parmesan cheese

In a saucepan, bring milk and 1/2 cup butter to a boil. Slowly stir in grits. Reduce heat; cook and stir for 5-7 minutes.

In a small bowl, whisk the eggs. Stir a small amount of hot grits into eggs; return all to the pan, stirring constantly. Melt remaining butter; stir into grits. Add the corn, chilies, cheese, salt and pepper.

Transfer to a greased 2-qt. baking dish. Sprinkle with Parmesan cheese. Bake, uncovered, at 350° for 35-40 minutes or until a knife inserted near the center comes out clean.

MARVELOUS SHELLS 'N' CHEESE

PREP: 25 min. | **BAKE:** 30 min. | **YIELD:** 6 servings.

This macaroni dish is so good! I adapted the recipe from one my mother makes, but she agrees that my version is rich and delicious. It's easy to assemble and always receives rave reviews.
LAUREN VERSWEYVELD DELAVAN, WISCONSIN

- 1 package (16 ounces) medium pasta shells
- 1 package (8 ounces) process cheese (Velveeta), cubed
- 1/3 cup 2% milk
- 2 cups (16 ounces) 2% cottage cheese
- 1 can (10-3/4 ounces) condensed cream of onion soup, undiluted
- 3 cups (12 ounces) shredded Mexican cheese blend
- 2/3 cup dry bread crumbs
- 1/4 cup butter, melted

Cook pasta according to package directions. Meanwhile, in a large saucepan, combine process cheese and milk; cook and stir over low heat until melted. Remove from the heat. Stir in cottage cheese and soup.

Drain pasta and add to cheese sauce; stir until coated. Transfer to a greased 13-in. x 9-in. baking dish. Sprinkle with Mexican cheese blend. Toss bread crumbs with butter; sprinkle over the top.

Bake, uncovered, at 350° for 30-35 minutes or until heated through.

BASIL TOMATO TART

PREP: 20 min. | **BAKE:** 20 min. | **YIELD:** 8 servings.

Here is an interesting and delicious way to serve garden-fresh tomatoes. Guests may say it reminds them of pizza.
CONNIE STUMPF NORTH MYRTLE BEACH, SOUTH CAROLINA

Pastry for a single-crust pie (9 inches)

1-1/2 cups (6 ounces) shredded part-skim mozzarella cheese, *divided*

5 to 6 fresh plum tomatoes

1 cup loosely packed fresh basil leaves

4 garlic cloves

1/2 cup mayonnaise

1/4 cup grated Parmesan cheese

1/8 teaspoon pepper

Roll pastry to fit a 9-in. tart pan or pie plate; place in pan. Do not prick. Line pastry shell with a double thickness of heavy-duty foil.

Bake at 450° for 5 minutes. Remove foil; bake 8 minutes more. Remove from the oven. Reduce heat to 375°. Sprinkle 1/2 cup mozzarella over the hot crust.

Cut each tomato into eight wedges; remove seeds. Arrange over cheese.

In a food processor, process the basil and garlic until coarsely chopped; sprinkle over tomatoes.

Combine the mayonnaise, Parmesan, pepper and the remaining mozzarella; spoon over basil. Bake, uncovered, for 20-25 minutes or until the cheese is browned and bubbly.

CAULIFLOWER CASSEROLE

PREP: 20 min. | **BAKE:** 20 min. | **YIELD:** 12 servings (3/4 cup each).

This comforting casserole is filled with tender cauliflower and topped with a sprinkling of stuffing mixture. I find the classic-style bake will appeal to kids and adults. **CAROL REX** OCALA, FLORIDA

3 packages (16 ounces *each*) frozen cauliflower

1/4 cup butter, cubed

1 cup stuffing mix

3/4 cup chopped walnuts

2 cups (16 ounces) sour cream

2 cups (8 ounces) shredded cheddar cheese

3 teaspoons chicken bouillon granules

1-1/2 teaspoons ground mustard

Boil cauliflower according to package directions. In a large skillet, melt butter; add stuffing mix and walnuts. Cook for 2-3 minutes or until butter is absorbed.

Drain cauliflower; place in a large bowl. Stir in the sour cream, cheese, bouillon and mustard until blended. Transfer to a greased 13-in. x 9-in. baking dish; sprinkle with stuffing mixture.

Bake, uncovered, at 375° for 18-22 minutes or until heated through.

COOKING WITH CAULIFLOWER

When purchasing fresh cauliflower, look for a head with compact florets that are free from yellow or brown spots. The leaves should be crisp and green, not withered or discolored. Tightly wrap an unwashed head of cauliflower and refrigerate for up to 5 days. Before using, wash and remove the leaves at the base and trim the stem. **TASTE OF HOME TEST KITCHEN**

CAULIFLOWER CASSEROLE

STEWED TOMATOES WITH DUMPLINGS

PREP/TOTAL TIME: 20 min. | **YIELD:** 2 servings.

When I was young and did not feel well, my mother would always make this because it was one of my favorite dishes. Just smelling it cook made me feel better, along with her tender loving care. **VIOLA STUTZ** GREENWOOD, DELAWARE

- 1 can (14-1/2 ounces) diced tomatoes, undrained
- 1 tablespoon sugar
- 1/4 teaspoon salt
- 1/4 teaspoon pepper
- 2 tablespoons butter
- 1/2 cup biscuit/baking mix
- 3 tablespoons milk

In a large saucepan, combine the tomatoes, sugar, salt, pepper and butter. Bring to a boil over medium heat, stirring occasionally.

In a small bowl, combine biscuit mix and milk. Drop batter in four mounds onto the tomatoes. Reduce heat; cover and simmer for 10 minutes or until a toothpick inserted in a dumpling comes out clean (do not lift cover while simmering).

WINTER ROASTED VEGETABLES

PREP: 10 min. | **BAKE:** 1 hour | **YIELD:** 6 servings.

Roasted vegetables and pears are scrumptious paired with blue cheese and toasted hazelnuts and then drizzled with balsamic vinegar.

SUSIE VAN ETTEN CHAPMANSBORO, TENNESSEE

- 1 medium acorn squash, seeded and cut into 8 wedges
- 1 pound fingerling potatoes, halved
- 1 medium onion, cut into wedges
- 3 tablespoons olive oil, *divided*
- 2 medium pears, cut into wedges
- 1/4 teaspoon minced fresh thyme
- 1/8 teaspoon salt
- 1/8 teaspoon pepper
- 2 tablespoons balsamic vinegar
- 1/2 cup crumbled blue cheese
- 1/4 cup chopped hazelnuts, toasted

Place the squash, potatoes and onion in a large resealable plastic bag. Add 2 tablespoons oil; seal bag and shake to coat. Place in a single layer in a greased 15-in. x 10-in. x 1-in. baking pan. Bake, uncovered, at 350° for 40-45 minutes or until golden brown, turning once.

Place pears in a large resealable plastic bag. Add the thyme, salt, pepper and remaining oil; seal bag and shake to coat. Arrange with vegetables. Bake 10-15 minutes longer or until tender. Arrange in an ovenproof dish; drizzle with vinegar and sprinkle with cheese. Bake for 2-3 minutes or until cheese is melted. Sprinkle with hazelnuts.

ROASTED NEW POTATOES

PREP: 15 min. | **BAKE:** 35 min.
YIELD: 4 servings.

These potatoes are anything but plain. The flavors of garlic and herbs combine to add extra zip to tender new potatoes. This side dish goes hand-in-hand with the delicate taste of fish.

ANN BERG CHESAPEAKE, VIRGINIA

- 1-1/2 pounds new potatoes, quartered
- 2 tablespoons olive oil
- 2 teaspoons minced garlic
- 1/2 teaspoon salt
- 1/2 teaspoon dried rosemary, crushed
- 1/2 teaspoon dried thyme
- 1/8 teaspoon pepper

In a resealable plastic bag, combine all ingredients; shake to coat. Pour into an ungreased 13-in. x 9-in. baking dish. Bake, uncovered, at 450° for 35 minutes or until potatoes are tender.

GRILLED ITALIAN EGGPLANT SLICES

PREP/TOTAL TIME: 25 min. | **YIELD:** 5 servings.

What a fabulous way to dress up eggplant! Piled high with herbs, cheese and fresh tomatoes, this fail-proof, grilled side nicely complements a variety of main dishes. **THERESA LASALLE** MIDLOTHIAN, VIRGINIA

- 1/4 cup shredded Parmesan cheese
- 3 tablespoons lemon juice
- 2 tablespoons minced fresh basil
- 5 teaspoons olive oil
- 3 garlic cloves, minced
- 1 teaspoon minced fresh oregano
- 1 large eggplant, cut into 10 slices
- 10 slices tomato
- 1/2 cup shredded part-skim mozzarella cheese

In a small bowl, combine the first six ingredients.

Grill eggplant, covered, over medium heat for 3 minutes. Turn slices; spoon Parmesan mixture onto each. Top with tomato; sprinkle with mozzarella cheese. Grill, covered, 2-3 minutes longer or until cheese is melted.

ASPARAGUS AND SUN-DRIED TOMATOES

PREP/TOTAL TIME: 25 min. | **YIELD:** 12 servings.

Crisp-tender asparagus is drizzled with lemon butter sauce and sprinkled with flavorful sun-dried tomatoes in this effortless, classic recipe.

PAT STEVENS GRANBURY, TEXAS

- 3 pounds fresh asparagus, trimmed
- 1/3 cup butter, cubed
- 1/3 cup chicken broth
- 3 tablespoons olive oil
- 4 teaspoons grated lemon peel
- 1/4 teaspoon salt
- 1/4 teaspoon pepper
- 1/3 cup oil-packed sun-dried tomatoes, patted dry and chopped
- 1/4 cup minced fresh basil

Place asparagus in a steamer basket; place in a large saucepan over 1 in. of water. Bring to a boil; cover and steam for 6-8 minutes or until crisp-tender.

Meanwhile, in a small saucepan, melt butter. Stir in the broth, oil, lemon peel and salt.

Transfer asparagus to a serving platter; drizzle with butter mixture. Sprinkle with pepper; top with tomatoes and basil.

SPICY SWEET POTATO CHIPS & CILANTRO DIP

PREP: 20 min. | **BAKE:** 25 min. | **YIELD:** 16 servings (3 cups dip).

This cool, creamy dip is a great partner for spicy chips. The flavors complement each other so well I can't imagine eating one without the other. **LIBBY WALP** CHICAGO, ILLINOIS

4 to 5 large sweet potatoes
(3-1/2 pounds), peeled and
cut into 1/8-inch slices

1/4 cup canola oil

2 teaspoons chili powder

1 teaspoon garlic powder

1 teaspoon taco seasoning

3/4 teaspoon salt

1/2 teaspoon ground cumin

1/2 teaspoon pepper

1/4 teaspoon cayenne pepper

DIP:

1-1/2 cups mayonnaise

1 cup (8 ounces) sour cream

4 ounces cream cheese, softened

3 tablespoons minced fresh cilantro

1 tablespoon lemon juice

1 teaspoon celery salt

1/4 teaspoon pepper

Place sweet potatoes in a large bowl. Combine the oil and seasonings; drizzle over potatoes and toss to coat.

Arrange in a single layer in two ungreased 15-in. x 10-in. x 1-in. baking pans. Bake at 400° for 25-30 minutes or until golden brown, turning once.

In a small bowl, beat the dip ingredients until blended. Serve with sweet potato chips.

BROCCOLI WITH LEMON SAUCE

PREP/TOTAL TIME: 20 min. | **YIELD:** 10 servings (1-1/4 cups sauce).

Enjoy this refreshing, delicious alternative to traditional cheese and broccoli. The lemon sauce is wonderful over cauliflower, too! **BARBARA FRASIER** FYFFE, ALABAMA

- 3 **pounds fresh broccoli spears**
- 1 **cup chicken broth**
- 1 **tablespoon butter**
- 4-1/2 **teaspoons cornstarch**
- 1/4 **cup cold water**
- 2 **egg yolks, lightly beaten**
- 3 **tablespoons lemon juice**
- 2 **tablespoons grated lemon peel**

Place broccoli in a large saucepan; add 1 in. of water. Bring to a boil. Reduce heat; cover and cook for 5-8 minutes or until crisp-tender.

Meanwhile, in a small heavy saucepan, heat broth and butter until butter is melted. Combine cornstarch and water until smooth; stir into broth mixture. Bring to a boil; cook and stir for 2 minutes or until thickened and bubbly.

Remove from the heat. Stir a small amount of hot mixture into egg yolks; return all to the pan, stirring constantly. Bring to a gentle boil; cook and stir 2 minutes longer. Remove from the heat. Gently stir in lemon juice and peel. Drain broccoli; serve with sauce.

HOPPIN' JOHN

PREP/TOTAL TIME: 15 min. | **YIELD:** 2 servings.

My family usually enjoys this mildly flavored rice dish on New Year's Eve, but it makes a great accompaniment to any entree, any time.

BETH WALL INMAN, SOUTH CAROLINA

- 1/4 cup chopped sweet red pepper
- 1/4 cup chopped green pepper
- 2 tablespoons chopped onion
- 1/4 teaspoon garlic powder
- 1/8 teaspoon salt
- 1 tablespoon butter
- 2/3 cup canned black-eyed peas, rinsed and drained
- 2/3 cup cooked rice

In a small skillet, saute the peppers, onion, garlic powder and salt in butter for 4-5 minutes or until vegetables are tender. Stir in the peas and rice; heat through, stirring occasionally.

HERBED GREEN BEANS

PREP/TOTAL TIME: 15 min.
YIELD: 4 servings.

An assortment of herbs adds a refreshing burst of flavor to this easy green bean dish. You can serve it in moments, and it goes so well with just about any main course.

ANN BASSETT NASHVILLE, TENNESSEE

- 1 small onion, chopped
- 2 teaspoons butter
- 1 package (16 ounces) frozen cut green beans, thawed
- 1/2 teaspoon garlic salt
- 1/2 teaspoon dried basil
- 1/4 teaspoon salt
- 1/4 teaspoon dried oregano
- 1/4 teaspoon dried marjoram

In a large nonstick skillet coated with cooking spray, cook onion in butter over medium heat for 2 minutes. Stir in green beans and seasonings. Cook and stir 6-8 minutes longer or until beans are tender.

DIRTY RICE

PREP/TOTAL TIME: 30 min. | **YIELD:** 10-12 servings.

This is an old Louisiana recipe that I've had longer than I can remember. It's a very popular dish in the South. To turn this into a main meal, simply add more sausage and chicken livers. **LUM DAY** BASTROP, LOUISIANA

1/2 pound bulk pork sausage

1/2 pound chicken livers, chopped

1 cup chopped onion

1/2 cup chopped celery

1/3 cup sliced green onions

2 tablespoons minced fresh parsley

3 tablespoons butter

1 garlic clove, minced

1 can (10-1/2 ounces) chicken broth

1/2 teaspoon dried basil

1/2 teaspoon dried thyme

1/2 teaspoon salt

1/4 teaspoon pepper

1/4 teaspoon hot pepper sauce

3 cups cooked rice

In a large skillet, cook sausage for 2-3 minutes; stir in chicken livers. Cook 5-7 minutes more or until sausage and chicken livers are no longer pink; drain and set aside.

In the same skillet, saute the onion, celery, green onions and parsley in butter until the vegetables are tender. Add garlic; cook 1 minute longer. Add broth, basil, thyme, salt, pepper and hot pepper sauce. Stir in rice, sausage and chicken livers. Heat through, stirring constantly.

FRIED GREEN TOMATOES

PREP: 20 min. | **COOK:** 25 min. | **YIELD:** 10 servings.

Panko bread crumbs have a coarser texture than ordinary bread crumbs, which you can also use to coat the tomatoes. However, the panko crumbs will give them a light and crispy texture. **JACQUELYNNE STINE** LAS VEGAS, NEVADA

3/4 cup all-purpose flour

3 eggs, lightly beaten

2 cups panko (Japanese) bread crumbs

5 medium green tomatoes, cut into 1/4-inch slices

Oil for deep-fat frying

Salt

In three separate shallow bowls, place the flour, eggs and bread crumbs. Dip tomatoes in flour, then in eggs; coat with bread crumbs.

In an electric skillet or deep-fat fryer, heat oil to 375°. Fry tomatoes, a few at a time, for 2-3 minutes on each side or until golden brown. Drain on paper towels. Sprinkle with salt. Serve immediately.

A SOUTHERN SPECIALTY

Fried green tomatoes are a popular side dish in the South, and can be served as an appetizer, side dish or a meal. They're made from sliced, unripened tomatoes coated with cornmeal, flour or bread crumbs and fried. Enjoy them with a platter of cheesy grits, on a sandwich or all on their own.
TASTE OF HOME TEST KITCHEN

FRIED GREEN TOMATOES

CORN FRITTERS WITH CARAMELIZED ONION JAM

TANGY PEAS AND CAULIFLOWER

PREP/TOTAL TIME: 20 min. | **YIELD:** 8-10 servings.

This pretty side dish gets it pleasant tangy flavor from silky yogurt. **MARIE HOYER** HODGENVILLE, KENTUCKY

- **4 cups fresh caulifiowerets**
- **1 package (16 ounces) frozen peas**
- **3/4 cup fat-free plain yogurt**
- **3 tablespoons minced fresh cilantro**
- **1 tablespoon lemon juice**
- **1/4 teaspoon ground cumin**
- **Dash salt-free lemon-pepper seasoning**

Place cauliflower in a saucepan with a small amount of water. Bring to a boil; cook for 6-8 minutes. Add peas; cook 2-4 minutes longer or until the vegetables are crisp-tender; drain.

Combine remaining ingredients; pour over vegetables and toss to coat.

CORN FRITTERS WITH CARAMELIZED ONION JAM

PREP: 30 min. | **COOK:** 15 min. | **YIELD:** 2 dozen (3/4 cup jam).

A friend's husband, who's a chef, came up with these light and fluffy fritters accompanied perfectly by a sweet-tart jam. I would never ask a chef to divulge his secrets, so I created my own version. **KIM CUPO** ALBANY, GEORGIA

- **1 large sweet onion, halved and thinly sliced**
- **1 tablespoon olive oil**
- **2 teaspoons balsamic vinegar**
- **1/3 cup apple jelly**
- **1/3 cup canned diced tomatoes**
- **1 tablespoon tomato paste**
- **1/8 teaspoon curry powder**
- **1/8 teaspoon ground cinnamon**
- **Dash salt and pepper**
- **FRITTERS:**
- **2 cups biscuit/baking mix**
- **1 can (11 ounces) gold and white corn, drained**
- **2 eggs, lightly beaten**
- **1/2 cup 2% milk**
- **1/2 cup sour cream**
- **1/2 teaspoon salt**
- **Oil for frying**

In a small skillet, saute onion in oil until golden brown. Add vinegar; cook and stir for 2-3 minutes. Set aside.

In a small saucepan, combine the jelly, tomatoes, tomato paste, curry powder, cinnamon, salt and pepper. Cook over medium heat for 5-7 minutes or until heated through. Add onion mixture. Cook and stir for 3 minutes; set aside and keep warm.

In a small bowl, combine the baking mix, corn, eggs, milk, sour cream and salt just until combined.

In a deep-fat fryer or electric skillet, heat oil to 375°. Drop batter by heaping tablespoonfuls, a few at a time, into hot oil; fry for 1-1/2 minutes on each side or until golden brown. Drain on paper towels. Serve warm with jam.

CRISPY CAJUN POTATO WEDGES

PREP: 15 min. | **BAKE:** 45 min. | **YIELD:** 2 servings.

A sprinkle of Cajun seasoning lends spunk to these hearty, cornflake-coated wedges. My husband, Jim, and I love potatoes, so I'm always trying to come up with new, lower-fat recipes.

LADONNA REED PONCA CITY, OKLAHOMA

- 1/4 cup 2% milk
- 1/4 cup mayonnaise
- 4-1/2 teaspoons ranch salad dressing mix
- 3/4 teaspoon Cajun seasoning, *divided*
- 3/4 cup crushed cornflakes
- 2 medium russet potatoes

In a shallow bowl, combine the milk, mayonnaise, dressing mix and 1/2 teaspoon Cajun seasoning. In another shallow bowl, combine cornflakes and remaining Cajun seasoning. Cut each potato into eight wedges; dip in mayonnaise mixture, then coat with crumbs.

Arrange in a single layer in a 15-in. x 10-in. x 1-in. baking pan coated with cooking spray. Bake at 375° for 45-50 minutes or until tender and lightly browned, turning once.

FRIED CABBAGE

PREP/TOTAL TIME: 20 min.
YIELD: 6 servings.

Fried cabbage is so good with potatoes, deviled eggs and corn bread. When I was young, my family grew our own cabbage and potatoes. It was fun to put them to use in the kitchen.

BERNICE MORRIS MARSHFIELD, MISSOURI

- 2 tablespoons butter
- 1 teaspoon sugar
- 1/2 teaspoon salt
- 1/4 teaspoon crushed red pepper flakes
- 1/8 teaspoon pepper
- 6 cups coarsely chopped cabbage
- 1 tablespoon water

In a skillet, melt butter over medium heat. Stir in the sugar, salt, pepper flakes and pepper. Add the cabbage and water. Cook for 5-6 minutes or until tender, stirring occasionally.

CREAMED SPINACH AND MUSHROOMS

PREP/TOTAL TIME: 10 min. | **YIELD:** 2 servings.

When my family was snowed in one time, we had to make do with what we had on hand. After looking through the pantry, I was able to put this recipe together. I find that it is very versatile and takes only 10 minutes to make from start to finish. **MICHELLE FERRARIO** IJAMSVILLE, MARYLAND

1-1/2 cups sliced fresh mushrooms

2 tablespoons olive oil

1/2 teaspoon butter

1 package (6 ounces) fresh baby spinach

3 ounces reduced-fat cream cheese, cubed

1/4 teaspoon salt

1/8 teaspoon pepper

In a small skillet, saute mushrooms in oil and butter until tender. Add spinach; cover and cook for 1 minute or until wilted.

Stir in the cream cheese, salt and pepper. Serve immediately.

VEGETABLE-STUFFED EGGPLANT

MARINATED LIMA BEAN SALAD

PREP: 10 min. + chilling | **YIELD:** 6-8 servings.

This salad is one of my family's favorites. It tastes even better the next day, after the lima beans have marinated in the dressing. **SUE THOMPSON** CHESTER, MARYLAND

1/3 cup canola oil

2 tablespoons red wine vinegar

2 teaspoons sugar

1/2 teaspoon salt

1/2 teaspoon ground mustard

1/2 teaspoon paprika

1/4 teaspoon dried tarragon

1/4 teaspoon dried oregano

1/4 teaspoon dried thyme

1/8 teaspoon pepper

Dash garlic powder

1 package (16 ounces) frozen baby lima beans, cooked and drained

1/2 cup sliced onions, halved

1/2 cup sliced fresh mushrooms

2 tablespoons diced pimiento

In a jar with a tight-fitting lid, combine the first 11 ingredients; shake well. Cover and refrigerate for at least an hour.

In a serving bowl, combine the lima beans, onion, mushrooms and pimientos. Add dressing and toss to coat. Cover and refrigerate for 1 hour.

VEGETABLE-STUFFED EGGPLANT

PREP: 20 min. | **BAKE:** 30 min. | **YIELD:** 2 servings.

A friend of mine is excellent at growing eggplant and shared this recipe with me. This fast and delicious side will complement most any entree. **DORIS HEATH** FRANKLIN, NORTH CAROLINA

1 small eggplant

1 medium ear sweet corn, husk removed

1 small onion, finely chopped

1 small tomato, chopped

1 garlic clove, minced

4-1/2 teaspoons canola oil

2 tablespoons minced fresh parsley

1/2 teaspoon salt

1/4 teaspoon minced fresh oregano

1/4 teaspoon pepper

1/2 cup water

1/3 cup shredded cheddar cheese

Cut eggplant in half lengthwise; remove pulp, leaving a 1/4-in. shell. Cube removed pulp; set shells aside. Cut corn off the cob.

In a large nonstick skillet, saute the eggplant pulp, corn, onion, tomato and garlic in oil until onion is tender. Stir in seasonings. Spoon mixture into reserved shells. Place in an ungreased 11-in. x 7-in. baking dish; pour water into dish.

Cover and bake at 350° for 25-30 minutes or until heated through. Uncover; sprinkle with cheese. Bake 5 minutes longer or until cheese is melted.

SALTING AN EGGPLANT
Salting an eggplant draws out moisture, gives the flesh a denser texture and reduces some of its bitterness. Sprinkle slices with 1/2 teaspoon salt and toss. Let stand for 30 minutes. Rinse, drain well and pat dry with paper towels. **TASTE OF HOME TEST KITCHEN**

CANDIED SWEET POTATOES

PREP: 40 min. + cooling
BAKE: 15 min.
YIELD: 8-10 servings.

I usually pair this side dish with baked ham or roasted turkey.
ESSIE NEALEY TABOR CITY, NORTH CAROLINA

   3 pounds sweet
      potatoes, peeled
1/2 cup packed brown sugar
  1 teaspoon ground cinnamon
1/4 cup butter, cubed
1/4 cup corn syrup

Place the sweet potatoes in a large kettle and cover with water. Cover and bring to a boil; boil gently for 30-45 minutes or until potatoes can be easily pierced with the tip of a sharp knife.

When cool enough to handle, peel potatoes and cut into wedges. Place in an ungreased 11-in. x 7-in. baking dish. Sprinkle with brown sugar and cinnamon. Dot with butter; drizzle with corn syrup.

Bake, uncovered, at 375° for 15-20 minutes or until bubbly, basting with sauce occasionally.

SLOW-COOKED SAUSAGE DRESSING

PREP: 20 min. | **COOK:** 3 hours | **YIELD:** 8 cups.

This dressing is so delicious no one will know it's lower in fat. And best of all, it cooks effortlessly in the slow cooker, so the stove and oven are free for other dishes. **RAQUEL HAGGARD** EDMOND, OKLAHOMA

1/2 pound reduced-fat bulk pork sausage
  2 celery ribs, chopped
  1 large onion, chopped
  7 cups seasoned stuffing cubes
  1 can (14-1/2 ounces) reduced-sodium chicken broth
  1 medium tart apple, chopped
1/3 cup chopped pecans
  2 tablespoons reduced-fat butter, melted
1-1/2 teaspoons rubbed sage
1/2 teaspoon pepper

In a large nonstick skillet, cook the sausage, celery and onion over medium heat until meat is no longer pink; drain. Transfer to a large bowl; stir in the remaining ingredients.

Transfer to a 5-qt. slow cooker coated with cooking spray. Cover and cook on low for 3-4 hours or until heated through and apple is tender, stirring once.

EDITOR'S NOTE: This recipe was tested with Land O'Lakes light stick butter.

CREAMY POTATOES 'N' PEAS

PREP/TOTAL TIME: 30 min. | **YIELD:** 6-8 servings.

One look at this side dish and you know you are in for some fabulous comfort food. It has great eye and appetite appeal, so I like to serve it in a pretty glass bowl. **DEBBIE TERENZINI-WILKERSON** LUSBY, MARYLAND

- 1 **pound small unpeeled red potatoes, cut into wedges**
- 1 **package (10 ounces) frozen peas**
- 2 **tablespoons chopped onion**
- 2 **tablespoons butter**
- 2 **tablespoons all-purpose flour**
- 3/4 **teaspoon salt**
- 1/4 **teaspoon pepper**
- 1-1/2 **cups milk**
- 1/2 **teaspoon dill weed**

Place potatoes in a large pot and cover with water. Bring to a boil. Reduce heat; cover and simmer for 15-20 minutes or until tender. Cook peas according to package directions.

Meanwhile, in a small saucepan, saute onion in butter until tender. Stir in the flour, salt and pepper until blended. Gradually stir in milk. Bring to a boil over medium heat; cook and stir for 2 minutes or until thickened. Add dill.

Drain potatoes and peas; place in a serving bowl. Top with sauce; stir to coat.

GRILLED CORN ON THE COB

PREP: 20 min. + soaking | **GRILL:** 25 min. | **YIELD:** 8 servings.

I'd never grilled corn until last summer when my sister-in-law served it for us. What a treat! So simple, yet delicious, grilled corn is now a must for my favorite summer menu. **ANGELA LEINENBACH** MECHANICSVILLE, VIRGINIA

8 medium ears sweet corn

1/2 cup butter, softened

2 tablespoons minced
fresh basil

2 tablespoons minced
fresh parsley

1/2 teaspoon salt

Soak the corn in cold water for 20 minutes. Meanwhile, in a small bowl, combine the butter, basil, parsley and salt. Carefully peel back corn husks to within 1 in. of bottoms; remove silk. Spread butter mixture over corn.

Rewrap corn in husks and secure with kitchen string. Grill corn, covered, over medium heat for 25-30 minutes or until tender, turning occasionally. Cut strings and peel back husks.

PICKLED BEETS

PREP: 20 min. + chilling | **YIELD:** 6-8 servings.

I grew up with my mother's pickled beets. The beets she used came from our garden and were canned for the winter months. Even as a child I loved beets because they brought so much color to our table. Their tangy flavor is a great complement to the rest of the foods in this meal. **SARA LINDLER** IRMO, SOUTH CAROLINA

- 8 medium fresh beets
- 1 cup vinegar
- 1/2 cup sugar
- 1-1/2 teaspoons whole cloves
- 1-1/2 teaspoons whole allspice
- 1/2 teaspoon salt

Remove and discard greens and all but 1/2 in. of the stems from beets. Cook beets in boiling water until tender; drain and cool. Peel and slice; place in a bowl and set aside.

In a small saucepan, combine vinegar, sugar, cloves, allspice and salt. Bring to a boil; boil for 5 minutes. Pour over beets. Refrigerate at least 1 hour. Drain before serving.

BARBECUED BEANS

PREP: 5 min. + standing | **COOK:** 10 hours
YIELD: 12-15 servings.

Most members of my family would agree that no picnic is complete until these delicious beans have made their appearance. Preparing them in a slow cooker makes them easy to transport to any gathering.
DIANE HIXON NICEVILLE, FLORIDA

- 1 pound dried navy beans
- 1 pound bacon strips, cooked and crumbled
- 1 bottle (32 ounces) tomato juice
- 1 can (8 ounces) tomato sauce
- 2 cups chopped onions
- 2/3 cup packed brown sugar
- 1 tablespoon reduced-sodium soy sauce
- 2 teaspoons garlic salt
- 1 teaspoon ground mustard
- 1 teaspoon Worcestershire sauce

Place beans in a large saucepan; add water to cover by 2 in. Bring to a boil; boil for 2 minutes. Remove from the heat; let stand for 1 hour. Drain beans and discard liquid.

In a 5-qt. slow cooker, combine remaining ingredients. Add the beans. Cover and cook on high for 2 hours. Reduce heat to low and cook 8-10 hours longer or until beans are tender.

OLD-FASHIONED MACARONI AND CHEESE

PREP: 15 min. | **BAKE:** 45 min. | **YIELD:** 12-16 servings.

Bring back the taste of days gone by with this ooey-gooey mac-and-cheese classic. A little ground mustard and hot pepper sauce give it just the right spice. **JAMES BACKMAN** CENTRALIA, WASHINGTON

3-1/2 cups uncooked elbow
    macaroni (about 12 ounces)

1/4 cup butter, cubed

1/4 cup all-purpose flour

1 teaspoon salt

3/4 teaspoon ground mustard

1/2 teaspoon pepper

Few dashes hot pepper sauce

3-1/2 cups milk

5 cups (20 ounces) shredded
    cheddar cheese, *divided*

Cook macaroni in boiling water until almost tender; drain. Meanwhile, in a Dutch oven, melt butter. Stir in the flour, salt, mustard, pepper and pepper sauce until smooth. Cook for 1 minute or until bubbly. Stir in the macaroni, milk and 4 cups cheese.

Transfer to an ungreased 13-in. x 9-in. baking dish. Cover and bake at 350° for 45-50 minutes or until bubbly. Uncover; sprinkle with the remaining cheese. Let stand for 5 minutes before serving.

SPICY SWEET POTATO FRIES

PREP: 25 min. | **BAKE:** 30 min. | **YIELD:** 5 servings.

Better pile these sweet and spicy orange fries high on the plate. Served with a thick dipping sauce, they create a craving for more. **MARY JONES** WILLIAMSTOWN, WEST VIRGINIA

1 teaspoon coriander seed

1/2 teaspoon fennel seed

1/2 teaspoon dried oregano

1/2 teaspoon crushed red
    pepper flakes

1/2 teaspoon salt

2 pounds sweet potatoes
    (about 4 medium), peeled
    and cut into wedges

2 tablespoons canola oil

SPICY MAYONNAISE DIP:

1-1/4 cups mayonnaise

2 tablespoons lime juice

2 tablespoons minced
    fresh cilantro

2 garlic cloves, minced

1 teaspoon ground mustard

1/4 teaspoon cayenne pepper

1/8 teaspoon salt

In a spice grinder or with a mortar and pestle, combine the coriander, fennel, oregano and pepper flakes; grind until mixture becomes a fine powder. Stir in salt.

In a large bowl, combine the potatoes, oil and ground spices; toss to coat. Transfer to a greased 15-in. x 10-in. x 1-in. baking pan.

Bake, uncovered, at 400° for 30-35 minutes or until crisp and golden brown, turning occasionally. Meanwhile, in a small bowl, combine the dip ingredients; chill until serving. Serve with fries.

IT'S A SLAM DUNK!

In addition to the Spicy Mayonnaise Dip recipe, dunk those sweet potato fries into any of the following suggestions: pure, sweet honey; a mixture of sour cream, lime juice and cilantro; buffalo wing sauce; or even ranch dressing!
TASTE OF HOME TEST KITCHEN

SPICY SWEET POTATO FRIES

FAMILY-FAVORITE BAKED BEANS

PREP: 20 min. | **BAKE:** 1 hour | **YIELD:** 8 servings.

Here's a quick-and-easy recipe that makes an appearance at most reunions and other large gatherings. The sweet and hearty dish includes three kinds of beans and plenty of beef and bacon. **LEA ANN ANDERSON** TULSA, OKLAHOMA

- **1/2** pound ground beef
- **1/2** pound bacon strips, diced
- **1** small onion, chopped
- **1/2** cup ketchup
- **1/2** cup barbecue sauce
- **1/3** cup packed brown sugar
- **2** tablespoons molasses
- **1** can (16 ounces) kidney beans, rinsed and drained
- **1** can (15-3/4 ounces) pork and beans
- **1** can (16 ounces) butter beans, rinsed and drained

In a Dutch oven, cook beef over medium heat until no longer pink; drain and set aside. In the same pan, cook bacon until crisp; drain.

Return beef to the pan. Add the onion, ketchup, barbecue sauce, brown sugar and molasses. Stir in the beans.

Transfer to a greased 3-qt. baking dish. Cover and bake at 350° for 1 hour or until beans reach desired thickness.

CHEESE 'N' GRITS CASSEROLE

PREP: 10 min. | **BAKE:** 30 min. + standing | **YIELD:** 8 servings.

Grits are a staple in Southern cooking. Serve this as a brunch item with bacon or as a side dish for dinner.
JENNIFER WALLIS GOLDSBORO, NORTH CAROLINA

- 4 cups water
- 1 cup uncooked old-fashioned grits
- 1/2 teaspoon salt
- 1/2 cup 2% milk
- 1/4 cup butter, melted
- 2 eggs, lightly beaten
- 1 cup (4 ounces) shredded cheddar cheese
- 1 tablespoon Worcestershire sauce
- 1/8 teaspoon cayenne pepper
- 1/8 teaspoon paprika

In a large saucepan, bring water to a boil. Slowly stir in grits and salt. Reduce heat; cover and simmer for 5-7 minutes or until thickened. Cool slightly. Gradually whisk in the milk, butter and eggs. Stir in the cheese, Worcestershire sauce and cayenne.

Transfer to a greased 2-qt. baking dish. Sprinkle with paprika. Bake, uncovered, at 350° for 30-35 minutes or until bubbly. Let stand 10 minutes before serving.

OKRA & CORN SAUTE

PREP/TOTAL TIME: 25 min. | **YIELD:** 12 servings (2/3 cup each).

My family loves the fresh-from-the-garden taste of this dish. The combination of the peppered bacon and the Italian seasoning adds just the right amount of zesty flavor. **KARIN CHRISTIAN** PLANO, TEXAS

- 8 cups fresh or frozen okra, thawed
- 6 thick-sliced peppered bacon strips, chopped
- 2 cups fresh whole kernel corn
- 4 teaspoons Italian seasoning

Cut okra lengthwise; set aside. In a large skillet, cook bacon over medium heat until crisp.

Stir in the corn, Italian seasoning and reserved okra; saute until okra is tender and corn is lightly browned.

CILANTRO CORN SAUTE

PREP/TOTAL TIME: 15 min.
YIELD: 4 servings.

This is an easy side dish that goes with most anything. Cilantro and cumin really perk up the flavor.
LISA LANGSTON CONROE, TEXAS

- 3-1/3 cups fresh or frozen corn, thawed
- 1 medium green pepper, chopped
- 1 tablespoon finely chopped onion
- 2 tablespoons butter
- 1/2 cup minced fresh cilantro
- 1-1/2 teaspoons ground cumin

In a skillet, saute the corn, green pepper and onion in butter until tender. Stir in cilantro and cumin; saute 1-2 minutes longer or until heated through.

LOADED RED POTATO CASSEROLE

PREP: 25 min. | **BAKE:** 20 min. | **YIELD:** 9 servings.

This potato casserole has the same flavor of the potato skins you can order as a restaurant appetizer. It's an ideal dish for tailgating and potlucks.

CHARLANE GATHY LEXINGTON, KENTUCKY

- 16 small red potatoes
- 1/2 cup 2% milk
- 1/4 cup butter, cubed
- 1/2 teaspoon pepper
- 1/8 teaspoon salt
- 1-1/2 cups (6 ounces) shredded cheddar cheese, *divided*
- 1/2 cup crumbled cooked bacon
- 1 cup (8 ounces) sour cream
- 2 tablespoons minced chives

Place potatoes in a Dutch oven and cover with water. Bring to a boil. Reduce heat; cover and cook for 15-20 minutes or until tender. Drain.

Mash potatoes with the milk, butter, pepper and salt. Transfer to a greased 13-in. x 9-in. baking dish. Sprinkle with 1 cup cheese and bacon.

Dollop with sour cream; sprinkle with chives and remaining cheese. Bake, uncovered, at 350° for 20-25 minutes or until cheese is melted.

CORN BREAD DRESSING WITH OYSTERS

PREP: 10 min. | **BAKE:** 45 min. | **YIELD:** 12-15 servings.

My father's dressing bakes separately from the turkey and is simply delicious. The secret is to prepare the corn bread first, let it cool and then crumble it to form the base for the rest of the ingredients. My father always added oysters to give the dressing a special flavor.

NELL BASS MACON, GEORGIA

- 8 to 10 cups coarsely crumbled corn bread
- 2 slices white bread, toasted and torn into small pieces
- 2 hard-cooked eggs, chopped
- 2 cups chopped celery
- 1 cup chopped onion
- 1 pint shucked oysters, drained and chopped, *or* 2 cans (8 ounces *each*) whole oysters, drained and chopped
- 1/2 cup egg substitute
- 1 teaspoon poultry seasoning
- 5 to 6 cups turkey *or* chicken broth

Combine the first eight ingredients in a large bowl. Stir in enough broth to make the mixture very wet. Pour into a greased 13-in. x 9-in. baking dish or shallow 3-qt. baking dish.

Bake, uncovered, at 400° for 45 minutes or until dressing is lightly browned.

CREAMY SUCCOTASH

PREP: 10 min. | **COOK:** 20 min. + cooling | **YIELD:** 10 servings.

When I first saw this dish being made, I didn't think the combination would be very tasty, but I changed my mind immediately upon tasting it. **SHANNON KOENE** BLACKSBURG, VIRGINIA

- 4 cups frozen lima beans
- 1 cup water
- 4 cups frozen corn
- 2/3 cup reduced-fat mayonnaise
- 2 teaspoons Dijon mustard
- 1/2 teaspoon onion powder
- 1/2 teaspoon garlic powder
- 1/4 teaspoon salt
- 1/4 teaspoon pepper

- 2 medium tomatoes,
  finely chopped
- 1 small onion, finely chopped

In a large saucepan, bring lima beans and water to a boil. Reduce heat; cover and simmer for 10 minutes. Add corn; return to a boil. Reduce heat; cover and simmer 5-6 minutes longer or until vegetables are tender. Drain; cool for 10-15 minutes.

Meanwhile, in a large bowl, combine the mayonnaise, mustard, onion powder, garlic powder, salt and pepper. Stir in the bean mixture, tomatoes and onion. Serve immediately or refrigerate.

TOMATOES ROCKEFELLER

FRIED PICKLE COINS

PREP: 20 min. | **COOK:** 5 min./batch | **YIELD:** 16 servings.

It took me several tries to create the ideal seasoning blend for my fried pickles. It is a hit with my group. Serve it as a side or as an appetizer with dips. **AMANDA THORNTON** ALEXANDRIA, KENTUCKY

2 cups all-purpose flour
1 teaspoon garlic powder
1 teaspoon ground mustard
1 teaspoon dill weed
1 teaspoon paprika
1/2 teaspoon garlic salt
1/2 teaspoon cayenne pepper
1/4 teaspoon pepper
2 eggs
3 tablespoons 2% milk

1 garlic clove, minced
3 cups dill pickle slices
Oil for deep-fat frying
Ranch salad dressing and prepared mustard, optional

In a shallow bowl, combine the first eight ingredients. In another shallow bowl, whisk the eggs, milk and garlic. Drain pickles and pat dry. Coat pickles with flour mixture, then dip in egg mixture; coat again with flour mixture.

In an electric skillet or deep-fat fryer, heat oil to 375°. Fry pickles, about 10 at a time, for 1-2 minutes or until golden brown, turning once. Drain on paper towels. Serve warm with ranch dressing and mustard if desired.

TOMATOES ROCKEFELLER

PREP: 20 min. | **BAKE:** 35 min. | **YIELD:** 6 servings.

You can serve these tomatoes with a variety of meats, especially beef. The topping freezes well and may be spread thinner to cover more tomato slices, if needed. **LINDA ROBERSON** COLLIERVILLE, TENNESSEE

3 eggs, lightly beaten
1 cup dry bread crumbs
3 green onions, chopped
1 tablespoon butter, melted
1 teaspoon Italian seasoning
1 garlic clove, minced
1/2 teaspoon minced fresh thyme
1/4 teaspoon salt
1/4 teaspoon pepper
1/8 teaspoon Worcestershire sauce
1/8 teaspoon hot pepper sauce
1 package (10 ounces) frozen creamed spinach
2 large tomatoes
1/4 cup shredded Parmesan cheese

In a large bowl, combine the first 11 ingredients. Cook spinach according to package directions; stir into egg mixture.

Cut each tomato into six slices; arrange in a single layer in a 13-in. x 9-in. baking dish coated with cooking spray. Mound 2 tablespoons of spinach mixture on each slice.

Bake, uncovered, at 350° for 30 minutes. Sprinkle with Parmesan cheese. Bake 5-10 minutes longer or until a thermometer reads 160°.

RIPEN GREEN TOMATOES

To ripen green garden tomatoes, put them in brown paper bags. Don't stack too many in one bag, or they might get bruised. Close the bags and check on them every few days. Remove the tomatoes as they ripen.
DELIA K. DEER PARK, WASHINGTON

LEMON MARMALADE, PG. 236

JAMS, PICKLES & MORE

Enjoy the taste of fresh produce long after the lazy days of summer with this treasured collection of homemade jams, jellies, preserves, sauces, pickles and more.

REFRIGERATOR PICKLES, PG. 238

ALMOST RASPBERRY JAM

PREP: 10 min. | **COOK:** 25 min. + chilling | **YIELD:** 7 cups.

You'll love this creative way to use up all those leftover green tomatoes in the garden.

SUE ELLEN DILLARD EL DORADO, ARKANSAS

- 5-1/2 cups chopped green tomatoes
- 5-1/2 cups sugar
- 1 package (6 ounces) raspberry gelatin

In a large kettle, combine tomatoes and sugar. Simmer for 25 minutes, stirring occasionally. Remove from the heat; stir in gelatin until dissolved, about 1 minute.

Pour mixture into jars or plastic containers; cool, stirring occasionally to prevent floating fruit. Top with lids. Refrigerate up to 3 weeks.

PEAR TOMATO PRESERVES

PREP: 1 hour 20 min. | **PROCESS:** 20 min. **YIELD:** 5 half-pints.

I have lived on a farm all my life so I always have had a garden. I can a lot of my garden-grown fruits and veggies and have made these wonderful preserves every year. **EVELYN STEARNS** ALTO PASS, ILLINOIS

- 4 cups sugar
- 1 tablespoon ground cinnamon
- 2 teaspoons ground cloves
- 1 teaspoon ground ginger
- 2 medium lemons, chopped
- 1 cup water
- 2 pounds yellow pear tomatoes, chopped

In a Dutch oven, combine sugar, cinnamon, cloves, ginger, lemons and water. Cook over medium heat for 15 minutes, stirring occasionally. Add the tomatoes. Reduce heat to low; continue cooking for 45-60 minutes or until tomatoes become transparent, stirring frequently.

Carefully ladle hot mixture into hot half-pint jars, leaving 1/4-in. headspace. Remove air bubbles, wipe rims and adjust lids. Process for 20 minutes in a boiling-water canner.

EDITOR'S NOTE: The processing time listed is for altitudes of 1,000 feet or less. Add 1 minute to the processing time for each 1,000 feet of additional altitude.

CORN RELISH IN PEPPER CUPS

PREP: 10 min. | **COOK:** 5 min. + chilling | **YIELD:** 8 servings.

This colorful, easy-to-fix side dish featuring flavorful veggies is a favorite at my house. I've made it on many special occasions for more than 30 years. What I like best about the recipe is that I can prepare it ahead of time and keep it in the fridge until company comes.

LOLA LANCE ZIRCONIA, NORTH CAROLINA

- 1/2 cup vinegar
- 1/4 cup sugar
- 1/2 teaspoon salt
- 1/4 teaspoon pepper
- 1/4 teaspoon celery seed
- 2 cans (15-1/4 ounces *each*) whole kernel corn, drained
- 3 tablespoons canola oil
- 2 tablespoons chopped sweet red pepper
- 4 bacon strips, cooked and crumbled
- 4 medium sweet red peppers, halved lengthwise and seeded

In a small saucepan, combine the first five ingredients; bring to a boil. Reduce heat; cover and simmer for 2 minutes. Cool.

Transfer to a bowl. Add corn, oil and chopped red pepper; toss to coat. Cover and refrigerate for 2 hours. Drain; stir in bacon. Spoon into pepper halves.

MUSTARD BARBECUE SAUCE

PREP/TOTAL TIME: 25 min. | YIELD: 2-1/3 cups.

I liked this zippy sauce from the first taste, as have my guests. It's not a thick sauce, but it coats meats very well. I use it on grilled barbecue ribs, and it's great with ham. **CLIFF MAYS** ST. ALBANS, WEST VIRGINIA

1 cup chicken *or* beef broth

1 cup prepared mustard

1/2 cup red wine vinegar

1/3 cup packed brown sugar

3 tablespoons butter

2 tablespoons Worcestershire sauce

2 tablespoons tomato paste

2 tablespoons molasses

1 tablespoon garlic powder

1 tablespoon onion powder

1-1/2 teaspoons cayenne pepper

1 teaspoon salt

1/4 teaspoon pepper

In a large saucepan, combine all ingredients. Bring to a boil. Reduce heat; simmer, uncovered, for 15-20 minutes or until the flavors are blended. Remove from the heat; cool.

SPICY PICKLED GREEN BEANS

PREP: 20 min. | **PROCESS:** 10 min. | **YIELD:** 4 pints.

A co-worker brought these pickled beans into work one day...I was hooked after one bite! And I was thrilled when a jar of my beans won first place at the local county fair. JILL DARIN GENESEO, ILLINOIS

1-3/4 pounds fresh green
    beans, trimmed

1 teaspoon cayenne pepper

4 garlic cloves, peeled

4 teaspoons dill seed *or*
    4 fresh dill heads

2-1/2 cups water

2-1/2 cups white vinegar

1/4 cup canning salt

Pack beans into four hot 1-pint jars to within 1/2 in. of the top. Add the cayenne, garlic and dill seed to jars.

In a large saucepan, bring the water, vinegar and salt to a boil.

Carefully ladle hot mixture over beans, leaving 1/2-in. headspace. Remove air bubbles; wipe rims and adjust lids. Process for 10 minutes in a boiling-water canner.

EDITOR'S NOTE: The processing time listed is for altitudes of 1,000 feet or less. For altitudes up to 3,000 feet, add 5 minutes; 6,000 feet, add 10 minutes; 8,000 feet, add 15 minutes; 10,000 feet, add 20 minutes.

YELLOW SUMMER SQUASH RELISH

PREP: 1 hour + marinating | **PROCESS:** 15 min. | **YIELD:** 6 pints.

My friends can barely wait for the growing season to arrive so I can make this incredible relish. The color really dresses up a hot dog.

RUTH HAWKINS JACKSON, MISSISSIPPI

- 10 cups shredded yellow summer squash (about 4 pounds)
- 2 large onions, chopped
- 1 large green pepper, chopped
- 6 tablespoons canning salt
- 4 cups sugar
- 3 cups cider vinegar
- 1 tablespoon *each* celery seed, ground mustard and ground turmeric
- 1/2 teaspoon ground nutmeg
- 1/2 teaspoon pepper

In a large container, combine the squash, onions, green pepper and salt. Cover and refrigerate overnight. Drain; rinse and drain again.

In a Dutch oven, combine the sugar, vinegar and seasonings; bring to a boil. Add squash mixture; return to a boil. Reduce heat; simmer for 15 minutes. Remove from the heat.

Carefully ladle hot mixture into six hot pint jars, leaving 1/2-in. headspace. Remove air bubbles; wipe rims and adjust lids. Process for 15 minutes in a boiling-water canner. Refrigerate remaining relish for up to 1 week.

EDITOR'S NOTE: The processing time listed is for altitudes of 1,000 feet or less. For altitudes up to 3,000 feet, add 5 minutes; 6,000 feet, add 10 minutes; 8,000 feet, add 15 minutes; 10,000 feet, add 20 minutes.

PLUM-APPLE BUTTER

PREP: 15 min. + chilling
COOK: 35 min. + cooling
YIELD: 5 cups.

I look forward to cooking up this fruity spread each December, using the plums I picked and froze during summer.

NANCY MICHEL LAKELAND, FLORIDA

- 2 pounds tart apples, peeled and quartered
- 2 pounds plums, pitted and quartered
- 1 cup water
- 3 cups sugar
- 1-1/2 teaspoons ground cinnamon
- 1 teaspoon ground nutmeg
- 1/4 teaspoon ground allspice

Place apples, plums and water in a large kettle; cover and simmer until tender, about 15 minutes. Cool.

Puree in batches in a food processor or blender; return all to the kettle. Add sugar and spices. Simmer, uncovered, for 20-30 minutes or until thickened, stirring frequently. Cool completely. Pour into jars.

Cover and store in the refrigerator for up to 3 weeks.

CARROT CAKE JAM

CHERRY PEAR CONSERVE

PREP: 1-1/4 hours + chilling | **PROCESS:** 10 min. + standing | **YIELD:** 10 pints.

I use pears harvested from my own trees to make this conserve. I love it combined with cream cheese and spread between two waffles that are topped with pure maple syrup. **RUTH BOLDUC** CONWAY, NEW HAMPSHIRE

- 2 medium lemons
- 2 medium limes
- 8 cups chopped peeled ripe pears
- 2 cans (16 ounces *each*) pitted tart cherries, drained
- 2 cans (20 ounces *each*) crushed pineapple, undrained
- 2 cups raisins
- 10 cups sugar
- 1-1/3 cups coarsely chopped walnuts

Grate peel from lemons and limes; set peel aside. Remove pith from lemons and limes; section the fruit and place in a large bowl. Add lemon and lime peel, pears, cherries, pineapple, raisins and sugar. Cover and refrigerate overnight.

Transfer to a large kettle or Dutch oven. Cook over medium heat for 50-60 minutes or until thickened. Stir in nuts; bring to a boil. Remove from the heat. Immediately ladle into hot sterilized jars, leaving 1/4-in. headspace. Adjust caps. Process for 10 minutes in a boiling water bath.

CARROT CAKE JAM

PREP: 20 min. | **COOK:** 25 min. | **YIELD:** 8 half-pints.

For a change of pace from berry jams, try this unique option. Spread on a bagel with cream cheese, it tastes almost as good as real carrot cake! **RACHELLE STRATTOIN** ROCK SPRINGS, WYOMING

- 1 can (20 ounces) unsweetened crushed pineapple, undrained
- 1-1/2 cups shredded carrots
- 1-1/2 cups chopped peeled ripe pears
- 3 tablespoons lemon juice
- 1 teaspoon ground cinnamon
- 1/4 teaspoon ground cloves
- 1/4 teaspoon ground nutmeg
- 1 package (1-3/4 ounces) powdered fruit pectin
- 6-1/2 cups sugar

In a large saucepan, combine the first seven ingredients. Bring to a boil. Reduce heat; cover and simmer for 15-20 minutes or until pears are tender, stirring occasionally. Remove from the heat; stir in pectin.

Bring to a full rolling boil over high heat, stirring constantly. Stir in sugar; return to a full rolling boil. Boil for 1 minute, stirring constantly. Remove from the heat; skim off foam.

Ladle hot mixture into hot sterilized half-pint jars, leaving 1/4-in. headspace. Remove air bubbles; wipe rims and adjust lids. Process in a boiling-water canner for 5 minutes.

> ## KITCHEN TIME-SAVER
> When a recipe requires shredded carrots, I put pieces of cut raw carrot into my blender, along with the eggs and oil called for in the recipe, then blend until they're finely chopped. **JUNE D.,** CANTON, OHIO

STRAWBERRY RHUBARB JAM

PREP: 30 min. + chilling | **YIELD:** 5-1/2 cups.

This tangy spread is a favorite with my family. They'll put it on almost anything, but especially like it on muffins or buttermilk biscuits.

DEB KOOISTRA KITCHENER, ONTARIO

- 2-1/2 cups fresh *or* frozen strawberries, crushed
- 1-1/2 cups finely diced fresh *or* frozen rhubarb
- 2-1/2 cups sugar
- 1 can (8 ounces) crushed pineapple, undrained
- 1 package (3 ounces) strawberry gelatin

In a large kettle, combine strawberries, rhubarb, sugar and pineapple. Bring to a boil; reduce heat and simmer for 20 minutes. Remove from the heat; stir in gelatin until dissolved. Pour into refrigerator containers, leaving 1/2-in. headspace. Let stand until cooled to room temperature. Top with lids. Refrigerate for 3-4 weeks.

FINE HERB BUTTER

PREP: 10 min. + freezing
YIELD: about 1 cup.

My dinner guests are impressed when they see these decorative flavorful butter pats on the table. I cut them in different shapes for variety. They're so easy to keep on hand, stored in the freezer, and make an attractive complement to rolls, bread or fish.

PAM DUNCAN SUMMERS, ARKANSAS

- 1 cup butter, softened
- 2 tablespoons minced fresh parsley
- 2 tablespoons minced chives
- 1 tablespoon minced fresh tarragon
- 1 tablespoon lemon juice
- 1/4 teaspoon pepper

In a small bowl, combine the butter, parsley, chives, tarragon, lemon juice and pepper; beat until well blended.

Spread on a baking sheet to 1/2-in. thickness. Freeze until firm. Cut into shapes with small cookie cutter.

SWEET HONEY ALMOND BUTTER

PREP/TOTAL TIME: 10 min. | **YIELD:** 2 cups.

This homemade butter makes a nice gift along with a loaf of fresh-from-the-oven bread.

EVELYN HARRIS WAYNESBORO, VIRGINIA

- 1 cup butter, softened
- 3/4 cup honey
- 3/4 cup confectioners' sugar
- 3/4 cup finely ground almonds
- 1/4 to 1/2 teaspoon almond extract

In a small bowl, combine all ingredients; mix well. Store in the refrigerator.

SAVORY STEAK RUB

PREP/TOTAL TIME: 5 min. | **YIELD:** 1/4 cup.

Marjoram stars in this rub that I use on a variety of beef cuts. It locks in the natural juices of the meat for mouthwatering results.

DONNA BROCKETT KINGFISHER, OKLAHOMA

- 1 tablespoon dried marjoram
- 1 tablespoon dried basil
- 2 teaspoons garlic powder
- 2 teaspoons dried thyme

- 1 teaspoon dried rosemary, crushed
- 3/4 teaspoon dried oregano

Combine all ingredients; store in a covered container. Rub over steaks before grilling or broiling. Will season four to five steaks.

PECAN BARBECUE SAUCE

PREP: 15 min. | **COOK:** 30 min. | **YIELD:** 3 cups.

After 18 years, I haven't found anything that this sauce doesn't taste great on. Pecans are the deliciously different ingredient.

VICKIE PATTERSON VINTA, OKLAHOMA

- 1 can (12 ounces) tomato paste
- 1 cup ground pecans
- 3/4 cup water
- 1/3 cup packed brown sugar
- 1/4 cup cider vinegar
- 1/4 cup chopped onion
- 1/4 cup honey
- 2 tablespoons lemon juice
- 1 tablespoon prepared mustard
- 1 teaspoon seasoned salt
- 2 garlic cloves, minced

In a large saucepan, combine all ingredients. Bring to a boil. Reduce heat; simmer, uncovered, for 20 minutes or until thickened, stirring occasionally.

SWEET DILL REFRIGERATOR PICKLES

PREP: 30 min. + chilling | **YIELD:** 3-1/2 quarts.

Dill and cucumbers are natural companions in a number of dishes. I turn to this recipe every summer when my garden is in full bloom. My family can hardly wait to eat these pickles. **KAY CURTIS, FIELD EDITOR** GUTHRIE, OKLAHOMA

> 2 cups sugar
> 2 cups vinegar
> 2 cups water
> 1/4 cup salt
> 3 quarts sliced unpeeled cucumbers
> 1 large onion, sliced
> 3/4 to 1 cup minced fresh dill

In a saucepan, combine sugar, vinegar, water and salt. Bring to a boil and boil 1 minute. In a large nonmetallic container, combine cucumbers, onion and dill.

Pour dressing over; cool. Cover and refrigerate at least 3 days before serving. Stir occasionally.

LEMON MARMALADE

PREP: 40 min. | **PROCESS:** 10 min. | **YIELD:** 6 half-pints.

Lemons and grapefruit combine to create a tantalizing spread for English muffins, toast and even shortbread cookies! I give away jars of this marmalade every Christmas. **BARBARA CARLUCCI** ORANGE PARK, FLORIDA

> 3 medium lemons
> 1 medium grapefruit
> 4 cups water
> 1 package (1-3/4 ounces) powdered fruit pectin
> 4 cups sugar

Peel rind from lemons and grapefruit; cut into thin strips, about 1 in. long. Set aside fruit.

In a Dutch oven, combine water and citrus peel. Bring to a boil. Reduce heat; cover and simmer for 5 minutes or until peel is softened. Remove from the heat and set aside.

Trim white pith from reserved lemons and grapefruit; discard pith. Cut lemons and grapefruit into segments, discarding membranes and seeds. Chop pulp, reserving juices; stir into reserved peel mixture.

Add pectin. Bring to a full rolling boil over high heat, stirring constantly.

Stir in sugar; return to a full rolling boil. Boil for 1 minute, stirring constantly.

Remove from the heat; skim off foam. Ladle hot mixture into hot half-pint jars, leaving 1/4-in. headspace. Remove air bubbles; wipe rims and adjust lids. Process for 10 minutes in a boiling-water canner.

EDITOR'S NOTE: The processing time listed is for altitudes of 1,000 feet or less. Add 1 minute to the processing time for each 1,000 feet of additional altitude.

A LESSON IN LEMONS
Look for lemons that are firm, feel heavy for their size and have a bright yellow color. Avoid any with bruises or wrinkles, and store them at room temperature for about 3 days. For longer storage, place in your refrigerator's crisper drawer for 2 to 3 weeks. Juice or grated peel can be frozen for up to 1 year. One medium lemon yields 3 tablespoons juice and 2 teaspoons grated peel.
TASTE OF HOME TEST KITCHEN

LEMON MARMALADE

REFRIGERATOR PICKLES

PREP: 25 min. + chilling | **YIELD:** 6 cups.

These pickles are so good and easy to prepare, you'll want to keep them on hand all the time. My in-laws send over produce just so I'll make more! **LOY JONES** ANNISTON, ALABAMA

3 cups sliced peeled cucumbers

3 cups sliced peeled yellow summer squash

2 cups chopped sweet onions

1-1/2 cups white vinegar

1 cup sugar

1/2 teaspoon salt

1/2 teaspoon celery seed

1/2 teaspoon mustard seed

Place the cucumbers, squash and onions in a large bowl; set aside. In a small saucepan, combine the remaining ingredients; bring to a boil. Cook and stir just until the sugar is dissolved. Pour over cucumber mixture; cool.

Cover tightly and refrigerate for at least 24 hours. Serve with a slotted spoon.

FRESH TOMATO RELISH

PREP: 30 min. + chilling | **YIELD:** about 6 pints.

My two grown sons actually eat this as a salad, but that's a bit too hot for me! I usually make a batch as soon as the first tomatoes of the season are ready and freeze some for later. It keeps for months in the freezer.

LELA BASKINS WINDSOR, MISSOURI

- 2 cups white vinegar
- 1/2 cup sugar
- 8 cups chopped tomatoes (about 11 large)
- 1/2 cup chopped onion
- 1 medium green pepper, diced
- 1 celery rib, diced
- 1/4 cup prepared horseradish
- 2 tablespoons salt
- 1 tablespoon mustard seed
- 1-1/2 teaspoons pepper
- 1/2 teaspoon ground cinnamon
- 1/2 teaspoon ground cloves

In a large saucepan, bring vinegar and sugar to a boil. Remove from the heat; cool completely.

In a large bowl, combine remaining ingredients; add vinegar mixture and mix well. Spoon into storage containers, allowing 1/2-in. headspace. Refrigerate up to 2 weeks or freeze up to 12 months. Serve with a slotted spoon.

PEACH CHUTNEY

PREP: 1 hour | **COOK:** 15 min. | **YIELD:** 7 half-pints.

Here's my take on several different chutney recipes combined. The sweet and spicy marmalade pairs well with just about any meat or poultry.

JOANNE SURFUS STURGEON BAY, WISCONSIN

- 2-1/2 cups white vinegar
- 1 cup packed brown sugar
- 3/4 cup sugar
- 1 medium sweet red pepper, finely chopped
- 1 small onion, finely chopped
- 1 banana pepper, seeded and finely chopped
- 2/3 cup golden raisins
- 1 tablespoon minced fresh gingerroot
- 1 teaspoon canning salt
- 6 whole cloves
- 1 cinnamon stick (3 inches), cut in half
- 3 pounds fresh peaches, peeled and chopped

In a Dutch oven, bring the vinegar, brown sugar and sugar to a boil. Add the red pepper, onion, banana pepper, raisins, ginger and salt.

Place cloves and cinnamon stick on a double thickness of cheesecloth; bring up corners of cloth and tie with string to form a bag. Add to the pan. Return to a boil. Reduce heat; simmer, uncovered, for 10 minutes.

Add peaches and return to a boil. Reduce heat; simmer, uncovered, for 25-30 minutes or until thickened. Discard spice bag.

Carefully ladle hot chutney into hot half-pint jars, leaving 1/2-in. headspace. Remove air bubbles; wipe rims and adjust lids. Process for 15 minutes in a boiling-water canner.

EDITOR'S NOTE: The processing time listed is for altitudes of 1,000 feet or less. For altitudes up to 3,000 feet, add 5 minutes; 6,000 feet, add 10 minutes; 8,000 feet, add 15 minutes; 10,000 feet, add 20 minutes.

PICKLED GREEN TOMATO RELISH

PREP: 1 hour + standing | **PROCESS:** 15 min./batch | **YIELD:** 8 pints.

When I'm left with green tomatoes at the end of summer, I reach for this recipe. Friends and family are so happy to receive the sweet-sour relish that they often return the empty jar and ask for a refill. **MARY GILL** FLORENCE, OREGON

7 pounds green tomatoes
(about 20 medium)

4 large onions

2 large red onions

3 large green peppers

2 large sweet red peppers

4 teaspoons canning salt

5 cups cider vinegar

4 cups sugar

2 tablespoons celery seed

4 teaspoons mustard seed

Cut the tomatoes, onions and peppers into wedges. In a food processor, cover and process vegetables in batches until finely chopped. Stir in salt. Divide mixture between two strainers and place each over a bowl. Let stand for 3 hours.

Discard liquid from bowls. Place vegetables in a stockpot; stir in the vinegar, sugar, celery seed and mustard seed. Bring to a boil. Reduce heat; simmer, uncovered, for 30-35 minutes or until thickened.

Carefully ladle hot mixture into hot pint jars, leaving 1/2-in. headspace. Remove air bubbles; wipe rims and adjust lids. Process for 15 minutes in a boiling-water canner.

EDITOR'S NOTE: The processing time listed is for altitudes of 1,000 feet or less. For altitudes up to 3,000 feet, add 5 minutes; 6,000 feet, add 10 minutes; 8,000 feet, add 15 minutes; 10,000 feet, add 20 minutes.

COFFEE BARBECUE SAUCE

PREP: 15 min. | **COOK:** 50 min. | **YIELD:** 4-1/2 cups.

Brewed coffee and instant coffee granules add rich color and depth to this sweet-and-sour sauce. It's wonderful spooned over grilled chicken or pork chops. **JULIA BUSHREE** GEORGETOWN, TEXAS

1 medium onion, finely chopped

2 tablespoons olive oil

8 garlic cloves, minced

2 cups ketchup

1 cup cider vinegar

1 cup honey

1/2 cup reduced-sodium
soy sauce

1/2 cup strong brewed coffee

2 teaspoons instant
coffee granules

1/4 teaspoon salt

1/4 teaspoon pepper

In a large saucepan, saute onion in oil until tender. Add garlic; cook 2 minutes longer. Stir in the remaining ingredients and bring to a boil. Reduce heat; simmer, uncovered, for 35-45 minutes or until desired consistency, stirring occasionally.

GRILLING WITH BARBECUE SAUCE

For best results when grilling with a barbecue sauce, be sure your grill is at the proper temperature before placing the food on the grill rack. Then wait to brush on thick or sweet sauces until the last 10 to 15 minutes of cooking; baste and turn every few minutes to prevent burning.
TASTE OF HOME TEST KITCHEN

COFFEE BARBECUE SAUCE

OZARK MOUNTAIN BERRY PIE, PG. 246

OLD-FASHIONED JAM CAKE, PG. 266

CAKES & PIES

Hope you saved room for dessert. If you didn't, you'll wish you had after browsing through this sinful selection of the very best cakes and pies south of the Mason-Dixon Line.

SOUTHERN SWEET POTATO PIE

PREP: 15 min. | **BAKE:** 55 min. + chilling | **YIELD:** 8 servings.

For a true taste of the South, try this popular pie. It's a particular favorite at our house because we always have plenty of sweet potatoes in our garden. Try it with a dollop of whipped cream. **BONNIE HOLCOMB** FULTON, MISSISSIPPI

3 tablespoons all-purpose flour
1-2/3 cups sugar
1/4 teaspoon ground nutmeg
Pinch salt
1 cup mashed sweet potatoes
2 eggs
1/4 cup light corn syrup
1/2 cup butter, softened
3/4 cup evaporated milk
1 unbaked pastry shell (9 inches)

In a small bowl, combine the flour, sugar, nutmeg and salt. In a large bowl, beat the potatoes, eggs, corn syrup, butter and sugar mixture. Gradually stir in milk. Pour into pastry shell.

Bake at 350° for 55-60 minutes. Cool on a wire rack for 1 hour. Refrigerate for at least 3 hours before serving. Refrigerate leftovers.

WALNUT CARROT CAKE

PREP: 15 min. | **BAKE:** 50 min. + cooling | **YIELD:** 12-16 servings.

This carrot cake is incredibly moist and very flavorful. It also has a nice texture and cuts beautifully for serving to your guests.

DARLENE BRENDEN SALEM, OREGON

- 1 cup butter, softened
- 1-2/3 cups sugar
- 4 eggs
- 1 teaspoon vanilla extract
- 1 teaspoon grated lemon peel
- 2-1/2 cups all-purpose flour
- 1 package (3.4 ounces) instant lemon pudding mix
- 1-1/2 teaspoons baking powder
- 1 teaspoon baking soda
- 1 teaspoon ground cinnamon
- 1/2 teaspoon salt
- 1 cup (8 ounces) plain yogurt
- 2-1/2 cups grated carrots
- 3/4 cup chopped walnuts
- 1 can (16 ounces) cream cheese frosting

In a large bowl, cream butter and sugar until light and fluffy. Add eggs, one at a time, beating well after each addition. Beat in the vanilla and lemon peel. Combine the flour, pudding mix, baking powder, baking soda, cinnamon and salt; gradually add to creamed mixture alternately with yogurt, beating well after each addition. Stir in carrots and nuts.

Transfer to a greased and floured 10-in. fluted tube pan. Bake at 350° for 50-55 minutes or until a toothpick inserted near the center comes out clean.

Cool for 10 minutes before removing from pan to a wire rack. Cool completely before frosting. Store in the refrigerator.

FREEZER PEANUT BUTTER PIE

PREP: 15 min. + freezing
YIELD: 6-8 servings.

If you like peanut butter, you're going to love this pie! It can be made ahead and frozen, so it's perfect for drop-in guests.

NINA RUFENER RITTMAN, OHIO

- 1 quart vanilla ice cream, softened
- 1 graham cracker crust (9 inches)
- 1/2 cup peanut butter
- 1/3 cup light corn syrup

Chocolate syrup

Chopped walnuts

Spread half of the ice cream into crust. Combine peanut butter and corn syrup; spread over ice cream. Top with remaining ice cream. Drizzle with chocolate syrup and sprinkle with nuts.

Cover and freeze for 3-4 hours. Remove from the freezer 15 minutes before serving.

OZARK MOUNTAIN BERRY PIE

PREP: 15 min. | **BAKE:** 55 min. + cooling | **YIELD:** 8 servings.

Slicing the berries will help them absorb more of the sugar or flavorings, but you still may want to taste the filling before adding it to the pie crust to make sure it's sweet enough. **ELAINE MOODY** CLEVER, MISSOURI

- 1 cup sugar
- 1/4 cup cornstarch
- 1/2 teaspoon ground cinnamon, optional
- Dash salt
- 1/3 cup water
- 1 cup fresh blueberries
- Pastry for a double-crust pie (9 inches)
- 1 cup halved fresh strawberries
- 1 cup fresh raspberries
- 3/4 cup fresh blackberries
- 1 tablespoon lemon juice
- 2 tablespoons butter

In a large saucepan, combine the sugar, cornstarch, cinnamon if desired, salt and water until smooth; add the blueberries. Bring to a boil; cook and stir for 2 minutes or until thickened. Set aside to cool slightly.

Line a 9-in. pie plate with bottom crust; trim pastry even with edge. Gently fold the strawberries, raspberries, blackberries and lemon juice into the blueberry mixture. Pour into pastry; dot with butter. Roll out remaining pastry; make a lattice crust. Trim, seal and flute edges.

Bake at 400° for 10 minutes. Reduce heat to 350°; bake for 45-50 minutes or until the crust is golden brown and filling is bubbly. Cool on a wire rack. Store in the refrigerator.

DEEP-FRIED CHERRY PIES

PREP/TOTAL TIME: 30 min. | **YIELD:** 4 servings.

These stuffed cherry pies with a wonderfully flaky crust always make a quick dessert. My family loves them after dinner, but they're also wonderful for my husband's take-along lunch. **MONICA LARKIN** SHINNSTON, WEST VIRGINIA

- 1 cup all-purpose flour
- 1/4 teaspoon baking powder
- 1/4 teaspoon salt
- 2 tablespoons shortening
- 1/3 cup boiling water
- 1 cup cherry pie filling
- Oil for frying
- 1/4 cup maple syrup
- 1/4 cup whipped topping

In a bowl, combine the flour, baking powder and salt. Cut in shortening until mixture resembles coarse crumbs. Stir in water just until moistened. Turn onto a lightly floured surface; knead 8-10 times.

Divide dough into four portions; roll each into an 8-in. circle. Place 1/4 cup of pie filling in the center of each circle. Fold dough over filling; secure with toothpicks.

In an electric skillet or deep-fat fryer, heat 1 in. of oil to 375°. Fry pies, folded side down, in oil for 2-3 minutes or until lightly browned. Turn and fry about 2-3 minutes longer. Drain on paper towels. Remove toothpicks. Serve with syrup and whipped topping.

FRYING BASICS
You'll soon be frying foods like a pro with these timely pointers: First, always follow the oil temperature recommended in recipes. If the oil is too hot, the foods will brown too fast and not be done in the center. If the oil is below the recommended temperature, the foods will absorb oil and taste greasy. Avoid splattering by carefully placing foods into the hot oil. And don't overload your fryer. You'll have better results if you fry in small batches.
TASTE OF HOME TEST KITCHEN

DEEP-FRIED CHERRY PIES

PEANUT BUTTER LOVER'S CAKE

PREP: 20 min. + cooling | **BAKE:** 25 min. + cooling
YIELD: 12-14 servings.

The combination of chocolate and peanut butter gives this cake the flavor of a popular candy bar. Folks will find it hard to resist a second slice of this decadent treat. **TERESA MOZINGO** CAMDEN, SOUTH CAROLINA

> 3 eggs
> 1-2/3 cups sugar, *divided*
> 1-1/2 cups milk, *divided*
> 3 ounces unsweetened chocolate, finely chopped
> 1/2 cup shortening
> 1 teaspoon vanilla extract
> 2 cups cake flour
> 1 teaspoon baking soda
> 1/2 teaspoon salt

PEANUT BUTTER FROSTING:

> 2 packages (8 ounces *each*) cream cheese, softened
> 1 can (14 ounces) sweetened condensed milk
> 1-1/2 cups peanut butter
> 1/4 cup salted peanuts, chopped
> 3 milk chocolate candy bars (1.55 ounces *each*), broken into squares

In a small saucepan, whisk 1 egg until blended. Stir in 2/3 cup sugar, 1/2 cup milk and chocolate. Cook and stir over medium heat until chocolate is melted and mixture just comes to a boil. Remove from the heat; cool to room temperature.

In a large bowl, cream shortening and remaining sugar until light and fluffy. Add remaining eggs, one at a time, beating well after each. Beat in vanilla. Combine the flour, baking soda and salt; gradually add to creamed mixture alternately with remaining milk, beating well after each addition. Stir in chocolate mixture.

Pour into three greased and floured 9-in. round baking pans. Bake at 325° for 25-30 minutes or until a toothpick inserted near the center comes out clean. Cool for 10 minutes before removing from pans to wire racks to cool completely.

For frosting, beat cream cheese in a large bowl until smooth. Gradually add milk and peanut butter until creamy. Spread between layers and over top and sides of cooled cake. Sprinkle with peanuts. Garnish with candy bars. Store in the refrigerator.

CREAMY PINEAPPLE PIE

PREP/TOTAL TIME: 10 min.
YIELD: 8 servings.

This light and refreshing pie is quick to make and impressive to serve. It's one of our favorite ways to complete a meal.

SHARON BICKETT
CHESTER, SOUTH CAROLINA

> 1 can (14 ounces) sweetened condensed milk
> 1 can (8 ounces) crushed pineapple, undrained
> 1/4 cup lemon juice
> 1 carton (8 ounces) frozen whipped topping, thawed
> 1 prepared graham cracker crust (9 inches)

In a bowl, combine the milk, pineapple and lemon juice. Fold in whipped topping. Pour into prepared crust. Chill until ready to serve.

RASPBERRY CHOCOLATE CAKE

PREP: 45 min. + standing | **BAKE:** 35 min. + cooling
YIELD: 16 servings.

Whenever I make this cake, I get rave reviews. It's impressive, and the raspberry filling is heavenly.

MARLENE SANDERS PARADISE, TEXAS

- 3 cups sugar
- 2-3/4 cups all-purpose flour
- 1 cup baking cocoa
- 2 teaspoons baking soda
- 1-1/2 teaspoons salt
- 3/4 teaspoon baking powder
- 1-1/4 cups buttermilk
- 3/4 cup canola oil
- 3 teaspoons vanilla extract
- 3 eggs
- 1-1/2 cups strong brewed coffee, room temperature

FILLING:

- 3 tablespoons all-purpose flour
- 6 tablespoons 2% milk
- 6 tablespoons shortening
- 3 tablespoons butter, softened
- 3 cups confectioners' sugar
- 2 tablespoons raspberry liqueur
- 1/4 teaspoon salt
- 2 drops red food coloring, optional
- 4 tablespoons seedless raspberry jam, melted

FROSTING:

- 1 package (8 ounces) cold cream cheese
- 1/3 cup butter, softened
- 1/2 cup baking cocoa
- 1 tablespoon raspberry liqueur
- 4 cups confectioners' sugar

Line three greased 9-in. round baking pans with waxed paper and grease paper; set aside. In a large bowl, combine the first six ingredients. Separately, combine the buttermilk, oil and vanilla; add to the dry ingredients. Add eggs, one at a time, beating well after each addition; beat for 2 minutes. Gradually add coffee (batter will be thin).

Pour batter into prepared pans. Bake at 350° for 35-40 minutes or until a toothpick inserted near the center comes out clean. Cool for 10 minutes before removing from pans to wire racks to cool completely.

For filling, in a small saucepan, whisk together flour and milk until smooth. Cook over medium heat for 1 minute or until thickened, stirring constantly. Remove from the heat and let stand until cool.

In a large bowl, cream shortening and butter until light and fluffy. Gradually add confectioners' sugar and mix well. Gradually add cooled milk mixture; beat for 4 minutes or until light and fluffy. Beat in liqueur, salt and food coloring if desired.

Level tops of cakes if necessary. Place one layer on a serving plate; spread with about 2 tablespoons jam. Place remaining layers on waxed paper; spread one of the remaining layers with remaining jam. Let stand for 30 minutes.

Spread 1/2 cup filling over cake on the plate to within 1/4 in. of edges. Top with jam-covered cake, then spread with remaining filling. Top with remaining cake layer.

In a large bowl, beat cream cheese and butter until smooth. Beat in cocoa and liqueur. Gradually beat in confectioners' sugar until light and fluffy. Frost top and sides of cake. Store in the refrigerator.

BERRY BEST FRIED PIES

PREP/TOTAL TIME: 30 min. | **YIELD:** 10 servings.

When I was growing up, we'd eat these wonderful fried pies faster than Mom could make them. The recipe has been handed down for generations in my family. **SHARON GARRISON** BELLA VISTA, ARKANSAS

1/2 cup sugar

1 tablespoon cornstarch

1/2 cup water

2 cups fresh *or* frozen blueberries

DOUGH:

2 cups all-purpose flour

1/4 teaspoon baking soda

1/4 teaspoon salt

1/2 cup canola oil

1/3 cup buttermilk

Oil for frying

In a saucepan, combine the sugar, cornstarch and water; add berries. Cook and stir over medium heat until the mixture comes to a boil. Cook and stir for 2 minutes; set aside to cool.

Combine the flour, baking soda and salt. Combine oil and buttermilk; stir into dry ingredients until mixture forms a ball. Roll on a floured surface to 1/8-in. thickness; cut into 4-1/2 in. circles. Place 1 tablespoon blueberry filling on each circle. Fold over; seal edges with fork.

In a skillet over medium heat, fry pies in 1/4 to 1/2 in. hot oil until golden brown, about 1-1/2 minutes on each side. Drain on paper towels.

ITALIAN CREAM CHEESE CAKE

PREP: 40 min. | **BAKE:** 20 min. + cooling | **YIELD:** 12 servings.

Buttermilk makes every bite of this awesome dessert moist and flavorful. I rely on this recipe year-round.
JOYCE LUTZ CENTERVIEW, MISSOURI

1/2 cup butter, softened

1/2 cup shortening

2 cups sugar

5 eggs, *separated*

1 teaspoon vanilla extract

2 cups all-purpose flour

1 teaspoon baking soda

1 cup buttermilk

1-1/2 cups flaked coconut

1 cup chopped pecans

CREAM CHEESE FROSTING:

2 packages (one 8 ounces, one 3 ounces) cream cheese, softened

3/4 cup butter, softened

6 cups confectioners' sugar

1-1/2 teaspoons vanilla extract

3/4 cup chopped pecans

In a large bowl, cream the butter, shortening and sugar until light and fluffy. Beat in egg yolks and vanilla. Combine flour and baking soda; add to the creamed mixture alternately with buttermilk. Beat just until combined. Stir in coconut and pecans.

In a small bowl, beat egg whites until stiff peaks form. Fold a fourth of the egg whites into batter, then fold in remaining whites. Pour into three greased and floured 9-in. round baking pans.

Bake at 350° for 20-25 minutes or until a toothpick inserted near the center comes out clean. Cool for 10 minutes before removing from pans to wire racks to cool completely.

In a large bowl, beat cream cheese and butter until smooth. Beat in the confectioners' sugar and vanilla until fluffy. Stir in pecans. Spread frosting between layers and over top and sides of cake. Store in the refrigerator.

ITALIAN CREAM CHEESE CAKE

KING CAKE WITH CREAM CHEESE FILLING

PREP: 25 min. | **BAKE:** 20 min. | **YIELD:** 16 servings.

A New Orleans tradition, King Cake is baked with a small plastic baby inside; the person who gets it hosts the next party. My recipe omits the baby, but you can still enjoy the cake. **ALICE LEJEUNE** VILLE PLATTE, LOUISIANA

- 2 tubes (8 ounces each) refrigerated reduced-fat crescent rolls
- 4 ounces reduced-fat cream cheese
- 2 tablespoons confectioners' sugar
- 1 teaspoon vanilla extract
- 1/3 cup light brown sugar
- 2 tablespoons butter, softened
- 3 teaspoons ground cinnamon

ICING:

- 1 cup confectioners' sugar
- 1/2 teaspoon vanilla extract
- 1 to 2 tablespoons 2% milk
- Red, blue, yellow and green food coloring

Unroll both tubes of crescent dough and separate into triangles. Place triangles on a greased 12-in. pizza pan, forming a ring with pointed ends facing toward the center and wide ends overlapping. Lightly press wide ends together.

In a small bowl, beat the cream cheese, confectioners' sugar and vanilla until smooth. Spoon over wide ends of ring. In another bowl, stir the brown sugar, butter and cinnamon until crumbly. Sprinkle over cream cheese mixture.

Fold points over filling and fold wide ends over points. Bake at 350° for 20-25 minutes or until golden brown. Cool for 5 minutes.

Meanwhile, combine the confectioners' sugar, vanilla and enough milk to achieve desired consistency. Divide icing among three bowls. Using red and blue food coloring, tint one portion purple. Tint another portion yellow and the remaining portion green. Drizzle over cake. Serve warm.

SWEET POTATO CAKE

PREP: 25 min. | **BAKE:** 40 min. | **YIELD:** 12-15 servings.

Just like my mom, I love to cook. I bake a lot for church dinners and homecomings, and many people have told me how much they like this cake. **WANDA ROLEN** SEVIERVILLE, TENNESSEE

- 1 cup canola oil
- 2 cups sugar
- 4 eggs
- 1-1/2 cups finely shredded uncooked sweet potato (about 1 medium)
- 1/4 cup hot water
- 1 teaspoon vanilla extract
- 2-1/2 cups self-rising flour
- 1 teaspoon ground cinnamon
- 1 cup sliced almonds

FROSTING:

- 1/2 cup butter, cubed
- 1 cup packed brown sugar
- 1 cup evaporated milk
- 3 egg yolks, lightly beaten
- 1-1/2 cups flaked coconut
- 1 cup sliced almonds
- 1 teaspoon vanilla extract

In a large bowl, beat oil and sugar. Add eggs, one at a time, beating well after each addition. Beat in the sweet potato, water and vanilla. Combine flour and cinnamon; gradually add to potato mixture until well blended. Stir in almonds.

Pour into a greased 13-in. x 9-in. baking pan. Bake at 350° for 40-45 minutes or until a toothpick inserted near the center comes out clean.

For frosting, melt butter in a saucepan; whisk in the brown sugar, milk and egg yolks until smooth. Cook and stir over medium heat until mixture reaches at least 160° and coats the back of a metal spoon. Remove from the heat; stir in coconut, almonds and vanilla. Spread over warm cake. Cool on a wire rack.

EDITOR'S NOTE: As a substitute for each cup of self-rising flour, place 1-1/2 teaspoons baking powder and 1/2 teaspoon salt in a measuring cup; add all-purpose flour to equal 1 cup. For 1/2 cup of self-rising flour, place 3/4 teaspoon baking powder and 1/4 teaspoon salt in a measuring cup; add all-purpose flour to equal 1/2 cup.

LEMONADE ICEBOX PIE

PREP: 15 min. + chilling
YIELD: 8 servings.

You will detect a definite lemonade flavor in this refreshing pie. High and fluffy, this dessert has a creamy smooth consistency.

CHERYL WILT EGLON, WEST VIRGINIA

- 1 package (8 ounces) cream cheese, softened
- 1 can (14 ounces) sweetened condensed milk
- 3/4 cup thawed lemonade concentrate
- 1 carton (8 ounces) frozen whipped topping, thawed
- Yellow food coloring, optional
- 1 graham cracker crust (9 inches)

In a large bowl, beat cream cheese and milk until smooth. Beat in lemonade concentrate. Fold in whipped topping and food coloring if desired. Pour into crust. Cover and refrigerate until set.

OLD-TIME BUTTERMILK PIE

PREP: 15 min. | **BAKE:** 45 min. + cooling | **YIELD:** 8-10 servings.

This recipe is older than I am. My mother and grandmother made this pie with buttermilk and eggs from our farm and set it on the tables at church meetings and gatherings. I did the same and now my children make it.

KATE MATHEWS SHREVEPORT, LOUISIANA

CRUST:

1-1/2 cups all-purpose flour

1 teaspoon salt

1/2 cup shortening

1/4 cup cold milk

1 egg, lightly beaten

FILLING:

1/2 cup butter

2 cups sugar

3 tablespoons all-purpose flour

3 eggs

1 cup buttermilk

1 teaspoon vanilla extract

1 teaspoon ground cinnamon

1/4 cup lemon juice

In a large bowl, mix flour and salt. Cut in shortening until smooth. Gradually add milk and egg and mix well. On a floured surface, roll dough out very thin. Place in a 10-in. pie pan; set aside.

For filling, cream butter and sugar in a bowl. Add flour. Add eggs, one at a time, beating well after each addition. Stir in remaining ingredients and mix well. Pour into crust.

Bake at 350° for 45 minutes. Cool completely before serving.

BUTTERSCOTCH PEACH PIE

PREP: 30 min. + chilling | **BAKE:** 45 min. + cooling | **YIELD:** 8 servings.

When peach season arrives, this great old-fashioned pie is sure to be on the table. The recipe has been in our family for more than 60 years, and I still make it every summer. Butterscotch buffs love it.

BARBARA MOYER TIFFIN, OHIO

2 cups all-purpose flour

1 teaspoon salt

3/4 cup shortening

4 to 5 tablespoons cold water

FILLING:

3/4 cup packed brown sugar

2 tablespoons all-purpose flour

1/3 cup light corn syrup

3 tablespoons butter, melted

2 tablespoons lemon juice

1/4 teaspoon almond extract

8 medium peaches, peeled and sliced

In a large bowl, combine flour and salt; cut in shortening until crumbly. Gradually add water, tossing with a fork until dough forms a ball. Cover and refrigerate for 30 minutes or until easy to handle.

For filling, in a small saucepan, combine brown sugar and flour. Stir in corn syrup and butter until blended. Bring to a boil; cook and stir for 2 minutes or until thickened. Remove from the heat; stir in lemon juice and extract. Place peaches in a large bowl; add syrup mixture and toss to coat.

Divide dough in half so one ball is slightly larger than the other. Roll out larger ball to fit a 9-in. pie plate. Transfer pastry to plate; trim pastry even with edge. Add filling. Roll out remaining pastry; make a lattice crust. Trim, seal and flute edges. Cover edges loosely with foil.

Bake at 375° for 25 minutes. Uncover; bake 20-25 minutes longer or until crust is golden brown and filling is bubbly. Cool on a wire rack.

BUTTERSCOTCH PEACH PIE

KENTUCKY CHOCOLATE WALNUT PIE

PREP: 15 min. | **BAKE:** 40 min. + cooling | **YIELD:** 6-8 servings.

This is our version of a Southern classic. Crunchy walnuts fill a rich bourbon and chocolate crust. You can use pecans in place of the walnuts if you prefer. TASTE OF HOME TEST KITCHEN

3 eggs

2 egg yolks

3/4 cup packed brown sugar

2/3 cup light corn syrup

1/3 cup butter, melted

2 tablespoons Kentucky bourbon, optional

1 teaspoon vanilla extract

Dash salt

1 cup coarsely chopped pecans *or* chopped walnuts

1 unbaked pastry shell (9 inches)

1 egg white, lightly beaten

3/4 cup semisweet chocolate chips

1 cup heavy whipping cream

2 tablespoons confectioners' sugar

In a large bowl, whisk the eggs, yolks, brown sugar, corn syrup, butter, bourbon if desired, vanilla and salt. Stir in nuts.

Brush pastry shell with egg white. Sprinkle with chocolate chips. Pour filling over chips. Bake at 350° for 40-45 minutes or until set. Cool on a wire rack.

In a small bowl, beat cream until it begins to thicken. Add confectioners' sugar; beat until stiff peaks form. Dollop whipped cream on pie just before serving. Refrigerate leftovers.

TRIPLE-LAYER LEMON CAKE

PREP: 30 min. + chilling | **BAKE:** 20 min. + cooling | **YIELD:** 12-14 servings.

A smooth and silky citrus filling separates three luscious layers of moist lemon cake. Each bite is simply divine. **CONNIE JURJEVICH** ATMORE, ALABAMA

- 2 cups sugar
- 3/4 cup canola oil
- 4 eggs, *separated*
- 1 teaspoon vanilla extract
- 3 cups all-purpose flour
- 3 teaspoons baking powder
- 1/4 teaspoon salt
- 1 cup 2% milk

FILLING:

- 3/4 cup sugar
- 2 tablespoons cornstarch
- 1/8 teaspoon salt
- 1/2 cup water
- 1 egg, lightly beaten
- 1/3 cup lemon juice
- 1-1/2 teaspoons grated lemon peel
- 1 tablespoon butter, softened

FROSTING:

- 1 cup butter, softened
- 6 cups confectioners' sugar
- 2 tablespoons lemon juice
- 1 teaspoon grated lemon peel
- 4 to 6 tablespoons heavy whipping cream

In a bowl, beat sugar and oil. Beat in yolks and vanilla. Combine dry ingredients; add to sugar mixture alternately with milk, beating well after each addition. In a large bowl, beat egg whites until stiff peaks form; fold into batter. Pour into three greased and waxed paper-lined 9-in. round baking pans. Bake at 350° for 20-25 minutes or until a toothpick comes out clean. Cool for 10 minutes; remove to wire racks to cool.

For filling, in a large saucepan, combine sugar, cornstarch and salt. Stir in water until smooth. Cook and stir over medium-high heat until thickened. Reduce heat; cook and stir 2 minutes longer. Stir a small amount of hot filling into egg; return all to pan, stirring constantly. Bring to a gentle boil; cook and stir 2 minutes longer. Remove from heat. Gently stir in lemon juice, peel and butter. Cool to room temperature without stirring. Cover and refrigerate.

In a large bowl, combine butter, confectioners' sugar, lemon juice, peel and enough cream to achieve desired spreading consistency. Spread filling between cake layers. Frost top and sides of cake. Store in the refrigerator.

STRAWBERRY RHUBARB PIE

PREP: 25 min. + chilling
YIELD: 8 servings.

My niece tasted this pie at a family dinner and urged me to enter it in our hometown pie contest. She said it would win the grand prize, and she was right!

JANICE SCHMIDT BAXTER, IOWA

- 2 tablespoons cornstarch
- 1 cup sugar
- 1 cup water
- 1 cup sliced rhubarb
- 3 tablespoons strawberry gelatin powder
- 1 pastry shell (9 inches), baked
- 2 pints fresh strawberries, halved

In a saucepan, mix cornstarch and sugar. Stir in water until smooth. Add rhubarb; cook and stir until clear and thickened. Add gelatin and stir until dissolved. Cool.

Pour about half of rhubarb sauce into pastry shell. Arrange berries over sauce; top with remaining sauce. Refrigerate for 3-4 hours.

SOUTHERN TEA CAKES

PREP/TOTAL TIME: 30 min. | **YIELD:** about 3 dozen.

There were nine children in our family and Mother had to stretch the budget, so she made these often for dessert. I loved them when I was a child, and they're still a special treat. In fact, I've never met anyone who doesn't like these cookies. They're so simple and quick to make. **MARY SINGLETARY** CONVERSE, LOUISIANA

1 cup shortening
1-3/4 cups sugar
2 eggs
1/2 cup milk
1/2 teaspoon vanilla extract
3 cups self-rising flour

In a bowl, cream together shortening and sugar. Beat in eggs. Add milk and vanilla; beat well. Stir in flour; mix well.

Drop by tablespoonfuls 2-1/2 in. apart onto greased baking sheets. Bake at 350° for 15-20 minutes.

APPLE PEAR CAKE

PREP: 25 min. | **BAKE:** 1 hour | **YIELD:** 12-15 servings.

When my sister Catherine made an apple cake for me, I asked her for the recipe because it was very moist and tasted so good. When I made it myself, I added some pears. Now every time I make it, people want the recipe—pears and all! **MARY ANN LEES** CENTREVILLE, ALABAMA

2 cups shredded peeled
   tart apple
2 cups shredded peeled pears
2 cups sugar
1-1/4 cups canola oil
1 cup raisins
1 cup chopped pecans
2 eggs, lightly beaten
1 teaspoon vanilla extract
3 cups all-purpose flour
2 teaspoons baking soda
2 teaspoons ground cinnamon
1/2 teaspoon ground nutmeg
1/2 teaspoon salt

CREAM CHEESE FROSTING:
1 package (3 ounces) cream cheese, softened
3 cups confectioners' sugar
1/4 cup butter, softened
2 tablespoons milk
1/2 teaspoon vanilla extract

In a large bowl, combine the first eight ingredients. Combine dry ingredients; stir into the fruit mixture.

Pour into a greased 13-in. x 9-in. baking pan. Bake at 325° for 1 hour or until a toothpick inserted near the center comes out clean. Cool on a wire rack.

For frosting, in a large bowl, beat the cream cheese, sugar and butter until smooth. Beat in the milk and vanilla; frost cake. Store in the refrigerator.

NO-STICK TRICK

Here's a tip that will make it easy to remove a cake from a baking pan: Before adding the batter, grease the pan. Line only the bottom with parchment paper, trimming the paper as needed to fit; grease the paper. Add batter as directed. Let cake cool in the pan for 10 minutes, then run a knife around the edges of the pan. Invert the pan onto a wire rack and lift up. **TASTE OF HOME TEST KITCHEN**

APPLE PEAR CAKE

PINEAPPLE UPSIDE-DOWN CAKE

CHOCOLATE PECAN PIE

PREP: 10 min. + chilling | **BAKE:** 40 min. | **YIELD:** 8 servings.

This recipe originated here in Louisville. It is often served during the famous Kentucky Derby, but it's good any other time of year, too! **MRS. JAY EVANS** LOUISVILLE, KENTUCKY

- 2 eggs
- 1 cup sugar
- 1/2 cup all-purpose flour

Pinch salt

- 1/2 cup butter, melted and cooled
- 1 cup semisweet chocolate chips
- 1 cup chopped pecans
- 2 teaspoons vanilla extract
- 1 unbaked pie shell (9 inches)

Whipped cream

In a bowl, beat eggs. Gradually add sugar and beat until smooth. Stir in flour, salt and butter. Fold in chips, nuts and vanilla. Pour into the pie shell.

Bake at 350° for 40 minutes or until set and golden brown. Chill for at least 4 hours. Serve with whipped cream.

PINEAPPLE UPSIDE-DOWN CAKE

PREP: 20 min. | **BAKE:** 30 min. + standing | **YIELD:** 9 servings.

A classic recipe like this never goes out of style! It's delicious with the traditional pineapple, but try it with peaches or a combination of cranberries and orange. **BERNARDINE MELTON** PAOLA, KANSAS

- 1/3 cup butter, melted
- 2/3 cup packed brown sugar
- 1 can (20 ounces) sliced pineapple
- 1/2 cup chopped pecans
- 3 eggs, *separated*
- 1 cup sugar
- 1 teaspoon vanilla extract
- 1 cup all-purpose flour
- 1 teaspoon baking powder
- 1/4 teaspoon salt
- 9 maraschino cherries

In an ungreased 9-in. square baking pan, combine butter and brown sugar. Drain pineapple, reserving 1/3 cup juice. Arrange 9 pineapple slices in a single layer over sugar (refrigerate any remaining slices for another use). Sprinkle pecans over pineapple; set aside.

In a large bowl, beat yolks until thick and lemon-colored. Gradually add sugar, beating well. Blend in vanilla and reserved pineapple juice. Combine flour, baking powder and salt; add to batter, beating well.

In a small bowl, beat egg whites on high speed until stiff peaks form; fold into batter. Spoon into pan. Bake at 375° for 30-35 minutes or until a toothpick inserted near the center comes out clean. Let stand for 10 minutes before inverting onto serving plate. Place a cherry in the center of each pineapple slice.

A FRESH IDEA

Want to use fresh pineapple instead? Slicing the tropical fruit is easier than you think. Cut off crown, then stand the pineapple upright and cut off the rind using a sharp knife. Cut off the base. Follow the pattern of the eyes to cut diagonal wedge-shaped grooves in pineapple. Remove the wedge.
TASTE OF HOME TEST KITCHEN

BLUE-RIBBON BUTTER CAKE

PREP: 20 min. | **BAKE:** 65 min. + cooling | **YIELD:** 12-16 servings.

I found this recipe in an old cookbook I bought at a garage sale and couldn't wait to try it. I knew it had been someone's favorite because of the well-worn page. **JOAN GERTZ** PALMETTO, FLORIDA

- 1 cup butter, softened
- 2 cups sugar
- 4 eggs
- 2 teaspoons vanilla extract
- 3 cups all-purpose flour
- 1 teaspoon baking powder
- 1/2 teaspoon baking soda
- 1/2 teaspoon salt
- 1 cup buttermilk

BUTTER SAUCE:

- 1 cup sugar
- 1/2 cup butter, cubed
- 1/4 cup water
- 1-1/2 teaspoons almond extract
- 1-1/2 teaspoons vanilla extract

In a large bowl, cream butter and sugar until light and fluffy. Add eggs, one at a time, beating well after each addition. Beat in vanilla. Combine the flour, baking powder, baking soda and salt; add to creamed mixture alternately with buttermilk, beating well after each addition.

Pour into a greased and floured 10-in. tube pan. Bake at 350° for 65-70 minutes or until a toothpick inserted near the center comes out clean. Cool for 10 minutes. Run a knife around edges and center tube of pan. Invert cake onto a wire rack over waxed paper.

For sauce, combine the sugar, butter and water in a small saucepan. Cook over medium heat just until butter is melted and sugar is dissolved. Remove from the heat; stir in extracts.

Poke holes in the top of the warm cake; spoon 1/4 cup sauce over cake. Let stand until sauce is absorbed. Repeat twice. Poke holes into sides of cake; brush remaining sauce over sides. Cool completely.

NEVER-FAIL PECAN PIE

PREP: 15 min.
BAKE: 45 min. + cooling
YIELD: 6-8 servings.

This incredible pecan pie recipe came from my mother-in-law. Her pies were a hit everywhere she took them!

BEVERLY MATERNE REEVES, LOUISIANA

- 1/2 cup sugar
- 1 tablespoon all-purpose flour
- 1/4 teaspoon salt
- 2 eggs, well beaten
- 1 cup dark corn syrup
- 1 teaspoon vanilla extract
- 1 cup pecan halves
- 1 unbaked pastry shell (9 inches)

In a large bowl, combine the sugar, flour, salt, eggs, corn syrup and vanilla. Stir in the pecan halves. Pour into pastry shell. Cover pastry edges with foil to prevent excess browning.

Bake at 350° for 30 minutes. Remove foil and bake another 15 minutes or until golden brown. Cool on a wire rack.

CARAMEL-CRUNCH APPLE PIE

PREP: 30 min. | **BAKE:** 40 min. + cooling | **YIELD:** 6-8 servings.

Hands down, this sweet apple pie will be the hit of every party. Slices are even better served warm with a scoop of vanilla ice cream. It's old-fashioned goodness with a twist. **BARBARA NOWAKOWSKI** MESA, ARIZONA

28 caramels

2 tablespoons water

5 cups thinly sliced peeled tart apples (about 2 pounds)

1 unbaked pastry shell (9 inches)

3/4 cup all-purpose flour

1/3 cup sugar

1/2 teaspoon ground cinnamon

1/3 cup cold butter, cubed

1/2 cup chopped walnuts

In a heavy saucepan, combine caramels and water. Cook and stir over low heat until melted; stir until smooth.

Arrange a third of the apples in pastry shell; drizzle with a third of the caramel mixture. Repeat layers twice. In a small bowl, combine the flour, sugar and cinnamon; cut in butter until crumbly. Stir in walnuts. Sprinkle over pie.

Bake at 375° for 40-45 minutes or until apples are tender (cover edges with foil during the last 15 minutes to prevent overbrowning, if necessary). Cool on a wire rack for 1 hour. Store in the refrigerator.

CHOCOLATE SHEET CAKE

PREP: 20 min. | **BAKE:** 20 min. + cooling | **YIELD:** 15 servings.

This chocolaty delight was one of my favorites growing up. The cake is so moist and the icing so sweet that everyone who samples it wants a copy of the recipe. **SUSAN ORMOND** JAMESTOWN, NORTH CAROLINA

1 cup butter, cubed
1 cup water
1/4 cup baking cocoa
2 cups all-purpose flour
2 cups sugar
1 teaspoon baking soda
1/2 teaspoon salt
1/2 cup sour cream

ICING:

1/2 cup butter, cubed
1/4 cup plus 2 tablespoons milk

3 tablespoons baking cocoa
3-3/4 cups confectioners' sugar
1 teaspoon vanilla extract

In a large saucepan, bring the butter, water and cocoa to a boil. Remove from the heat. Combine the flour, sugar, baking soda and salt; add to cocoa mixture. Stir in the sour cream until smooth.

Pour into a greased 15-in. x 10-in. x 1-in. baking pan. Bake at 350° for 20-25 minutes or until a toothpick inserted near the center comes out clean.

In a small saucepan, melt butter; add milk and cocoa. Bring to a boil. Remove from the heat. Whisk in confectioners' sugar and vanilla until smooth. Pour over warm cake. Cool completely on a wire rack.

EDITOR'S NOTE: This recipe does not use eggs.

GRAPEFRUIT MERINGUE PIE

PREP: 15 min. | **BAKE:** 15 min. + chilling
YIELD: 6-8 servings.

There's a grapefruit tree in our backyard, so I like to use fresh grapefruit juice when I make this pie. I just love the unique citrus flavor of this dessert.
BARBARA SOLIDAY WINTER HAVEN, FLORIDA

- 1-1/3 cups sugar
- 1/3 cup cornstarch
- 2 cups pink grapefruit juice
- 3/4 cup water
- 3 egg yolks, lightly beaten
- 2 tablespoons butter
- 1/2 teaspoon lemon extract
- 1 pastry shell (9 inches), baked

MERINGUE:

- 3 egg whites
- 1/4 teaspoon cream of tartar
- 6 tablespoons sugar

In a large saucepan, combine the sugar and cornstarch. Stir in grapefruit juice and water until smooth. Cook and stir over medium-high heat until thickened and bubbly. Reduce heat; cook and stir 2 minutes longer. Remove from the heat.

Stir 1/2 cup of hot filling into egg yolks; return all to pan, stirring constantly. Bring to a gentle boil; cook and stir 2 minutes longer. Remove from the heat. Gently stir in butter and extract. Pour hot filling into pastry shell.

In a large bowl, beat egg whites and cream of tartar on medium speed until soft peaks form. Gradually beat in sugar, 1 tablespoon at a time, on high until stiff glossy peaks form and sugar is dissolved. Spread evenly over hot filling, sealing edges to crust.

Bake at 350° for 12-15 minutes or until the meringue is golden brown. Cool on a wire rack for 1 hour. Refrigerate for at least 3 hours before serving. Store leftovers in the refrigerator.

DEVIL'S FOOD CAKE WITH CHOCOLATE FUDGE FROSTING

PREP: 45 min. | **BAKE:** 25 min. + cooling
YIELD: 12 servings.

I won several blue ribbons at our state fair thanks to this incredible dessert. The made-from-scratch chocolate layer cake topped with a fudgy homemade frosting is truly a can't-miss dessert.
DONNA CARMAN TULSA, OKLAHOMA

- 3 ounces unsweetened chocolate, chopped
- 1/2 cup butter, softened
- 2-1/4 cups packed brown sugar
- 3 eggs
- 1-1/2 teaspoons vanilla extract
- 2-1/4 cups cake flour
- 1 teaspoon baking soda
- 1/2 teaspoon salt
- 1/2 teaspoon baking powder
- 1 cup water
- 1 cup (8 ounces) sour cream

FROSTING:

- 1/2 cup butter, cubed
- 4 ounces unsweetened chocolate, chopped
- 3-3/4 cups confectioners' sugar
- 1/2 cup milk
- 2 teaspoons vanilla extract

In a microwave, melt chocolate; stir until smooth. Set aside. In a large bowl, cream butter and brown sugar until light and fluffy. Add eggs, one at a time, beating well after each addition. Beat in vanilla and melted chocolate.

Combine the flour, baking soda, salt and baking powder; add to the creamed mixture alternately with water and sour cream. Transfer to two greased and floured 9-in. round baking pans. Bake at 350° for 25-30 minutes or until a toothpick inserted near the center comes out clean. Cool for 10 minutes before removing from pans to wire racks to cool completely.

For frosting, in a small heavy saucepan, melt butter and chocolate over low heat. Remove from the heat; cool for 5 minutes. In a large bowl, beat the confectioners' sugar, milk and vanilla until smooth. Gradually beat in chocolate mixture until frosting is light and fluffy. Spread between layers and over top and sides of cake. Refrigerate leftovers.

PECAN POUND CAKE

PREP: 20 min. | **BAKE:** 1 hour + cooling
YIELD: 12-16 servings.

A slice of this rich and buttery cake is wonderful with a steaming cup of coffee on a chilly winter day.

FLETA WEST HAYES, VIRGINIA

- 1-1/2 cups butter, softened
- 3-3/4 cups confectioners' sugar
- 6 eggs
- 1 tablespoon vanilla extract
- 2-1/2 cups all-purpose flour
- 1/2 teaspoon salt
- 1 cup flaked coconut
- 2/3 cup chopped pecans, toasted

In a large bowl, cream butter and confectioners' sugar until light and fluffy. Add eggs, one at a time, beating well after each addition. Add vanilla. Combine flour and salt; stir into creamed mixture just until combined. Stir in coconut and pecans.

Pour into a greased and floured 10-in. tube pan; spread evenly. Bake at 325° for 60-65 minutes or until a toothpick inserted near the center comes out clean. Cool for 10 minutes before removing from pan to a wire rack to cool completely.

OLD-FASHIONED JAM CAKE

PREP: 25 min. + standing | **BAKE:** 40 min. + cooling
YIELD: 12-16 servings.

I remember my Aunt Murna telling me she made this cake often when she was a young girl. Through the years, she made improvements to it, and her cake became a real family favorite. It has been a popular staple at our reunions.

JANET ROBINSON LAWRENCEBURG, KENTUCKY

- 1 cup raisins
- 1 can (8 ounces) crushed pineapple, undrained
- 1 cup butter, softened
- 1 cup sugar
- 4 eggs
- 3 cups all-purpose flour
- 1/3 cup baking cocoa
- 1 teaspoon baking soda
- 1 teaspoon ground cinnamon
- 1 teaspoon ground nutmeg
- 1/2 teaspoon ground cloves
- 1 jar (12 ounces) *or* 1 cup blackberry jam
- 2/3 cup buttermilk
- 1 cup chopped pecans

CARAMEL ICING:

- 1 cup butter, cubed
- 2 cups packed brown sugar
- 1/2 cup 2% milk
- 3-1/2 to 4 cups confectioners' sugar

In a small bowl, combine raisins and pineapple; let stand for at least 30 minutes.

In a large bowl, cream butter and sugar until light and fluffy. Add eggs, one at a time, beating well after each addition. Combine dry ingredients; gradually add to creamed mixture alternately with jam and buttermilk, beating well after each addition. Stir in raisin mixture and nuts.

Spread into two greased and floured 9-in. round baking pans. Bake at 350° for 40-45 minutes or until a toothpick inserted near the center comes out clean. Cool for 10 minutes before removing from pans to wire racks to cool completely.

For icing, in a large saucepan, melt butter over medium heat. Stir in sugar and milk. Bring to a boil. Remove from the heat; cool until just warm. Pour into a large bowl; beat in enough confectioners' sugar to achieve a spreading consistency. Spread frosting between layers and over the top and sides of cake.

IF COOKING FOR TWO: Prepare and frost entire cake, then freeze serving-size portions to enjoy for months to come.

GEORGIA PECAN CAKE

PREP: 15 min. | **BAKE:** 1 hour + cooling | **YIELD:** 12-16 servings.

My mother handed down this recipe, which always has been a hit with our family. One taste and you'll see why!
CAROLYN GRIFFIN MACON, GEORGIA

1 cup butter, softened

2 cups sugar

4 eggs

1 teaspoon vanilla extract

1/2 teaspoon lemon extract

3 cups all-purpose flour

3/4 teaspoon salt

1/2 teaspoon baking powder

1/2 teaspoon baking soda

1 cup buttermilk

1 cup chopped pecans

In a large bowl, cream butter and sugar until light and fluffy. Add the eggs one at a time, beating well after each addition. Beat in extracts. Combine the flour, salt, baking powder and baking soda; set 1/4 cup aside. Add the remaining flour mixture to the creamed mixture alternately with buttermilk. Toss pecans with the reserved flour mixture; fold into batter.

Pour into a greased and floured 10-in. tube pan. Bake at 325° for 60-70 minutes or until a toothpick inserted near the center comes out clean. Cool for 10 minutes before removing from pan to a wire rack to cool completely.

HUMMINGBIRD CAKE

PREP: 40 min. | **BAKE:** 25 min. + cooling | **YIELD:** 12-14 servings.

This impressive cake is my dad's favorite, so I always make it for his birthday. It also makes a great Easter dessert and is lovely with a summer meal. **NANCY ZIMMERMAN** CAPE MAY COURT HOUSE, NEW JERSEY

2 cups mashed ripe bananas

1-1/2 cups canola oil

3 eggs

1 can (8 ounces) unsweetened crushed pineapple, undrained

1-1/2 teaspoons vanilla extract

3 cups all-purpose flour

2 cups sugar

1 teaspoon salt

1 teaspoon baking soda

1 teaspoon ground cinnamon

1 cup chopped walnuts

PINEAPPLE FROSTING:

1/4 cup shortening

2 tablespoons butter, softened

1 teaspoon grated lemon peel

1/4 teaspoon salt

6 cups confectioners' sugar

1/2 cup unsweetened pineapple juice

2 teaspoons half-and-half cream

Chopped walnuts, optional

In a large bowl, beat the bananas, oil, eggs, pineapple and vanilla until well blended. In another bowl, combine the flour, sugar, salt, baking soda and cinnamon; gradually beat into banana mixture until blended. Stir in walnuts.

Pour into three greased and floured 9-in. round baking pans. Bake at 350° for 25-30 minutes or until a toothpick inserted near the center comes out clean. Cool for 10 minutes before removing from pans to wire racks to cool completely.

For frosting, in a large bowl, beat the shortening, butter, lemon peel and salt until fluffy. Add confectioners' sugar alternately with pineapple juice. Beat in cream. Spread between layers and over top and sides of cake. Sprinkle with walnuts if desired.

OLD-FASHIONED COCONUT PIE

PREP: 20 min. | **BAKE:** 15 min. + cooling
YIELD: 6-8 servings.

This is an old-fashioned way of making coconut pie from scratch. **BARBARA SMITH** FRANKLIN, GEORGIA

- 1 cup sugar
- 1/4 cup all-purpose flour
- Dash salt
- 3 eggs, *separated*
- 2 cups milk
- 1-1/2 teaspoons vanilla extract
- 1-1/4 cups flaked coconut, *divided*
- 1 pie shell (9 inches), baked

MERINGUE:

- 3 egg whites
- 6 tablespoons sugar

In a large saucepan, combine the sugar, flour and salt. Combine egg yolks and milk; stir into dry ingredients until smooth. Cook and stir over medium heat until mixture is thickened and bubbly. Reduce heat to low; cook and stir 2 minutes longer. Remove from the heat; stir in vanilla and 1 cup coconut. Pour hot filling into pie shell.

For meringue, beat egg whites in a bowl until soft peaks form. Gradually beat in sugar until mixture forms stiff glossy peaks and sugar is dissolved. Spread meringue over hot filling. Sprinkle with remaining coconut.

Bake at 350° for 12-15 minutes or until golden. Cool. Store in the refrigerator.

MISSISSIPPI MUD CAKE

PREP: 20 min. | **BAKE:** 35 min. + cooling
YIELD: 16-20 servings.

Make this tempting cake and you'll satisfy kids of all ages! A fudgy brownie-like base is topped with marshmallow creme and a nutty frosting.

TAMMI SIMPSON GREENSBURG, KENTUCKY

- 1 cup butter, softened
- 2 cups sugar
- 4 eggs
- 1-1/2 cups self-rising flour
- 1/2 cup baking cocoa
- 1 cup chopped pecans
- 1 jar (7 ounces) marshmallow creme

FROSTING:

- 1/2 cup butter, softened
- 3-3/4 cups confectioners' sugar
- 3 tablespoons baking cocoa
- 1 tablespoon vanilla extract
- 4 to 5 tablespoons 2% milk
- 1 cup chopped pecans

In a large bowl, cream butter and sugar until light and fluffy. Add eggs, one at a time, beating well after each addition. Combine flour and cocoa; gradually add to creamed mixture until blended. Fold in the pecans.

Transfer to a greased 13-in. x 9-in. baking pan. Bake at 350° for 35-40 minutes or until a toothpick inserted near the center comes out clean. Cool for 3 minutes (cake will fall in the center). Spoon the marshmallow creme over cake; carefully spread to cover top. Cool completely.

For frosting, in a bowl, cream butter and confectioners' sugar until light and fluffy. Beat in the cocoa, vanilla and enough milk to achieve frosting consistency. Fold in pecans. Spread over marshmallow creme layer. Store in the refrigerator.

EDITOR'S NOTE: As a substitute for 1-1/2 cups self-rising flour, place 2-1/4 teaspoons baking powder and 3/4 teaspoon salt in a measuring cup. Add all-purpose flour to measure 1 cup. Combine with an additional 1/2 cup all-purpose flour.

LEMON CHESS PIE

PREP: 15 min.
BAKE: 35 min. + chilling
YIELD: 6 servings.

This creamy, lemony pie cuts beautifully and has a smooth texture. It's one of my favorites.
HANNAH LARUE RIDER
EAST POINT, KENTUCKY

- 1 sheet refrigerated pie pastry
- 4 eggs
- 1-1/2 cups sugar
- 1/2 cup lemon juice
- 1/4 cup butter, melted
- 1 tablespoon cornmeal
- 2 teaspoons all-purpose flour
- 1/8 teaspoon salt

Unroll pastry on a lightly floured surface. Transfer to a 9-in. pie plate. Trim pastry to 1/2 in. beyond edge of plate; flute edges.

In a bowl, beat eggs for 3 minutes. Gradually add sugar; beat for 2 minutes or until mixture becomes thick and lemon-colored. Beat in the lemon juice, butter, cornmeal, flour and salt.

Pour into pastry shell. Bake at 350° for 35-40 minutes or until a knife inserted near the center comes out clean. Cool on a wire rack for 1 hour. Refrigerate for at least 3 hours before serving.

MARDI GRAS KING CAKE

PREP: 40 min. + rising | **BAKE:** 20 min. + cooling
YIELD: 2 cakes (12 servings each).

This frosted yeast bread is the highlight of our annual Mardi Gras party. If you want to hide a token inside, do so by cutting a small slit in the bottom of the baked cake—and be sure to warn your guests!
LISA MOUTON ORLANDO, FLORIDA

- 1 package (1/4 ounce) active dry yeast
- 1/2 cup warm water (110° to 115°)
- 1/2 cup warm milk (110° to 115°)
- 1/3 cup shortening
- 1/3 cup sugar
- 1 teaspoon salt
- 1 egg
- 4 to 4-1/2 cups all-purpose flour
- 2 cans (12-1/2 ounces *each*) almond cake and pastry filling

GLAZE:
- 3 cups confectioners' sugar
- 1/2 teaspoon vanilla extract
- 3 to 4 tablespoons water

Purple, green and gold colored sugar

In a large bowl, dissolve yeast in warm water. Add the milk, shortening, sugar, salt, egg and 2 cups flour. Beat on medium speed for 3 minutes. Beat until smooth. Stir in enough remaining flour to form a soft dough (dough will be sticky).

Turn onto a floured surface; knead until smooth and elastic, about 6-8 minutes. Place in a greased bowl, turning once to grease top. Cover and let rise in a warm place until doubled, about 1 hour.

Punch dough down. Turn onto a lightly floured surface; divide in half. Roll one portion into a 16-in. x 10-in. rectangle. Spread almond filling to within 1/2 in. of edges. Roll up jelly-roll style, starting with a long side; pinch seam to seal. Place seam side down on a greased baking sheet; pinch ends together to form a ring. Repeat with remaining dough and filling. Cover and let rise until doubled, about 1 hour.

Bake at 375° for 20-25 minutes or until golden brown. Cool on a wire rack. For glaze, combine the confectioners' sugar, vanilla and enough water to achieve desired consistency. Spread over cooled cakes. Sprinkle with colored sugars.

EDITOR'S NOTE: This recipe was tested with Solo brand cake and pastry filling. Look for it in the baking aisle.

CARAMEL BANANA ICE CREAM PIE

PREP: 20 min. + freezing | **YIELD:** 8 servings.

With six ingredients and a prepared graham cracker crust, this pie is easy to make and luscious, too. Guests will enjoy the symphony of caramel, banana and toffee bits. **APRIL TIMBOE** SILOAM SPRINGS, ARKANSAS

- 1/4 cup plus 1 tablespoon caramel ice cream topping, *divided*
- 1 graham cracker crust (9 inches)
- 1 cup cold 2% milk
- 2 packages (3.4 ounces *each*) instant banana cream pudding mix
- 1 quart vanilla ice cream, softened
- 1-3/4 cups whipped topping
- 1 English toffee candy bar (1.4 ounces), chopped

Spread 1/4 cup caramel topping into crust. In a large bowl, beat milk and pudding mix on low speed for 2 minutes. Add ice cream; mix well.

Spoon into prepared crust. Top with whipped topping. Drizzle with remaining caramel topping; sprinkle with chopped candy bar.

Cover and freeze for 2 hours or until firm. Remove from the freezer 15 minutes before serving.

CARAMEL-CHOCOLATE ICE CREAM PIE: Substitute chocolate pudding for the banana pudding.

TRIPLE-CHOCOLATE ICE CREAM PIE: Substitute chocolate ice cream topping for the caramel topping, chocolate pudding for the banana pudding and chocolate ice cream for the vanilla.

LEMON-FILLED COCONUT CAKE

PREP: 35 min. | **BAKE:** 25 min. + cooling | **YIELD:** 16 servings.

Around 1970, one of my co-workers brought this cake to a luncheon. It was so delicious that I have baked it for nearly every special occasion since. It's that good. **JACKIE BERGENHEIER** WICHITA FALLS, TEXAS

1 cup butter, softened

2 cups sugar

3 eggs

2 teaspoons vanilla extract

3-1/4 cups all-purpose flour

3-1/4 teaspoons baking powder

3/4 teaspoon salt

1-1/2 cups 2% milk

FILLING:

1 cup sugar

1/4 cup cornstarch

1 cup water

4 egg yolks, lightly beaten

1/3 cup lemon juice

2 tablespoons butter

FROSTING:

1-1/2 cups sugar

2 egg whites

1/3 cup water

1/4 teaspoon cream of tartar

1 teaspoon vanilla extract

3 cups flaked coconut

In a large bowl, cream butter and sugar until light and fluffy. Add eggs one at a time, beating well after each addition. Beat in vanilla. Combine the flour, baking powder and salt; add to creamed mixture alternately with milk, beating well after each addition.

Transfer to three greased and floured 9-in. round baking pans. Bake at 350° for 25-30 minutes or until a toothpick inserted near the center comes out clean. Cool for 10 minutes before removing from pans to wire racks to cool completely.

For filling, in a small saucepan, combine the sugar, cornstarch and water until smooth. Bring to a boil; cook and stir 2 minutes longer or until thickened and bubbly. Remove from the heat.

Stir a small amount of hot mixture into egg yolks; return all to the pan, stirring constantly. Bring to a gentle boil; cook and stir 2 minutes longer. Remove from the heat; gently stir in lemon juice and butter. Cool to room temperature without stirring.

Place one cake on serving plate; spread with half of the filling. Repeat layers. Top with remaining cake.

For frosting, in a large heavy saucepan, combine the sugar, egg whites, water and cream of tartar. With a portable mixer, beat on low speed for 1 minute. Continue beating on low over low heat until frosting reaches 160°, about 10 minutes.

Transfer to a large bowl; add vanilla. Beat on high until stiff peaks form, about 7 minutes. Frost top and sides of cake. Sprinkle with coconut. Store the frosted cake in the refrigerator.

CREATING BAKERY-PERFECT LAYER CAKES

Stacking layers for a layered cake is easier when the layers are level. When the cake is cool, use a long serrated knife to slice the high spot from the bottom layer of a two-layer cake or the bottom and middle layers of a three-layer cake. You can trim off the crown of the top layer or leave it for a domed effect.
TASTE OF HOME TEST KITCHEN

SHOOFLY PIE

PREP: 30 min. | **BAKE:** 45 min. | **YIELD:** 6-8 servings.

The distinctive tastes of molasses and brown sugar come out in this traditional pie recipe from my grandmother. **MARK MORGAN** WATERFORD, WISCONSIN

- 1 unbaked pastry shell (9 inches)
- 1 egg yolk, lightly beaten

FILLING:

- 1/2 cup packed brown sugar
- 1/2 cup molasses
- 1 egg
- 1-1/2 teaspoons all-purpose flour
- 1/2 teaspoon baking soda
- 1 cup boiling water

TOPPING:

- 1-1/2 cups all-purpose flour
- 3/4 cup packed brown sugar
- 3/4 teaspoon baking soda
- Dash salt
- 6 tablespoons cold butter

Line pastry with a double thickness of heavy-duty foil. Bake at 350° for 10 minutes. Remove foil; brush crust with egg yolk. Bake 5 minutes longer; cool on a wire rack.

For filling, in a small bowl, combine the brown sugar, molasses, egg, flour and baking soda; gradually add boiling water. Cool to room temperature; pour into prepared crust.

For topping, in a large bowl, combine the flour, brown sugar, baking soda and salt. Cut in butter until crumbly. Sprinkle over filling.

Bake at 350° for 45-50 minutes or until golden brown and filling is set. Cool on a wire rack. Store in the refrigerator.

MARSHMALLOW-ALMOND KEY LIME PIE

PREP: 40 min. | **BAKE:** 15 min. + chilling | **YIELD:** 8 servings.

It's great to see that many supermarkets now carry key limes, which give this pie its sweet-tart flavor.
JUDY CASTRANOVA NEW BERN, NORTH CAROLINA

- 1 cup all-purpose flour
- 3 tablespoons brown sugar

- 1 cup slivered almonds, toasted, *divided*
- 1/4 cup butter, melted
- 1 tablespoon honey
- 1 can (14 ounces) sweetened condensed milk
- 1 package (8 ounces) cream cheese, softened, *divided*
- 1/2 cup key lime juice
- 1 tablespoon grated key lime peel
- Dash salt
- 1 egg yolk
- 1-3/4 cups miniature marshmallows
- 4-1/2 teaspoons butter
- 1/2 cup heavy whipping cream

Place flour, brown sugar and 1/2 cup almonds in a food processor. Cover and process until blended. Add melted butter and honey; cover and process until crumbly. Press onto the bottom and up the sides of a greased 9-in. pie plate. Bake at 350° for 8-10 minutes or until crust is lightly browned. Cool on a wire rack.

In a bowl, beat the milk, 5 ounces cream cheese, lime juice, peel and salt until blended. Add egg yolk; beat on low speed just until combined. Pour into crust. Bake for 15-20 minutes or until center is almost set. Cool on a wire rack.

In a large saucepan, combine marshmallows and butter. Cook and stir over medium-low heat until melted. Remove from the heat and transfer to a bowl. Add cream and remaining cream cheese; beat until smooth. Cover and refrigerate until chilled.

Beat marshmallow mixture until light and fluffy. Spread over pie; sprinkle with remaining almonds.

LEMON MERINGUE PIE

PREP: 35 min. | **BAKE:** 15 min. + chilling | **YIELD:** 8 servings.

I think of my grandmother every time I enjoy this refreshing pie. It's a lovely, special dessert that feels like home.

MERLE DYCK ELKFORD, BRITISH COLUMBIA

1/2 cup sugar

1/4 cup cornstarch

Pinch salt

2 cups cold water

2 egg yolks, lightly beaten

3 tablespoons lemon juice

1 teaspoon grated lemon peel

1 teaspoon butter

MERINGUE:

3 egg whites

1/8 teaspoon cream of tartar

6 tablespoons sugar

Pastry for single-crust pie
(9 inches), baked

In a large saucepan, combine the sugar, cornstarch and salt. Stir in water until smooth. Cook and stir over medium heat until thickened and bubbly, about 2 minutes. Reduce heat; cook and stir 2 minutes longer.

Remove from the heat. Gradually stir 1 cup hot filling into egg yolks; return all to the pan. Bring to a gentle boil; cook and stir for 2 minutes. Remove from the heat. Gently stir in lemon juice, peel and butter until butter is melted. Set aside and keep warm.

For meringue, in a small bowl, beat egg whites and cream of tartar on medium speed until soft peaks form. Gradually beat in sugar, 1 tablespoon at a time, on high until stiff glossy peaks form and sugar is dissolved.

Pour filling into crust. Spread meringue over hot filling, sealing edges to crust. Bake at 350° for 15 minutes or until meringue is golden brown. Cool on a wire rack for 1 hour; refrigerate for at least 3 hours before serving.

SOUTH CAROLINA COBBLER, PG. 287

OTHER SWEET TREATS

Look no further for some sweet inspiration. Fruit-filled cobblers, decadent homemade candies, rich and chewy brownies, creamy bananas Foster and more await to tempt your sweet tooth.

BUCKEYES, PG. 279

GINGER FRUIT CRISP

PREP: 20 min. | **BAKE:** 30 min. | **YIELD:** 9 servings.

Our B&B guests tell us this fun breakfast crisp is one of the most enjoyable parts of their stay. There's seldom a crumb left in the bowl. **ELINOR STABILE** CANMORE, ALBERTA

1/3 cup packed brown sugar

2 tablespoons plus 1-1/2
   teaspoons cornstarch

2 cups sliced fresh plums

1 cup sliced peeled peaches

1 cup sliced nectarines

TOPPING:

1 cup crushed gingersnap
   cookies (about 20 cookies)

1/2 cup old-fashioned oats

1/3 cup packed brown sugar

1/2 teaspoon ground ginger

1/2 teaspoon ground cinnamon

1/4 teaspoon salt

1/3 cup cold butter, cubed

1/2 cup sliced almonds

Whipped cream, optional

In a bowl, combine brown sugar and cornstarch. Add the plums, peaches and nectarines; gently toss to coat. Transfer to a greased 8-in. square baking dish.

For topping, in a small bowl, combine the gingersnap crumbs, oats, brown sugar, ginger, cinnamon and salt. Cut in butter until crumbly. Stir in almonds; sprinkle over fruit.

Bake at 350° for 30-35 minutes or until filling is bubbly and topping is browned. Serve warm with whipped cream if desired.

MARBLE BROWNIES

PREP: 20 min. | **COOK:** 15 min. | **YIELD:** 1 dozen.

I like to bake and enjoy trying new recipes. The cream cheese topping in these delights made them a fast favorite in my house.
DIANA COPPERNOLL LINDEN, NORTH CAROLINA

- 5 tablespoons butter
- 2 ounces unsweetened chocolate
- 2/3 cup sugar
- 2 eggs
- 1 teaspoon vanilla extract
- 2/3 cup all-purpose flour
- 1/2 teaspoon baking powder

CHEESECAKE LAYER:

- 1 package (8 ounces) cream cheese, softened
- 1/2 cup sugar
- 1 egg
- 1 teaspoon vanilla extract
- 1 cup (6 ounces) semisweet chocolate chips

In a large microwave-safe bowl, combine butter and chocolate. Cover and microwave on high for 30-60 seconds; stir until smooth. Beat in sugar, eggs and vanilla. Combine flour and baking powder; gradually add to chocolate mixture until blended. Spread into a greased microwave-safe 8-in. square dish; set aside.

In a large bowl, beat cream cheese until fluffy. Beat in the sugar, egg and vanilla until smooth. Spoon over brownie batter; cut through batter with a knife to swirl. Sprinkle with chocolate chips.

Cook, uncovered, at 70% power for 8-10 minutes or until a toothpick comes out clean. Cook on high for 1 minute longer. Remove to a wire rack to cool completely. Store in the refrigerator.

EDITOR'S NOTE: This recipe was tested in a 1,100-watt microwave.

BUCKEYES

PREP: 15 min. + chilling
YIELD: about 5-1/2 dozen.

I make these peanut butter candies for my church's annual Christmas fundraiser. They're a quick sell!
MERRY KAY OPITZ ELKHORN, WISCONSIN

- 5-1/2 cups confectioners' sugar
- 1-2/3 cups peanut butter
- 1 cup butter, melted
- 4 cups (24 ounces) semisweet chocolate chips
- 1 teaspoon shortening

In a large bowl, beat the sugar, peanut butter and butter until smooth. Shape into 1-in. balls; set aside.

In a microwave, melt chocolate chips and shortening; stir until smooth. Dip balls in chocolate, allowing excess to drip off. Place on a wire rack over waxed paper; refrigerate for 15 minutes or until firm. Cover and store in the refrigerator.

PUNCH BOWL TRIFLE

PREP: 20 min. | **BAKE:** 20 min. | **YIELD:** 24-28 servings.

I threw this dessert together when I needed something quick to take to my in-laws' house. Because it's beautiful, everyone thought I fussed over it, but it's really very easy.

KRISTI JUDKINS MORRISON, TENNESSEE

- 1 package (18-1/4 ounces) chocolate cake mix
- 1 quart fresh whole strawberries
- 1 carton (15 ounces) strawberry glaze
- 2 cartons (12 ounces *each*) frozen whipped topping, thawed, *divided*
- 1 cup chocolate frosting

Shaved chocolate

Prepare and bake cake according to package directions, using a 13-in. x 9-in. baking pan. Cool completely on a wire rack.

Set aside five strawberries for garnish. Slice remaining strawberries. Cut cake into 1-in. cubes. Place half of the cubes in a 6-qt. glass punch bowl. Top with half of the sliced strawberries; drizzle with half of the strawberry glaze. Spread with 3-1/2 cups whipped topping.

In a microwave-safe bowl, heat frosting on high for 20-30 seconds or until pourable, stirring often; cool slightly. Drizzle half over the whipped topping. Repeat layers of cake, berries, glaze, whipped topping and frosting. Top with remaining whipped topping. Cover and refrigerate until serving. Garnish with shaved chocolate and reserved strawberries.

RICH LUSCIOUS LEMON CHEESECAKE

PREP: 20 min. | **BAKE:** 1 hour + chilling
YIELD: 12-14 servings.

I'm always greeted with oohs and aahs when I bring out this exquisite dessert. It has a wonderful lemony flavor, silky texture and rich sour cream topping.

KAAREN JURACK MANASSAS, VIRGINIA

CRUST:

- 1-1/4 cups graham cracker crumbs (about 20 squares)
- 3/4 cup finely chopped nuts
- 1/4 cup sugar
- 1/3 cup butter, melted

FILLING:

- 4 packages (8 ounces *each*) cream cheese, softened
- 1-1/4 cups sugar
- 4 eggs
- 1 tablespoon lemon juice
- 2 teaspoons grated lemon peel
- 1 teaspoon vanilla extract

TOPPING:

- 2 cups (16 ounces) sour cream
- 1/4 cup sugar
- 1 teaspoon grated lemon peel
- 1 teaspoon vanilla extract

In a bowl, combine the crumbs, nuts and sugar; stir in butter. Press onto the bottom of a greased 10-in. springform pan; set aside. In a large bowl, beat cream cheese and sugar until smooth. Add eggs, beating on low speed just until combined. Stir in the lemon juice, peel and vanilla; beat just until blended. Pour into crust.

Bake at 350° for 55 minutes or until center is almost set. Remove from the oven; let stand for 5 minutes. Combine topping ingredients; spread over filling. Return to the oven for 5 minutes. Cool on a wire rack for 10 minutes.

Carefully run a knife around edge of pan to loosen; cool 1 hour longer. Refrigerate overnight. Remove sides of pan. Let stand at room temperature for 30 minutes before slicing.

CHOCOLATE TEMPTATION BROWNIES

PREP: 20 min. | **BAKE:** 25 min. + chilling | **YIELD:** 3 dozen.

Chocolate lovers will stand in line for these rich three-layer squares, which have a peanut butter filling and decadent glaze. They're heavenly! **IOLA EGLE** BELLA VISTA, ARKANSAS

1 cup butter, cubed

1 ounce bittersweet
  chocolate, chopped

3/4 cup sugar

3/4 cup packed light brown sugar

2 teaspoons vanilla extract

3 eggs

1-1/4 cups all-purpose flour

3/4 teaspoon salt

1 cup chopped salted peanuts

PEANUT BUTTER FILLING:

12 ounces cream
  cheese, softened

1 cup creamy peanut butter

1 cup confectioners' sugar

CHOCOLATE GLAZE:

8 ounces bittersweet chocolate, finely chopped

1/4 cup butter, cubed

1/2 cup heavy whipping cream

1/2 cup confectioners' sugar

In a large saucepan, melt butter and chocolate over medium heat. Remove from the heat; stir in sugars and vanilla. Add eggs one at a time, stirring well after each addition. Combine flour and salt; stir into butter mixture just until combined. Stir in peanuts.

Transfer to a greased 13-in. x 9-in. baking pan. Bake at 350° for 25-30 minutes or until a toothpick inserted near the center comes out clean. Cool completely on a wire rack.

In a small bowl, beat the cream cheese, peanut butter and confectioners' sugar until light and fluffy; spread over brownie layer. Chill until firm.

In a microwave, melt chocolate and butter with cream; stir until smooth. Stir in confectioners' sugar. Spread over peanut butter layer. Chill until firm.

1-2-3 BLACKBERRY SHERBET

PREP: 10 min. + freezing
YIELD: 1 quart.

My mom gave me this recipe, which was a favorite when I was young. Now when I make it, I'm reminded of those sweet memories.

LISA EREMIA IRWIN, PENNSYLVANIA

- **4 cups fresh *or* frozen blackberries, thawed**
- **2 cups sugar**
- **2 cups buttermilk**

In a food processor, combine the blackberries and sugar. Cover; process until smooth. Strain and discard seeds and pulp. Stir in buttermilk.

Transfer puree to a 13-in. x 9-in. dish. Freeze for 1 hour or until edges begin to firm. Stir and return to freezer. Freeze 2 hours longer or until firm.

Just before serving, transfer to a food processor; cover and process for 2-3 minutes or until smooth.

CHOCOLATE STRAWBERRY TRUFFLE BROWNIES

PREP: 30 min. | **BAKE:** 30 min. + chilling | **YIELD:** about 2 dozen.

Every summer I make strawberry jam, and one day I decided to add some to a batch of brownies. They were a hit with my family! I also like to treat the students in my special ed classes to these delectable treats.

TERESA JANSEN ADVANCE, MISSOURI

- **1-1/4 cups semisweet chocolate chips**
- **1/2 cup butter, cubed**
- **3/4 cup packed brown sugar**
- **2 eggs**
- **1 teaspoon instant coffee granules**
- **2 tablespoons water**
- **3/4 cup all-purpose flour**
- **1/2 teaspoon baking powder**

TRUFFLE FILLING:

- **1 cup (6 ounces) semisweet chocolate chips**
- **1/4 teaspoon instant coffee granules**
- **1 package (8 ounces) cream cheese, softened**
- **1/4 cup sifted confectioners' sugar**
- **1/3 cup strawberry jam *or* preserves**

GLAZE:

- **1/4 cup semisweet chocolate chips**
- **1 teaspoon shortening**

In a microwave, melt chocolate and butter; stir until smooth. Cool slightly. In a large bowl, beat brown sugar and eggs. Stir in chocolate mixture. Dissolve coffee in water; add to chocolate mixture. Combine flour and baking powder; gradually add to batter.

Spread evenly in a greased and floured 9-in. square baking pan. Bake at 350° for 30-35 minutes or until a toothpick inserted near the center comes out clean. Cool.

Meanwhile, for filling, melt chocolate chips and coffee granules; stir until smooth. Set aside.

In a small bowl, beat cream cheese until smooth. Add confectioners' sugar and jam; mix well. Beat in melted chocolate mixture until well blended. Spread over brownies.

For glaze, in a microwave, melt semisweet chocolate chips and shortening; stir until smooth. Drizzle over filling. Chill at least 1-2 hours.

SHORTBREAD LEMON TART

PREP: 20 min. | **BAKE:** 25 min. + cooling
YIELD: 10-12 servings.

For a change from ordinary lemon bars, we added orange peel to both the crust and filling and turned the recipe into a tart. It's a refreshing finish to heavy meals. **TASTE OF HOME TEST KITCHEN**

- 3 eggs
- 1/4 cup lemon juice
- 1-1/4 cups sugar
- 1 tablespoon grated orange peel
- 1/4 cup butter, melted

CRUST:

- 1 cup all-purpose flour
- 1/3 cup confectioners' sugar
- 1/2 cup ground almonds
- 1 teaspoon grated lemon peel
- 1 teaspoon grated orange peel
- 1/2 cup cold butter, cubed

Additional confectioners' sugar

For filling, in a blender, combine the eggs, lemon juice, sugar and orange peel. Cover and blend on high until smooth. Add butter; cover and process on high just until smooth. Set aside.

In a food processor, combine the flour, confectioners' sugar, almonds, lemon peel, orange peel and butter; cover and process until mixture forms a ball. Press pastry onto the bottom and up the sides of an ungreased 9-in. tart pan with removable bottom.

Pour filling into crust. Bake at 350° for 25-30 minutes or until center is almost set. Cool tart on a wire rack. Just before serving, sprinkle with confectioners' sugar.

OLD-FASHIONED WHOOPIE PIES

PREP: 35 min. + chilling | **BAKE:** 10 min./batch + cooling
YIELD: 2 dozen.

Who can resist soft chocolate sandwich cookies filled with a layer of fluffy white frosting? Mom has made these for years, and now I make them for my family.
MARIA COSTELLO MONROE, NORTH CAROLINA

- 1/2 cup baking cocoa
- 1/2 cup hot water
- 1/2 cup shortening
- 1-1/2 cups sugar
- 2 eggs
- 1 teaspoon vanilla extract
- 2-2/3 cups all-purpose flour
- 1 teaspoon baking powder
- 1 teaspoon baking soda
- 1/4 teaspoon salt
- 1/2 cup buttermilk

FILLING:

- 3 tablespoons all-purpose flour

Dash salt

- 1 cup 2% milk
- 3/4 cup shortening
- 1-1/2 cups confectioners' sugar
- 2 teaspoons vanilla extract

In a small bowl, combine cocoa and water. Cool for 5 minutes. In a large bowl, cream shortening and sugar until light and fluffy. Beat in the eggs, vanilla and cocoa mixture. Combine dry ingredients; gradually add to creamed mixture alternately with buttermilk, beating well after each addition.

Drop by rounded tablespoonfuls 2 in. apart onto greased baking sheets. Flatten slightly with a spoon. Bake at 350° for 10-12 minutes or until firm to the touch. Remove to wire racks to cool.

In a small saucepan, combine flour and salt. Gradually whisk in milk until smooth; cook and stir over medium-high heat until thick, 5-7 minutes. Remove from heat. Cover and refrigerate until completely cool.

In a small bowl, cream the shortening, sugar and vanilla until light and fluffy. Add milk mixture; beat for 7 minutes or until fluffy. Spread filling on half of the cookies; top with remaining cookies. Store in the refrigerator.

GINGERED MOLASSES COOKIES

PREP: 15 min. | **BAKE:** 10 min./batch | **YIELD:** 5-1/2 dozen.

A nice blend of spices and grated orange peel makes these a little different from your basic molasses cookies. My son loved these when he was growing up. **DONALD MITCHELL** FREDERICKSBURG, TEXAS

- 1/2 cup butter, softened
- 1/4 cup shortening
- 1-1/4 cups sugar, *divided*
- 1 egg
- 1/4 cup molasses
- 1/2 teaspoon grated orange peel
- 2 cups all-purpose flour
- 2 teaspoons baking soda
- 1/2 teaspoon salt
- 1/2 teaspoon ground ginger
- 1/2 teaspoon ground cinnamon
- 1/4 teaspoon ground cloves

In a large bowl, cream the butter, shortening and 1 cup sugar until light and fluffy. Beat in egg, molasses and orange peel. Combine the dry ingredients; gradually add to creamed mixture and mix well.

Roll into 1-1/4-in. balls, then in remaining sugar. Place 2 in. apart on ungreased baking sheets. Bake at 350° for 10-12 minutes or until edges are firm and surface cracks. Remove to wire racks to cool.

BANANAS FOSTER

PREP/TOTAL TIME: 25 min. | **YIELD:** 4 servings.

Guests are always impressed when I ignite the rum in this delicious dessert. Use perfectly ripe bananas for best results. **MARY LOU WAYMAN** SALT LAKE CITY, UTAH

- 1/3 cup butter, cubed
- 3/4 cup packed dark brown sugar
- 1/4 teaspoon ground cinnamon
- 3 medium bananas
- 2 tablespoons creme de cacao
  or banana liqueur
- 1/4 cup dark rum
- 2 cups vanilla ice cream

In a skillet or flambe pan, melt butter over medium-low heat. Stir in brown sugar and cinnamon until combined. Cut each banana lengthwise and then widthwise into quarters; add to butter mixture. Cook, stirring gently, for 3-5 minutes or until glazed and slightly softened. Stir in creme de cacao; heat through.

In a small saucepan, heat rum over low heat until vapors form on surface. Carefully ignite rum and slowly pour over bananas, coating evenly.

Leaving skillet or pan on the cooking surface, gently shake pan back and forth until flames are completely extinguished.

Spoon ice cream into fluted glasses; top with the bananas and sauce. Serve immediately.

EDITOR'S NOTE: Keep liquor bottles and other flammables at a safe distance when preparing this dessert. We do not recommend using a nonstick skillet.

NO-STICK MOLASSES

When a recipe calls for molasses, spray the inside of the measuring cup with nonstick cooking spray. The molasses will flow out of the cup without sticking to the sides. **TASTE OF HOME TEST KITCHEN**

BANANAS FOSTER

PECAN CARAMELS

PREP: 20 min. | **COOK:** 35 min. + cooling | **YIELD:** about 2-1/2 pounds.

I altered the original recipe for these creamy caramels by substituting condensed milk for part of the whipping cream and cutting back on the sugar. Everybody raves about them, and they make a great holiday gift. You can't eat just one! **PATSY HOWELL** PERU, INDIANA

- 1 tablespoon butter, softened
- 1 cup sugar
- 1 cup light corn syrup
- 2 cups heavy whipping cream, *divided*
- 1 can (14 ounces) sweetened condensed milk
- 2 cups chopped pecans
- 1 teaspoon vanilla extract

Line a 13-in. x 9-in. pan with foil; grease the foil with butter. Set aside.

In a large heavy saucepan, combine the sugar, corn syrup and 1 cup cream. Bring to a boil over medium heat. Cook and stir until smooth and blended, about 10 minutes. Stir in milk and remaining cream. Bring to a boil over medium-low heat, stirring constantly. Cook and stir until a candy thermometer reads 238° (soft-ball stage), about 25 minutes.

Remove from the heat; stir in pecans and vanilla. Pour into prepared pan (do not scrape saucepan). Cool. Using foil, lift candy out of pan; cut into 1-in. squares. Wrap individually in waxed paper.

EDITOR'S NOTE: We recommend that you test your candy thermometer before each use by bringing water to a boil; the thermometer should read 212°. Adjust your recipe temperature up or down based on your test.

SOUTHERN-STYLE SOFT CUSTARD

PREP/TOTAL TIME: 30 min. | **YIELD:** 8 servings.

Custard is one of our favorite desserts for holidays and other special family gatherings. **MARGARET ALLEN** ABINGDON, VIRGINIA

- 3 egg yolks
- 1/4 cup sugar
- 1/8 teaspoon salt
- 2 cups whole milk
- 1/2 teaspoon vanilla extract

Sliced pound cake

Fresh berries of choice

Beat together eggs, sugar and salt. Scald milk (heat to 180°) and pour slowly over egg mixture. Return mixture to top of double boiler and cook over simmering (not boiling) water; stir constantly until mixture reaches 160° or is thick enough to coat the back of a spoon.

Mixture will not have the consistency of a firm baked custard. Cool over ice water, stirring occasionally. Add vanilla. If mixture separates, beat with egg beater until smooth. Serve chilled over slice pound cake; top with berries.

TEA CAKES

PREP: 10 min. | **BAKE:** 10 min./batch | **YIELD:** 9 dozen.

I've baked many batches of different cookies through the years, but family and friends tell me these are the best. The simple buttery flavor appeals to all. **DORIS MCGOUGH** DOTHAN, ALABAMA

- 1 cup butter, softened
- 1-1/2 cups sugar
- 3 eggs
- 1 tablespoon vanilla extract
- 3 cups all-purpose flour
- 1 tablespoon baking powder
- 1/4 teaspoon salt

In a bowl, cream butter and sugar until light and fluffy. Add eggs, one at a time, beating well after each addition. Beat in vanilla. Combine the flour, baking powder and salt; gradually add to the creamed mixture (the dough will be soft).

Drop by teaspoonfuls 2 in. apart onto greased baking sheets. Bake at 375° for 7-8 minutes or until the edges are golden brown. Remove to wire racks to cool.

SOUTH CAROLINA COBBLER

PREP: 10 min. | **BAKE:** 50 min. **YIELD:** 8 servings.

With peach orchards just a couple miles from home, I'm happy to treat family to this traditional dessert.
MATTIE CARTER
ROCK HILL, SOUTH CAROLINA

- 4 cups sliced peeled fresh *or* frozen peaches, thawed
- 1 cup sugar, *divided*
- 1/2 teaspoon almond extract
- 1/3 cup butter, melted
- 3/4 cup all-purpose flour
- 2 teaspoons baking powder

Pinch salt

- 3/4 cup milk

Vanilla ice cream, optional

In a bowl, gently toss peaches, 1/2 cup sugar and extract; set aside. Pour butter into a 2-qt. baking dish.

In a small bowl, combine the flour, baking powder, salt and remaining sugar; stir in milk until smooth. Pour evenly over butter (do not stir). Top with peach mixture.

Bake at 350° for 50-55 minutes or until golden brown and bubbly. Serve with ice cream if desired.

HOMEMADE LEMON BARS

PREP: 25 min. | **BAKE:** 20 min. | **YIELD:** 9 servings.

Memorable family meals were complete as soon as these tangy bars were served. Their sweetness rounds out the meal, but the lemony flavor keeps them light. Don't expect many leftovers once family and friends taste these bars! **DENISE BAUMERT** DALHART, TEXAS

CRUST:

- 1 cup all-purpose flour
- 1/3 cup butter, softened
- 1/4 cup confectioners' sugar

TOPPING:

- 1 cup sugar
- 2 eggs
- 2 tablespoons all-purpose flour
- 2 tablespoons lemon juice
- 1/2 teaspoon lemon extract
- 1/2 teaspoon baking powder
- 1/4 teaspoon salt

Confectioners' sugar

Orange peel strips (1 to 3 inches), optional

In a large bowl, combine the flour, butter and confectioners' sugar; press into an ungreased 8-in. square baking pan. Bake at 375° for 15 minutes or until lightly browned.

Meanwhile, in a large bowl, beat the sugar, eggs, flour, lemon juice, extract, baking powder and salt until frothy; pour over crust.

Bake for 18-22 minutes or until light golden brown. Dust with confectioners' sugar. Sprinkle with orange peel strips if desired.

BUTTER PECAN CHEESECAKE

PREP: 30 min. | **BAKE:** 70 min. + chilling
YIELD: 16 servings.

Fall always makes me yearn for this pecan cheesecake, but it's welcomed any time of year. You'll want to put it on your list of favorite special-occasion desserts.
LAURA SYLVESTER MECHANICSVILLE, VIRGINIA

- 1-1/2 cups graham cracker crumbs
- 1/2 cup finely chopped pecans
- 1/3 cup sugar
- 1/3 cup butter, melted

FILLING:

- 3 packages (8 ounces *each*) cream cheese, softened
- 1-1/2 cups sugar
- 2 cups (16 ounces) sour cream
- 1 teaspoon vanilla extract
- 1/2 teaspoon butter flavoring
- 3 eggs, lightly beaten
- 1 cup finely chopped pecans

In a large bowl, combine the cracker crumbs, pecans, sugar and butter; set aside 1/3 cup for topping. Press remaining crumb mixture onto the bottom and 1 in. up the sides of a greased 9-in. springform pan.

Place springform pan on a double thickness of heavy-duty foil (about 18 in. square). Securely wrap foil around pan.

In a large bowl, beat cream cheese and sugar until smooth. Beat in the sour cream, vanilla and butter flavoring. Add eggs; beat on low speed just until combined. Fold in pecans. Pour into crust; sprinkle with reserved crumb mixture. Place springform pan in a large baking pan; add 1 in. of hot water to larger pan.

Bake at 325° for 70-80 minutes or until center is almost set. Remove springform pan from water bath. Cool on a wire rack for 10 minutes. Carefully run a knife around edge of pan to loosen; cool 1 hour longer. Refrigerate overnight. Remove sides of pan.

PINWHEEL MINTS

PREP: 45 min. + chilling | **YIELD:** about 3 dozen.

Both my grandmother and my mom used to make these eye-catching confections as a replacement for ordinary mints at Christmas. When I offer them at parties, guests tell me the mints are wonderful, and then ask how I create the pretty swirl pattern. **MARILOU ROTH** MILFORD, NEBRASKA

1 package (8 ounces) cream cheese, softened

1/2 to 1 teaspoon mint extract

7-1/2 to 8-1/2 cups confectioners' sugar

Red and green food coloring

Additional confectioners' sugar

In a large bowl, beat cream cheese and mint extract until smooth. Gradually beat in as much confectioners' sugar as possible; knead in the remaining confectioners' sugar until a firm mixture is achieved. Divide mixture in half; with food coloring, tint half pink and the other light green.

On waxed paper, lightly sprinkle remaining confectioners' sugar into a 12-in. x 5-in. rectangle. Divide pink portion in half; shape each portion into a 10-in. log.

Place one log on sugared waxed paper and flatten slightly. Cover with waxed paper; roll into a 12-in. x 5-in. rectangle. Repeat with remaining pink portion; set aside. Repeat with light green portion.

Remove top piece of waxed paper from one pink and one green rectangle. Place one over the other. Roll up jelly-roll style, starting with a long side. Wrap in waxed paper; twist ends. Repeat. Chill overnight.

To serve, cut into 1/2-in. slices. Store in an airtight container in the refrigerator for up to 1 week.

BERRY SHORTBREAD DREAMS

PREP: 20 min. + chilling | **BAKE:** 15 min. | **YIELD:** about 3-1/2 dozen.

Raspberry jam adds fruity sweetness to these rich-tasting cookies. They will absolutely melt in your mouth!
MILDRED SHERRER FORT WORTH, TEXAS

1 cup butter, softened

2/3 cup sugar

1/2 teaspoon almond extract

2 cups all-purpose flour

1/3 to 1/2 cup seedless raspberry jam

GLAZE:

1 cup confectioners' sugar

1/2 teaspoon almond extract

2 to 3 teaspoons water

In a bowl, cream butter and sugar until light and fluffy. Beat in extract; gradually add flour until dough forms a ball. Cover and refrigerate for 1 hour or until dough is easy to handle.

Roll into 1-in. balls. Place 1 in. apart on ungreased baking sheets. Using the end of a wooden spoon handle, make an indentation in the center. Fill with jam.

Bake at 350° for 14-18 minutes or until edges are lightly browned. Remove to wire racks to cool.

Spoon additional jam into cookies if desired. Combine confectioners' sugar, extract and enough water to achieve drizzling consistency; drizzle over cookies.

SHORTBREAD SECRETS

For melt-in-your-mouth shortbread cookies, make sure the butter is at room temperature. Cold, hard butter will cause you to overwork the batter and will take away from the cookies' melt-in-your-mouth quality. Melted butter isn't good either, as it will make your cookies tough. **TASTE OF HOME TEST KITCHEN**

CHOCOLATE PECAN TORTE

PREP: 1 hour | **BAKE:** 20 min. + cooling | **YIELD:** 12-16 servings.

This impressive dessert looks lovely on a buffet table. It requires several steps but is worth the effort for milestone occasions.

LOIS SCHLICKAU HAVEN, KANSAS

8 eggs, *separated*

1-1/2 cups sugar, *divided*

1-1/2 cups ground pecans

2/3 cup all-purpose flour

2/3 cup baking cocoa

1 teaspoon baking soda

1/2 teaspoon salt

1/2 cup water

2 teaspoons vanilla extract

CHOCOLATE FROSTING:

3 cups heavy whipping cream

1 cup confectioners' sugar

1/2 cup baking cocoa

2 teaspoons vanilla extract

CHOCOLATE GLAZE:

2 tablespoons baking cocoa

2 tablespoons water

1 tablespoon butter

1 cup confectioners' sugar

1/4 teaspoon vanilla extract

Let eggs stand at room temperature for 30 minutes. In a large bowl, beat egg yolks. Gradually add 1 cup sugar, beating until thick and lemon-colored. Combine pecans, flour, cocoa, baking soda and salt; add to yolk mixture alternately with water. Stir in vanilla.

In another large bowl, beat egg whites until foamy. Gradually add remaining sugar, 1 tablespoon at a time, beating until stiff peaks form; fold into batter.

Spoon into two greased and floured 9-in. round baking pans. Bake at 375° for 20-22 minutes or until cake springs back when lightly touched. Cool for 10 minutes before removing from pans to wire racks to cool completely.

For frosting, in a large bowl, beat cream until soft peaks form. Beat in confectioners' sugar, cocoa and vanilla until stiff peaks form. Cut each cake horizontally into two layers. Place bottom layer on a serving plate; top with about 1 cup frosting. Repeat layers twice. Top with remaining layer.

For glaze, in a small saucepan, combine cocoa, water and butter. Cook and stir over medium heat until butter is melted. Remove from the heat; stir in confectioners' sugar and vanilla until smooth. Spread over top cake layer. Spread remaining frosting over sides of cake. Store in the refrigerator.

PEANUT MERINGUES

PREP: 20 min.
BAKE: 1 hour + standing
YIELD: 8 servings.

I live in the peanut capital of the world, and this is one of the recipes I get the most compliments on.

CLARA GIBERSON DOTHAN, ALABAMA

4 egg whites

1/4 teaspoon cream of tartar

1/4 teaspoon vanilla extract

1/8 teaspoon salt

1 cup sugar

1/2 cup finely chopped roasted peanuts

Ice cream of your choice

In a bowl, beat egg whites, cream of tartar, vanilla and salt on medium speed until soft peaks form. Gradually beat in sugar, 1 tablespoon at a time, on high until stiff peaks form. Fold in peanuts.

Drop eight mounds onto a baking sheet lined with parchment paper. Shape into 3-in. cups with the back of a spoon. Bake at 250° for 1 hour or until set and dry. Turn oven off; leave meringues in oven for 1 hour. To serve fill meringues with ice cream.

BROWNIE BOURBON BITES

PREP: 25 min. + chilling | **BAKE:** 10 min. + cooling | **YIELD:** about 2 dozen.

Chocolate and chopped pecans flavor these simple, spirited treats. Make a double batch so you can give some as gifts and savor the rest! **PAULA KIRCHENBAUER** NEWTON, NEW JERSEY

1/2 cup butter, softened
1/2 cup packed brown sugar
1/4 cup bourbon
1 cup all-purpose flour
3 tablespoons baking cocoa
1/2 cup miniature semisweet chocolate chips
1 cup coarsely chopped pecans

In a bowl, cream butter and brown sugar until light and fluffy. Beat in bourbon. Combine flour and cocoa; gradually add to creamed mixture, beating until smooth. Stir in chocolate chips. Cover and refrigerate for 1-2 hours.

Shape into 1-in. balls; roll in pecans. Place 2 in. apart on ungreased baking sheets. Bake at 350° for 8-10 minutes or until cookies are set. Cool for 5 minutes before carefully removing from pans to wire racks to cool completely. Store in an airtight container.

LEMON RICE PUDDING BRULEE

PREP: 30 min. + cooling | **BROIL:** 5 min. | **YIELD:** 6 servings.

You can make the lemonade from frozen concentrate to speed up the assembly of this delicious and easy rice pudding and creme brulee hybrid. **HELEN CONWELL** PORTLAND, OREGON

1-1/3 cups lemonade
1/2 cup uncooked long grain rice
1 teaspoon grated lemon peel
1/3 cup plus 3 tablespoons sugar, *divided*
1 tablespoon all-purpose flour
1/2 teaspoon salt
2 cups milk
2 eggs, lightly beaten
1/4 cup dried cranberries
3 tablespoons brown sugar
1/3 cup chopped pecans, toasted

In a small saucepan, bring lemonade and rice to a boil. Reduce heat; cover and simmer for 20 minutes. Remove from the heat; stir in lemon peel. Cover and let stand for 5 minutes. Cool to room temperature.

In a saucepan, combine 1/3 cup sugar, flour and salt. Stir in milk until smooth. Cook and stir over medium-high heat until thickened and bubbly. Reduce heat; cook and stir 2 minutes longer.

Remove from the heat. Stir a small amount of hot filling into eggs; return all to the pan, stirring constantly. Bring to a gentle boil; cook and stir 2 minutes longer. Remove from the heat. Gently stir in cranberries and cooled rice.

Divide among six 8-oz. ramekins. Place on a baking sheet. Combine brown sugar and remaining sugar. If using a creme brulee torch, sprinkle puddings with sugar mixture. Heat sugar with the torch until caramelized. Sprinkle with pecans. Serve immediately.

If broiling the puddings, place ramekins on a baking sheet; let stand at room temperature for 15 minutes. Sprinkle with sugar mixture. Broil 8 in. from the heat for 4-7 minutes or until sugar is caramelized. Sprinkle with pecans. Serve warm.

ADD SOME ZEST
Grated lemon peel adds a wallop of bright citrus flavor to desserts. If you do not have a citrus zester, use a vegetable peeler or a small, sharp knife. You can also use a cheese grater to remove the peel. When removing the skin from lemons or other citrus fruits, be sure to take only the thin outer zest or colored portion. The white pith will give your dish a bitter taste. **TASTE OF HOME TEST KITCHEN**

LEMON RICE PUDDING BRULEE

BREAD PUDDING WITH BUTTER SAUCE

PECAN DIVINITY

PREP/TOTAL TIME: 25 min. | **YIELD:** 4 dozen.

The table at our Sunday school Christmas party has a spot reserved for my divinity. I love making candy and have recruited my husband to help...between nibbles. **CAOLYN WEBER** VICKSBURG, MISSISSIPPI

- 2 cups sugar
- 1 cup water
- 1 jar (7 ounces) marshmallow creme
- 1 teaspoon vanilla extract
- 1-1/2 cups chopped pecans

In a large heavy saucepan, combine the sugar and water. Cook over medium heat, without stirring, until a candy thermometer reads 250° (hard-ball stage).

Remove from the heat; stir in the marshmallow creme, vanilla and pecans. Continue stirring until candy cools and begins to hold its shape when dropped from a spoon.

Quickly drop by heaping teaspoonfuls onto waxed paper-lined baking sheet. Store in an airtight container at room temperature.

EDITOR'S NOTE: We recommend that you test your candy thermometer before each use by bringing water to a boil; the thermometer should read 212°. Adjust your recipe temperature up or down based on your test.

BREAD PUDDING WITH BUTTER SAUCE

PREP: 15 min. | **BAKE:** 35 min. + cooling | **YIELD:** 2 servings.

When we went out to eat, bread pudding was my choice dessert. I eventually found out how it was made and have enjoyed making, eating and serving it since. **NORMA BURGGRAF** MARSHFIELD, OHIO

- 2 slices white bread, cubed
- 2 tablespoons raisins
- 1 egg
- 1/2 cup evaporated milk
- 3 tablespoons water
- 2 tablespoons sugar
- 1/4 teaspoon ground cinnamon
- 1/4 teaspoon ground nutmeg

BUTTER SAUCE:

- 2 tablespoons butter
- 2 tablespoons sugar
- 1 egg yolk, beaten
- 1 tablespoon water
- 1 tablespoon bourbon, optional

Divide the bread cubes and raisins between two greased 8-oz. ramekins or custard cups.

In a small bowl, whisk the egg, milk, water, sugar, cinnamon and nutmeg. Pour over bread mixture.

Bake, uncovered, at 350° for 35-40 minutes or until a knife inserted near the center comes out clean. Cool for 15 minutes.

Meanwhile, in a small saucepan, melt butter. Stir in the sugar, egg yolk and water. Cook and stir over medium-low heat for 4 minutes or until sugar is dissolved and mixture comes to a boil. Remove from the heat; stir in bourbon if desired. Serve warm with bread pudding.

A TASTY TWIST

Ordinary bread pudding becomes a distinctive treat when you use angel food cake instead of bread, and substitute dried cranberries for raisins. You can also try substituting chunks of apples or pears in place of raisins, or tempt chocolate-lovers by replacing the dried fruit with chocolate chips and miniature marshmallows. **TASTE OF HOME TEST KITCHEN**

PECAN SANDIES

PREP/TOTAL TIME: 25 min. | **YIELD:** about 3-1/2 dozen.

My family prefers these pecan cookies to any store-bought variety. Self-rising flour makes them a little different from most cookie recipes.
JEANIE HANNA RUSTBURG, VIRGINIA

- 1/3 cup butter, softened
- 1/3 cup shortening
- 1/2 cup sugar
- 1/2 cup packed brown sugar
- 1 egg
- 1 teaspoon vanilla extract
- 1-1/2 cups self-rising flour
- 1/2 cup chopped pecans

In a large bowl, cream the butter, shortening and sugars until light and fluffy. Beat in egg and vanilla. Gradually add flour and mix well. Stir in pecans.

Drop by rounded teaspoonfuls 2 in. apart onto ungreased baking sheets. Bake at 375° for 9-11 minutes or until edges are lightly browned. Cool for 1-2 minutes before removing to wire racks.

HONEY PEACH FREEZE

PREP: 10 min. + freezing
YIELD: 4 servings.

Want a cool and refreshing dessert? This slightly sweet treat, which is big on peach flavor, will be the perfect answer.
DOROTHY SMITH EL DORADO, ARKANSAS

- 1/4 cup honey
- 2 tablespoons orange juice
- 1 tablespoon lemon juice
- 1 package (20 ounces) frozen sliced peaches, partially thawed

Set aside a few peach slices for garnish. In a blender, combine the honey, juices and peaches. Cover and process until mixture is smooth.

Pour into four freezerproof dishes. Freeze. Remove from the freezer 5 minutes before serving. Garnish with reserved peaches.

GEORGIA PEACH ICE CREAM

PREP: 45 min. + chilling | **PROCESS:** 20 min./batch + freezing
YIELD: 3-3/4 quarts.

This frosty recipe has been a family favorite for almost 50 years.
MARGUERITE ETHRIDGE AMERICUS, GEORGIA

- 1 quart milk
- 2-1/4 cups sugar, *divided*
- 1/2 teaspoon salt
- 4 eggs, lightly beaten
- 2 cans (14 ounces *each*) sweetened condensed milk
- 1-3/4 pounds fresh peaches, peeled and sliced

In a large heavy saucepan, heat milk to 175°; stir in 1 cup sugar and salt until dissolved. Whisk in a small amount of the hot mixture to the eggs. Return all to the pan, whisking constantly. Cook and stir over low heat until mixture reaches at least 160° and coats the back of a metal spoon. Remove from the heat.

Cool quickly by placing pan in a bowl of ice water; stir for 2 minutes. Stir in sweetened condensed milk. Press plastic wrap onto surface of custard. Refrigerate for several hours or overnight.

When ready to freeze, mash peaches with remaining sugar in a small bowl; let stand for 30 minutes. Combine milk mixture and peaches in an ice cream freezer. Freeze according to manufacturer's directions.

PEANUT BUTTER BROWNIE BARS

PREP: 20 min. | **BAKE:** 25 min. + chilling | **YIELD:** 3 dozen.

A brownie mix base makes this a no-fuss treat that will appeal to adults and children alike. Creamy peanut butter, crunchy nuts and crisp cereal make the bars fun to bite into. **RADELLE KNAPPENBERGER** OVIEDO, FLORIDA

1 package fudge brownie mix
(13-inch x 9-inch pan size)

12 peanut butter cups, chopped

1/2 cup salted peanuts, chopped

2 cups (12 ounces) semisweet
chocolate chips

1-1/4 cups creamy peanut butter

1 tablespoon butter

1-1/2 cups crisp rice cereal

1 teaspoon vanilla extract

1/8 teaspoon salt

Prepare brownie batter according to package directions. Spread into a greased 13-in. x 9-in. baking pan. Bake at 350° for 20-25 minutes or until a toothpick inserted near the center comes out with moist crumbs.

Sprinkle with peanut butter cups and peanuts. Bake 4-6 minutes longer or until chocolate is melted. Cool on a wire rack.

Meanwhile, in a microwave-safe bowl, melt the chocolate chips, peanut butter and butter; stir until smooth. Stir in the cereal, vanilla and salt. Carefully spread over brownies. Cover and refrigerate for at least 2 hours before cutting.

PEACH BLACKBERRY COBBLER

BOURBON BALLS

PREP: 30 min. + chilling | **YIELD:** 4 dozen.

You'll remember the days at Grandma and Grandpa's house when you make these wonderfully traditional treats. The blended taste of bourbon and pecans is irresistible! **TASTE OF HOME TEST KITCHEN**

- 1-1/4 cups finely chopped pecans, *divided*
- 1/4 cup bourbon
- 1/2 cup butter, softened
- 3-3/4 cups confectioners' sugar
- 1 pound dark chocolate candy coating, melted

Combine 1 cup pecans and bourbon; cover and let stand for 8 hours or overnight.

In a large bowl, cream butter and confectioners' sugar until light and fluffy; stir in pecan mixture. Cover and refrigerate for 45 minutes or until firm enough to shape into 1-in. balls. Place on waxed paper-lined baking sheets. Chill for 1 hour or until firm.

Dip in chocolate coating; allow excess to drip off. Sprinkle with remaining pecans. Let stand until set.

PEACH BLACKBERRY COBBLER

PREP: 40 min. | **BAKE:** 40 min. | **YIELD:** 12 servings.

This is great for a large family group or church dinner during peach season. The rest of the year canned peaches are fine, but, of course, fresh is best. **MARGUERITE SHAEFFER** SEWELL, NEW JERSEY

- 12 medium peaches, peeled and sliced
- 1/3 cup all-purpose flour
- 1/4 cup honey
- 3 tablespoons lemon juice
- 1/4 teaspoon salt
- 3 cups fresh blackberries

TOPPING:

- 2 cups all-purpose flour
- 1/2 cup sugar
- 1 teaspoon baking powder
- 1/2 teaspoon salt
- 1/4 teaspoon baking soda
- 1/3 cup cold butter, cubed
- 1-1/4 cups buttermilk
- 1 tablespoon coarse sugar

In a large bowl, combine the peaches, flour, honey, lemon juice and salt; let stand for 15 minutes. Fold in blackberries. Transfer to a 13-in. x 9-in. baking dish coated with cooking spray.

For topping, in a large bowl, combine the flour, sugar, baking powder, salt and baking soda. Cut in butter until crumbly. Make a well in the center; pour in buttermilk. Stir just until a soft dough forms. Drop by tablespoonfuls over fruit mixture; sprinkle with coarse sugar.

Bake at 400° for 40-45 minutes or until filling is bubbly and a toothpick inserted into topping comes out clean. Serve warm.

PERFECTLY PEELED PEACHES

Follow these simple tips to make peeling peaches, well...a real peach! First, place peaches in a large pot of boiling water for 10-20 seconds or until the skin splits. Remove with a slotted spoon, and immediately place in an ice water bath to cool the peaches and stop the cooking process. Use a paring knife to peel off the skin. If stubborn areas won't peel, return fruit to the boiling water for a few more seconds.

TASTE OF HOME TEST KITCHEN

CARAMEL PECAN SHORTBREAD

PREP: 30 min. + chilling | **BAKE:** 15 min./batch + cooling
YIELD: about 4 dozen.

My grandchildren look for Grandma's "candy bar cookies" every Christmas. I recommend doubling the recipe for these sweet treats because they disappear quickly. **DOROTHY BUITER** WORTH, ILLINOIS

- 3/4 cup butter, softened
- 3/4 cup confectioners' sugar
- 2 tablespoons evaporated milk
- 1 teaspoon vanilla extract
- 2 cups all-purpose flour
- 1/4 teaspoon salt

FILLING:

- 28 caramels
- 6 tablespoons evaporated milk
- 2 tablespoons butter
- 1/2 cup confectioners' sugar
- 3/4 cup finely chopped pecans

ICING:

- 1 cup (6 ounces) semisweet chocolate chips
- 3 tablespoons evaporated milk
- 2 tablespoons butter
- 1/2 cup confectioners' sugar
- 1/2 teaspoon vanilla extract

Pecan halves

In a large bowl, cream butter and confectioners' sugar until light and fluffy. Beat in milk and vanilla. Combine flour and salt; gradually add to creamed mixture. Cover and refrigerate for 1 hour or until easy to handle.

On a lightly floured surface, roll out the dough to 1/4-in. thickness. Cut into 2-in. x 1-in. strips. Place 1 in. apart on greased baking sheets.

Bake at 325° for 12-14 minutes or until lightly browned. Remove to wire racks to cool.

For filling, combine caramels and milk in a large saucepan. Cook and stir over medium-low heat until caramels are melted and smooth. Remove from the heat; stir in the butter, sugar and pecans. Cool for 5 minutes. Spread 1 teaspoon over each cookie.

For icing, in a microwave-safe bowl, melt chips and milk; stir until smooth. Stir in the butter, sugar and vanilla. Cool for 5 minutes.

Spread 1 teaspoon icing on each cookie; top each with a pecan half. Let stand until set. Store in an airtight container.

MACADAMIA FUDGE

PREP: 20 min. + chilling
YIELD: about 2 pounds.

There are a few recipes I just have to pull out every holiday season, and this fudge is one of them. It couldn't be easier or better!

TINA JACOBS WANTAGE, NEW JERSEY

- 1-1/2 teaspoons butter, softened
- 3 cups (18 ounces) semisweet chocolate chips
- 1 can (14 ounces) sweetened condensed milk

Pinch salt

- 1 cup chopped macadamia nuts
- 1-1/2 teaspoons vanilla extract

Line an 8-in. square pan with foil and grease the foil with butter; set aside.

In a heavy saucepan, combine the chocolate chips, milk and salt. Cook and stir over low heat until chips are melted. Remove from the heat; stir in nuts and vanilla. Pour into prepared pan. Chill for 2 hours or until firm.

Using foil, lift fudge out of pan. Gently peel off foil; cut fudge into 1-in. squares.

BOURBON PECAN PRALINES

PREP: 15 min. | **COOK:** 25 min. + standing | **YIELD:** 1 pound.

Like authentic pralines found in New Orleans, these treats are sweet, crunchy and rich. But beware: You won't be able to stop after eating just one! **TASTE OF HOME TEST KITCHEN**

1/4 cup butter, cubed
1/2 cup sugar
1/2 cup packed brown sugar
3/4 cup heavy whipping cream
1 cup pecan halves, toasted
1/2 cup chopped pecans, toasted
1 tablespoon bourbon

Grease two baking sheets; set aside. In a large heavy saucepan over medium heat, melt butter. Stir in the sugars, then cream; cook and stir until mixture comes to a boil. Cook, stirring occasionally, until a candy thermometer reads 236° (soft-ball stage), about 20 minutes.

Remove from the heat; stir in the pecan halves, chopped pecans and bourbon. Immediately drop by tablespoonfuls onto prepared baking sheets. Let stand until pralines are set and no longer glossy. Store in an airtight container.

EDITOR'S NOTE: We recommend that you test your candy thermometer before each use by bringing water to a boil; the thermometer should read 212°. Adjust your recipe temperature up or down based on your test.

MARDI GRAS CUPCAKES

PREP: 25 min. | **BAKE:** 20 min. + cooling | **YIELD:** 2 dozen.

Take these simple gems to a Mardi Gras get-together and watch them disappear. Kids will love helping decorate them. **TASTE OF HOME TEST KITCHEN**

- 1 package (18-1/4 ounces) white cake mix
- 1 cup (8 ounces) sour cream
- 2/3 cup canola oil
- 1/3 cup sugar
- 4 eggs
- 3 tablespoons *each* lemon, lime and grape gelatin powder
- 1 can (16 ounces) cream cheese frosting

Purple, green and yellow sprinkles

In a large bowl, combine the cake mix, sour cream, oil, sugar and eggs; beat on low speed for 30 seconds. Beat on medium for 2 minutes. Divide evenly among three bowls.

Stir one flavor of gelatin powder into each bowl until blended. Fill paper-lined muffin cups with 2 tablespoons of each flavored batter.

Bake at 350° for 18-22 minutes or until a toothpick inserted near the center comes out clean. Cool for 10 minutes before removing from pans to wire racks to cool completely. Frost with cream cheese frosting. Decorate with sprinkles.

CARAMEL APPLE CHEESECAKE

PREP: 45 min. | **BAKE:** 50 min. + chilling
YIELD: 12 servings.

This won the grand prize in an apple recipe contest! With caramel both on the bottom and over the top, the cheesecake is ooey-gooey good.

LISA MORMAN MINOT, NORTH DAKOTA

- 1-1/2 cups cinnamon graham cracker crumbs (about 8 whole crackers)
- 3/4 cup sugar, *divided*
- 1/4 cup butter, melted
- 1 package (14 ounces) caramels
- 2/3 cup evaporated milk
- 1/2 cup chopped pecans, *divided*
- 2 packages (8 ounces *each*) cream cheese, softened
- 2 tablespoons all-purpose flour, *divided*
- 2 eggs, lightly beaten
- 1-1/2 cups chopped peeled apples
- 1/2 teaspoon ground cinnamon

Place a greased 9-in. springform pan on a double thickness of heavy-duty foil (about 18 in. square). Securely wrap foil around pan.

In a small bowl, combine the cracker crumbs, 1/4 cup sugar and butter. Press onto the bottom and 1 in. up the sides of prepared pan. Place on a baking sheet. Bake at 350° for 10 minutes or until lightly browned. Cool on a wire rack.

In a heavy saucepan over medium-low heat, cook and stir caramels and milk until melted and smooth. Pour 1 cup over crust; sprinkle with 1/4 cup pecans. Set remaining caramel mixture aside.

In a large bowl, beat the cream cheese, 1 tablespoon flour and remaining sugar until smooth. Add eggs; beat on low speed just until combined. Combine the apples, cinnamon and remaining flour; fold into cream cheese mixture. Pour into crust.

Place springform pan in a large baking pan; add 1 in. of hot water to larger pan. Bake for 40 minutes. Reheat reserved caramel mixture if necessary; gently spoon over cheesecake. Sprinkle with remaining pecans.

Bake 10-15 minutes longer or until center is just set. Remove pan from water bath. Cool on a wire rack for 10 minutes. Carefully run a knife around edge of pan to loosen; cool 1 hour longer. Refrigerate overnight.

SOUTHERN BANANA PUDDING

PREP: 30 min. | **BAKE:** 15 min. + chilling
YIELD: 8 servings.

This is an old Southern recipe, featuring a comforting custard layered with bananas and vanilla wafers, then topped with a meringue. I serve it all year-round— it's a nice ending to most any meal.

JAN CAMPBELL HATTIESBURG, MISSISSIPPI

- 3/4 cup sugar
- 1/3 cup all-purpose flour
- 2 cups 2% milk
- 2 egg yolks, lightly beaten
- 1 tablespoon butter
- 1 teaspoon vanilla extract
- 36 vanilla wafers
- 3 medium ripe bananas, cut into 1/4-inch slices

MERINGUE:

- 2 egg whites
- 1 teaspoon vanilla extract
- 1/8 teaspoon cream of tartar
- 3 tablespoons sugar

In a large saucepan, combine sugar and flour. Stir in milk until smooth. Cook and stir over medium-high heat until thickened and bubbly. Reduce heat; cook and stir 2 minutes longer.

Remove from the heat. Stir a small amount of hot filling into egg yolks; return all to the pan, stirring constantly. Bring to a gentle boil; cook and stir 2 minutes longer. Remove from the heat. Gently stir in butter and vanilla.

In an ungreased 8-in. square baking dish, layer a third of the vanilla wafers, banana slices and filling. Repeat layers twice.

For meringue, in a large bowl, beat the egg whites, vanilla and cream of tartar on medium speed until soft peaks form. Gradually beat in sugar, 1 tablespoon at a time, on high until stiff peaks form. Spread evenly over hot filling, sealing edges to sides of baking dish.

Bake at 350° for 12-15 minutes or until meringue is golden. Cool on a wire rack for 1 hour. Refrigerate for at least 3 hours before serving. Refrigerate leftovers.

VERY CHERRY ICE CREAM

PREP: 20 min. + chilling | **PROCESS:** 20 min./batch + freezing | **YIELD:** 2 quarts.

This recipe is a favorite at family get-togethers...everyone, from my 80-year-old grandmother to my 2-year-old daughter, enjoys it. I usually mix and chill the ingredients early in the day, then later everyone gets in on cranking the ice cream! **SANDY HOLD** SAPULPA, OKLAHOMA

- 1 pound fresh *or* frozen pitted dark sweet cherries, coarsely chopped (about 1-3/4 cups)
- 1/2 cup sugar
- 1 package (3 ounces) cherry gelatin
- 1 cup boiling water
- 1 package (3 ounces) cook-and-serve vanilla pudding mix
- 3-1/2 cups milk
- 2 cups heavy whipping cream
- 2 teaspoons vanilla extract

In a large bowl, combine cherries and sugar; set aside. Dissolve gelatin in boiling water; set aside. Cook pudding according to package directions, using 3-1/2 cups milk. Add to cherries. Stir in cream, vanilla and prepared gelatin. Refrigerate, stirring occasionally, until cold.

Fill cylinder of ice cream freezer two-thirds full; freeze according to manufacturer's directions. Refrigerate remaining mixture until ready to freeze. When ice cream is frozen, transfer to a freezer container; freeze for 2-4 hours before serving.

NEW ORLEANS BREAD PUDDING

PREP: 35 min. | **BAKE:** 35 min. | **YIELD:** 12 servings.

For an extra-special treat, try this sweet and buttery bread pudding. When we serve it to guests from the South, they say it tastes like home. **LINDA WIESE** PAYETTE, IDAHO

- 1/2 cup raisins
- 1/4 cup brandy *or* unsweetened apple juice
- 1/2 cup butter, melted, *divided*
- 1 tablespoon sugar
- 4 eggs, lightly beaten
- 2 cups half-and-half cream
- 1 cup packed brown sugar
- 2 teaspoons vanilla extract
- 1/2 teaspoon salt
- 1/2 teaspoon freshly ground nutmeg
- 10 slices day-old French bread (1 inch thick), cubed

SAUCE:
- 1/2 cup packed brown sugar
- 2 tablespoons cornstarch

Dash salt
- 1 cup cold water
- 1 tablespoon butter
- 2 teaspoons vanilla extract

In a small saucepan, combine raisins and brandy. Bring to a boil. Remove from the heat; cover and set aside. Brush a shallow 2-1/2-qt. baking dish with 1 tablespoon butter; sprinkle with sugar and set aside.

In a large bowl, combine the eggs, cream, brown sugar, vanilla, salt and nutmeg. Stir in remaining butter and reserved raisin mixture. Gently stir in bread; let stand for 15 minutes or until bread is softened.

Transfer to prepared dish. Bake, uncovered, at 350° for 35-40 minutes or until a knife inserted near the center comes out clean.

For sauce, in a small saucepan, combine the brown sugar, cornstarch and salt; gradually add water. Bring to a boil; cook and stir for 1-2 minutes or until thickened. Remove from the heat; stir in butter and vanilla. Serve with bread pudding.

NEW ORLEANS BREAD PUDDING

GENERAL RECIPE INDEX

ALPHABETICAL RECIPE INDEX

PHOTO CREDITS

SUBSTITUTIONS & EQUIVALENTS

EQUIVALENT MEASURES

3 teaspoons	=	1 tablespoon	16 tablespoons	=	1 cup
4 tablespoons	=	1/4 cup	2 cups	=	1 pint
5-1/3 tablespoons	=	1/3 cup	4 cups	=	1 quart
8 tablespoons	=	1/2 cup	4 quarts	=	1 gallon

FOOD EQUIVALENTS

Grains

Macaroni	1 cup (3-1/2 ounces) uncooked	=	2-1/2 cups cooked
Noodles, Medium	3 cups (4 ounces) uncooked	=	4 cups cooked
Popcorn	1/3 to 1/2 cup unpopped	=	8 cups popped
Rice, Long Grain	1 cup uncooked	=	3 cups cooked
Rice, Quick-Cooking	1 cup uncooked	=	2 cups cooked
Spaghetti	8 ounces uncooked	=	4 cups cooked

Crumbs

Bread	1 slice	=	3/4 cup soft crumbs, 1/4 cup fine dry crumbs
Graham Crackers	7 squares	=	1/2 cup finely crushed
Buttery Round Crackers	12 crackers	=	1/2 cup finely crushed
Saltine Crackers	14 crackers	=	1/2 cup finely crushed

Fruits

Bananas	1 medium	=	1/3 cup mashed
Lemons	1 medium	=	3 tablespoons juice, 2 teaspoons grated peel
Limes	1 medium	=	2 tablespoons juice, 1-1/2 teaspoons grated peel
Oranges	1 medium	=	1/4 to 1/3 cup juice, 4 teaspoons grated peel

Vegetables

Cabbage	1 head	= 5 cups shredded	Green Pepper	1 large	= 1 cup chopped
Carrots	1 pound	= 3 cups shredded	Mushrooms	1/2 pound	= 3 cups sliced
Celery	1 rib	= 1/2 cup chopped	Onions	1 medium	= 1/2 cup chopped
Corn	1 ear fresh	= 2/3 cup kernels	Potatoes	3 medium	= 2 cups cubed

Nuts

Almonds	1 pound	= 3 cups chopped	Pecan Halves	1 pound	= 4-1/2 cups chopped
Ground Nuts	3-3/4 ounces	= 1 cup	Walnuts	1 pound	= 3-3/4 cups chopped

EASY SUBSTITUTIONS

WHEN YOU NEED...		USE...
Baking Powder	1 teaspoon	1/2 teaspoon cream of tartar + 1/4 teaspoon baking soda
Buttermilk	1 cup	1 tablespoon lemon juice or vinegar + enough milk to measure 1 cup (let stand 5 minutes before using)
Cornstarch	1 tablespoon	2 tablespoons all-purpose flour
Honey	1 cup	1-1/4 cups sugar + 1/4 cup water
Half-and-Half Cream	1 cup	1 tablespoon melted butter + enough whole milk to measure 1 cup
Onion	1 small, chopped (1/3 cup)	1 teaspoon onion powder or 1 tablespoon dried minced onion
Tomato Juice	1 cup	1/2 cup tomato sauce + 1/2 cup water
Tomato Sauce	2 cups	3/4 cup tomato paste + 1 cup water
Unsweetened Chocolate	1 square (1 ounce)	3 tablespoons baking cocoa + 1 tablespoon shortening or oil
Whole Milk	1 cup	1/2 cup evaporated milk + 1/2 cup water